THE IMPERIAL AFRICAN COOKERY BOOK

Recipes from English-speaking Africa

Featuring memories from

Inkosi Dr Mangosuthu Buthelezi MP
Adelaine Hain
The Rt Hon Peter Hain MP
Chenjerai Hove
Lord Joffe CBE
Dr Roger Leakey
Prue Leith CBE
Dame Monica Mason DBE
HE Dr Festus Mogae
Matthew Parris
Rupert Pennant-Rea
The Most Rev and Rt Hon John Sentamu
Sylvester Stein

Also available from Jeppestown Press

Where the Lion Roars: An 1890 African Colonial Cookery Book

The Bulawayo Cookery Book and Household Guide

The Anglo-African Who's Who 1907

Matabeleland and the Victoria Falls

With Captain Stairs to Katanga

The Ghana Cookery Book

Cooking in West Africa

The Imperial African Cookery Book

Recipes from English-speaking Africa

by

Will Sellick

First published 2010 by Jeppestown Press, London.
www.jeppestown.com

ISBN 0-9553936-8-X
ISBN-13 978-0-9553936-8-6

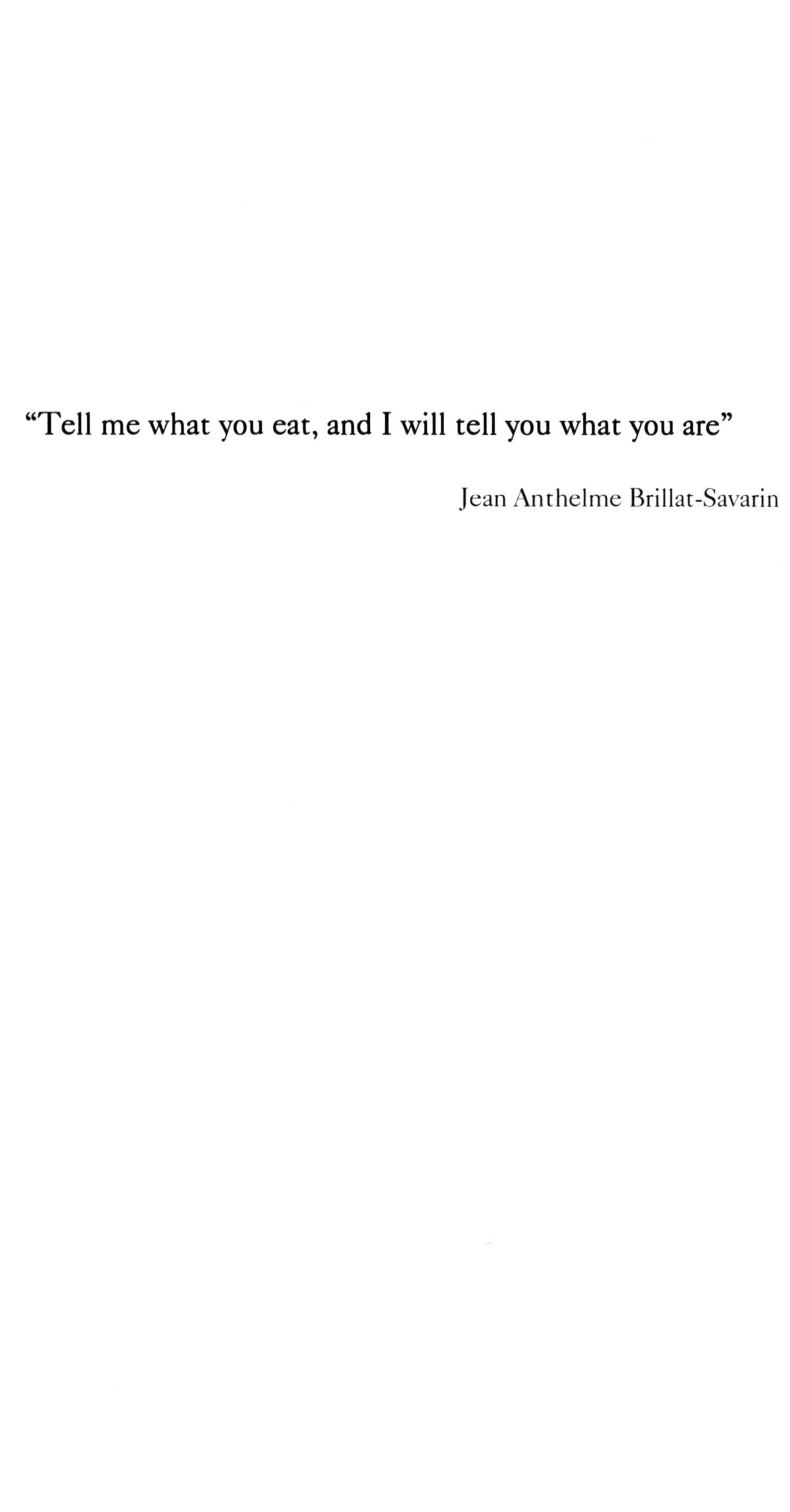

"Tell me what you eat, and I will tell you what you are"

Jean Anthelme Brillat-Savarin

Contents

Introduction

"African cookery? Great! I love African food," said the charming American woman. "Moroccan food is just the best, and there's an amazing Ethiopian restaurant in Portland..."

I explained that this book would focus on the colonial cookery of British Africa, and the woman looked puzzled before asking, "If you're writing about Africa, why do you want a book about white folks' food?"

It is a valid question. The answer lies in the colonial history of Africa and its population, which includes communities of immigrant European, Indonesian, Indian, Chinese, and Middle Eastern origin. For motivation to record this history, one has only to examine—or, better still, taste—the distinctive foods which each community brought with it.

> "Two fruits I can never get in England, and I only have to think of them to be filled with a nostalgic longing for the sun, and the innocence of childhood, and the pleasure of scoffing straight from the tree—and those two are mulberries and tree tomatoes. I've had blackberries and blueberries, blackcurrants and redcurrants, in some pretty fancy places at very fancy prices—but nothing to touch a mulberry. We ate them till our tongues were black with their juice, and our lips too, and hands—and clothes. And we gorged ourselves on tree tomatoes, spitting out the skin. Happy days."
>
> *Rupert Pennant-Rea, Zimbabwe-born former Deputy Governor of the Bank of England and Editor,* The Economist

Sometimes dishes associated with a specific group of settlers have been adopted by the wider population: the golden yellow custard tarts (*pasteis de natas*) of the Portuguese, still enjoyed with morning coffee in Luanda and Maputo; iced *Lebkuchen* and slabs of *Weihnachtsstollen*, rich with candied peel and marzipan, piled on the shelves of bakeries in Namibia at Christmas; while at the Curry Tavern in the Carlton Centre in Johannesburg I used to queue for a platter of fiery, aniseed-scented mutton curry alongside Zulu police officers and blonde secretaries chatting in Afrikaans.

Equally, as communities become assimilated into other groups, or emigrate from the region, their unique foodstuffs and recipes may disappear. French Huguenot settlers' recipes such as *oblietjies* (waffles) remained popular in South Africa long after their descendants had embraced an Afrikaans-speaking cultural identity, but were all but unknown by the Second World War. Further north, Jewish emigration to Zambia and Zimbabwe brought the Mediterranean traditions of Sephardic cookery to European settler communities along the Copperbelt and in the cities of Lusaka, Salisbury (now Harare) and Bulawayo; and gave rise to a generation of African domestic servants trained in the Jewish dietary laws of *kashrut*.

> "On patrol in the Zambezi Valley we would sit around the fire at night, taking turns stirring the *sadza* pot. It was good, wholesome food."
>
> *Jock Hutton,*
> *Regimental Sergeant-Major,*
> *1 (Rhodesian) S.A.S. Regiment*

I began to write this book out of a desire to record a sample of traditional recipes inextricably linked with colonial life in British Africa. Some recipes in this book are for dishes still widely known and popular: others are less familiar. What they all share is a foundation in or adaptation to British colonial Africa, or a strong historical link with the settler past.

These recipes' common association with British Africa does not mean that they are British—far from it. After 350 years of settlement, British African cookery emerged from a mix of Tudor spices, Indian feasting, Malaysian gastronomy, Victorian gentlemen's club dinners, and Boer survival foods. This unique and, in the final analysis, ephemeral cuisine reached its zenith during the brief period of African colonial rule—the "imperial intermission", as it has been called—from about 1880 to 1965.

Since then, it has largely been abandoned. In South Africa, the African country with the largest white population, colonial cookery styles cling on among the elderly and in conservative communities, particularly in rural farming districts. In the rest of Africa, British-style cookery is usually regarded at best as an amusing anachronism and at worst as a tangible hangover of colonial rule.

However, African colonial cooking thrives in the white African diaspora outside Africa. The race for national independence in the years after the Second World War, and the consequent political upheavals, resulted in a worldwide dispersal of the white populations of many African countries. From Nyasaland, Northern Rhodesia and Kenya we went to Australia, Europe and the USA; and, wherever we went, we took our foodstuffs and our family recipes.

I have eaten spiced oxtail in Washington, DC; buttermilk rusks in Brussels and mutton curry in Brooklyn; drunk rooibos tea in the Ottawa Valley and Tusker beer in Paris. As the child of South African political refugees living in London in the 1970s, I remember my parents' glee when my grandmother smuggled a couple of sticks of illicit beef biltong through Customs as a belated birthday present for my father; and my mother's despair when import sanctions meant that she could no longer buy IXL Export Grade Whole Apricot Jam. Today African settler cookery is used in the post-colonial context as a signifier of cultural identity, a tangible demonstration of membership of a particular community within the wider African diaspora. This is reflected by developments in Africa itself, where the post-colonial political desire for a single, national cultural identity is expressed in the recent efforts of some African states to define and label a national cuisine.

Notably, in most instances this new national cuisine incorporates significant influences from the period of colonial rule—whether by British, Belgian, Portuguese or French administrations. For example, although the textbook approved in 1985 for teaching cookery in Zimbabwean schools includes a large number of traditional recipes from black Zimbabwean cultures, the majority of the recipes are in fact for European dishes. Instructions for preparing flans and sponge cakes sit, perhaps incongruously, alongside recipes for goat's tripe and *ishwa* (white ants).

At its peak in the late 1950s the white African population consisted of about 6,500,000 whites living in various colonies and imperial possessions. About 2% of the people living in Africa were white—a proportion roughly equivalent to the percentage of people of black African and African-Caribbean descent living in England and Wales today. These European settlers, missionaries, merchants, engineers and

EASY CARE
WASH & WEAR
ARCHER
LEISURE SUITS
AVAILABLE IN
VARIOUS
STYLES
COLOURS
AND SIZES.
Meikles
BULAWAYO Tel.65101
BARKER McCORMAC

administrators were widely scattered, from two million French *pieds-noirs* in the ports and vineyards of North Africa to the tiny British protectorate of Zanzibar, with its population of just over 500 Europeans.

Only a handful of African territories, however, were ever settled in the sense of white colonists and their families making a permanent home there. It is this settlement—the notion of homemaking, and reliance on local resources and produce—which provided the first steps towards the development of a distinctive colonial cuisine in sub-Saharan Africa; and its roots lay in the British colonies in the south.

In fact, the most widespread influence on British African cookery came, paradoxically, from one of Britain's chief competitors in international trade: the Dutch and their tropical colonies in South Asia and the East Indies—Sri Lanka, the Moluccas, Bengal, Malaysia and Indonesia. The Cape of Good Hope was set up as a provision station in the 1650s to serve Dutch ships sailing to Europe with cargoes of aromatic, tropical spices like cloves, cinnamon and nutmeg: flavourings which are still used in meat dishes, fruit preserves and milk puddings. The slaves whom the Dutch brought from the east imported their own traditional recipes and cooking techniques, and these laid the foundations for the highly-spiced, piquant Cape dishes that were such a strong influence on colonial cookery across Africa.

> Food is a strong cultural identifier and how all countries' dishes evolve, reflecting migration and immigration, is certainly an interesting topic. Just look at Britain: our favourite remains curry—a dish which is now considered almost unrecognisable from the Bangladeshi dish.
>
> *Helen Burt, Commission for Racial Equality, London*

This is the first book to explore and record the cookery of British Africa in a single volume: it contains 180 recipes—discovered, developed and recorded by bachelors, housewives, club secretaries and big-game hunters across the continent from the lush green jungles of West Africa to the snow-dusted mountains of Uganda. Some are more elaborate than others, but all are delicious.

British people in Africa

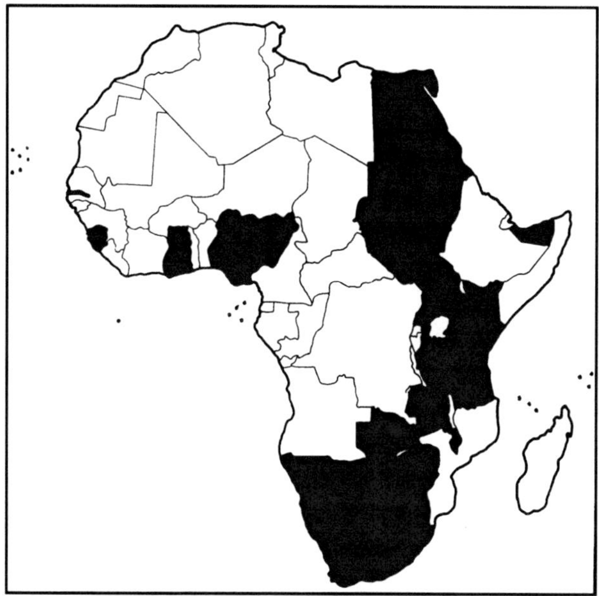

Figure 1. British possessions in Africa.

British colonial rule in Africa came officially to an end in 1980, when the Union flag was lowered in Salisbury, the capital of the rogue colony of Southern Rhodesia, and was replaced by the yellow, green, scarlet and black standard of the new republic of Zimbabwe. British influence in Africa began three hundred years earlier, with the building of trading outposts in the steamy mangrove swamps at the mouth of the Gambia River. The earliest West African trading station was Fort James, settled in Gambia in 1689, and these outposts included the later colonies of Gold Coast, Sierra Leone and The Gambia. However, although a handful of English-speaking colonists and tradesmen had

> We want breakfast at six o'clock; make Indian meal porridge and boil some sweet potatoes.
>
> *'English—Luganda useful and idiomatic phrases'*
> *Handbook to East Africa and Uganda*
> *1900*

settled at the Cape of Good Hope since the 1750s, arriving in increasing numbers after the Cape came under British rule in 1806, British settlement in Africa did not begin in earnest until 1820, when ships containing parties of English settlers and their families landed to support the process of consolidating British rule and settlement in the Eastern Cape.

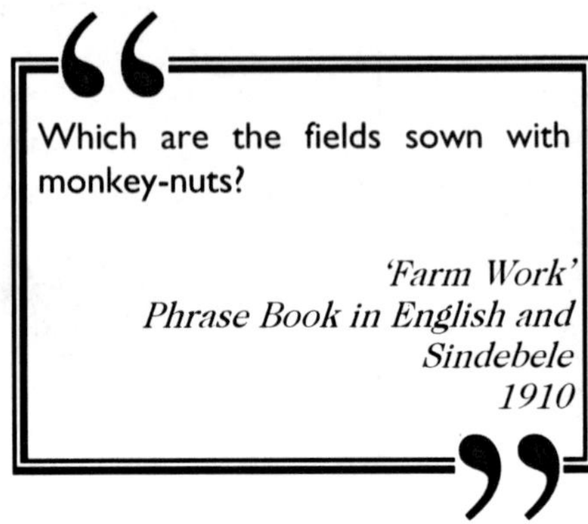
Which are the fields sown with monkey-nuts?

'Farm Work'
Phrase Book in English and Sindebele
1910

Over the following hundred years a vast proportion of Africa was conquered, swapped, taken over, traded, occupied and ruled by the British during what has become known as 'the scramble for Africa'. Often brutal, violent and coercive, the rules of the game were set at the 1884-5 Berlin Conference, where representatives of Turkey, the USA and the European powers met to agree the conditions under which African territorial annexations might be recognised. No representatives from Africa were invited to attend. Over the following fifteen years the remaining land in Africa, with the exception of Ethiopia and Liberia, was divided between the European powers.

At its peak in the late 1940s and early 1950s, when 80% of the population of Africa lived under European rule, British colonies, dominions, protectorates and UN-mandated territories in Africa consisted of the following countries:

South Africa
South-West Africa (now Namibia)
Swaziland
Basutoland (now Lesotho)
Bechuanaland (now Botswana)
Southern Rhodesia (now Zimbabwe)
Northern Rhodesia (now Zambia)
Nyasaland (now Malawi)
Tanganyika (now part of Tanzania)
Zanzibar (now part of Tanzania)
Kenya
Uganda
British Cameroons (now divided between Cameroun and Nigeria)
Nigeria

Gold Coast (now Ghana)
Sierra Leone
The Gambia (now Gambia)
British Somaliland (now part of Somalia but a disputed territory; Somaliland declared itself independent in 1991)
Anglo-Egyptian Sudan (now Sudan)

In the Protectorates the British government discouraged or forbade European settlement, and so English-speaking European colonists were concentrated in South Africa, the Rhodesias, Kenya and Tanganyika, with significant minority communities living in the Portuguese colonies of Angola and Mozambique and in the Belgian Congo.

The rise of African nationalism after the Second World War was one of the major factors in the dismantling of the European empires in Africa and the transformation of former imperial colonies into independent states. The twin objectives of nationalism were to bring an end to European rule in Africa and to forge the disparate populations in each colonial territory into a single, unified, nation-state. From the late 1950s, and with the strong support of the United Nations and the United States of America, Britain's African colonies were each in turn granted independence.

In each possession, British Colonial Office employees handed over their responsibilities to African administrators and returned to Britain. Yet, in every one of Britain's African colonies that had been settled by Europeans, a number of white colonists and their families remained; citizens of the new, independent nation under a nationalist government—determined to build their lives in Africa.

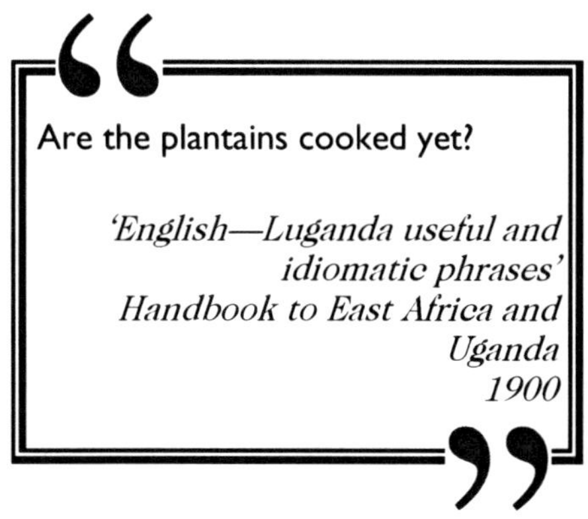

Are the plantains cooked yet?

'English—Luganda useful and idiomatic phrases'
Handbook to East Africa and Uganda
1900

Indigenous cookery

The diversity of Africa's ecological systems ranges from the Mediterranean climate of the Cape of Good Hope to the Sahara desert, and from tropical rain forest like the lush, green forests of Gabon to the savannah lands of Mozambique; meaning that there were and still are many crops and game restricted to a specific, narrow, latitude or growing area. This in turn influenced the settlement and development of different parts of Africa and, of course, had a significant effect on indigenous cookery styles.

> "One of the most mouth-watering experiences of my youth was the food we children ate when we joined the servants at quarters at the back of the house. We would sit on our haunches with them in the dusty space outside, and eat their incredibly savoury stew, simply cooked over a wood fire. We dipped balls of dough-like *sadza* into that stew, took a bite and then dipped again, picking up a piece of *nyama*. Thinking back, this consumption of their food rations was cheeky to say the least, but I recollect always feeling welcome."
>
> *Zimbabwe-born artist Trevor Southey*

Before the first European colonial exploration of Africa it is suggested that there may have been as many as 10,000 different political states across the continent: ranging from small, family units of San nomadic hunter-gatherers in southern Africa to the rich and glorious Bantu-speaking kingdoms of Central and West Africa, and the sophisticated city-states of southern and East Africa—whose trading networks are known to have reached as far as China.

Around 2,000 years ago some African people began to herd goats and cattle, and this provided a source not only of fresh meat, but also of dairy products like milk, butter and curds. Five hundred years ago maize was introduced to Africa and quickly became a popular crop among farmers, while the introduction of bananas and plantains from Asia also widened the scope of available staple foodstuffs.

Until several hundred years ago in sub-Saharan Africa, the staple foods of many African people in farming regions consisted of sorghum and millet and beans like cow-pea and ground-nut, with yams common in Equatorial Africa. Many meals consisted (and often still consist) of a stiff grain or starch porridge served with one of dozens of hot sauces or stews, often served with a piquant and highly-flavoured relish. This model has migrated and been adopted in a variety of forms right across sub-Saharan Africa, so that in southern Africa maize porridge or *puthu* is accompanied by meat gravy; in West Africa *fufu* is made from cassava, yams or plantain and served with stew or hot pepper sauce, and in East Africa maize porridge is known by names including *ugali* and *posho*, and is often served with a spicy meat casserole known in Swahili as *sukuma wiki*.

However, just as traditional British 'meat and two veg' meals form only one aspect of European cookery, it would be a mistake to imagine that a dish like *sadza nenyama* ("mielie-meal and meat": a Zimbabwean favourite of maize porridge served with a rich stew) is fully representative of the breadth and complexity of African cookery. A popular reference guide to useful plants of southern Africa lists vast numbers of common wild and cultivated indigenous plants commonly eaten cooked or raw—sixteen cereals; eighteen nuts and beans; 65 fruits and berries and about 50 leaf vegetables—and its authors admit that not all plants have been included. That just one region of Africa can provide such a

> "A cooked dish that reflects what I view as our national or family heritage is sour milk with either boiled mielies or mielie bread. This was the most important meal in our society from time immemorial."
>
> *Zulu politician*
> *Dr Mangosuthu Buthelezi*

massive range of different indigenous food plants gives an indication of the breadth of different ingredients, flavours and textures available to pre-colonial African cooks.

> As a young man I especially looked forward to any meal with meat (usually beef or goat), more so as meat was not served as commonly back then as now.
>
> *Festus Mogae, former President of B* 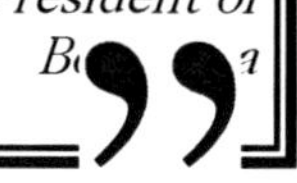 *a*

It is notable that, at the time when white African cookery was simultaneously developing and being recorded (the first English-language cookery book was published in Africa in 1889), black African women, especially, were suffering as a result of shortages of energy, money and time. Land seizure across the continent discouraged traditional farming and cultivation systems, reduced the amount of land available to black farmers and narrowed the range of farmed and wild foods available. Systematic hunting with firearms wiped out game animals across Africa: slaughtered either for their trophies, meat and hides, or in order to preserve grazing for settler livestock.

Simultaneously, increasing urbanisation and close control over agricultural production led black African people to rely more and more on expensive, industrially-processed foodstuffs like wheat flour, white rice, mielie (maize) meal and sugar. Often these foods were imported by colonial wholesalers, processed by settler-owned mills and factories or bought and sold in settler-owned trading stores, diminishing the potential for small-scale production and trade. As a consequence, indigenous cookery during the colonial period—particularly in urban areas—was characterised by a drastically restricted range of ingredients and cooking styles.

KIZITO BAKERY

Bakers & Confectioners

TEA ROOM

at

40 KAMPALA ROAD

(Near Drapers (1943) Ltd.)

Our Bread and Cakes are made in our own Modern, Hygienic, Electrically Operated Bakery at Seventh Street, Kampala

Box No. 1667 Phone 56247

KAMPALA

Sole Proprietor : E. Kizito

This restriction is reflected both in the paucity of resources relating to indigenous African recipes across sub-Saharan Africa, and in the patronising and dismissive approach that white cookery writers took until comparatively recently to African food. Even the usually even-handed Robin Howe, in *Cooking from the Commonwealth*, describes African menu as 'monotonous' and writes critically of kapenta ('dried fish, looking dark and evil, and smelling even worse') just 50 pages after nostalgically detailing a Northern Irish soup made from red herring—a British dried and smoked fish delicacy which could be described in exactly the same negative terms as kapenta.

> "Childhood memories are brisket cooked together with *rape* (a green vegetable); mushrooms in a peanut butter sauce (still my favourite) and, of course, *sadza*. Pumpkin leaves cooked in peanut butter sauce (yummy)!"
>
> *Wilf Mbanga,*
> *Editor,* The Zimbabwean

Selborne Hotel
L ★ ★
Bulawayo
Tonight!
Club Sheridan
8.00 - midnight. Cover Charge
JACKET AND TIE
PEOPLE WITHOUT PARTNERS ARE WELCOME!
e77676/W-tc

African food overseas

Jambalaya; collard greens; fufu; hominy grits; rice and peas; gumbo; *vatapa*; akra fritters. All these New World dishes descend from traditional African dishes taken to North and South America and the Caribbean by slaves.

Jambalaya, which seems to have been adopted as representing the Cajun tradition of Louisiana, and which became known worldwide during the explosion of interest in Cajun cookery in the 1980s, is simply jollof rice—a West African dish originally made from nutty African rice cooked with spiced meat and vegetables. Collard greens find their African equivalents in *moroko* in southern Africa, Congolese *mfumbwa* and Nigerian *akasi*, and countless other African dishes made from different greenstuffs. These are often given a thick, protein-rich sauce by being cooked with ground-nuts or crushed peanuts.

> I always enjoyed chicken stew with *amadumbe* (a traditional root vegetable) or dumplings.
>
> *Zulu politician Dr Mangosuthu Buthelezi describes a favourite dish from his childhood*

In the United States, the West African starch staple *fufu* (called coocoo in some parts of the Caribbean) was made from cornflour, and was probably the ancestor of Southern cornbread and corn pone, while hominy grits are identical to South African and Zimbabwean *umngqusho*, or samp. Rice and peas (the common name in the Caribbean for this dish, although it is often called Hopping John in the United States) is traditionally made with pigeon peas, which are also known as Congo peas. The dish is known as *wakye* in Ghana.

Gumbo, the slightly gelatinous, spicy soup thickened with okra, demonstrates its origins from *ngumbo*, the word used by the Luba people of the Congo for okra; the word goober, used in the southern United States as a slang name for peanuts, is a corruption of the Congolese word *nguba*, or ground-nut. *Vatapa* is a hot and piquant Brazilian peanut sauce traditionally served with meat or fish, and is very closely related to some ground-nut stews and sauces from West and Central Africa; you will find two recipes for peanut soup in this book, along with a Mozambican recipe for chicken in peanut sauce. Meanwhile akras, the Jamaican fritters made from black-eyed peas, are kin to the Ghanaian and Nigerian fried *akara* patties made from cowpeas or black-eyed beans.

It is bitterly ironic that, with the opening of a handful of Cajun-style restaurants in Africa over the last ten years ("The sights, sounds and flavours of the New Orleans French Quarter burst into life at Morton's", the web site of the Victoria and Alfred Waterfront in Cape Town brightly informs prospective diners), styles of cuisine transported forcibly to the New World through the slave trade have now been returned to their continent of origin.

There is a curious sort of reverse migration in the form of chilli peppers. These originated in South and Central America and were brought from the Caribbean to Europe by Columbus. They are said to have been introduced to Africa by the navigator Ferdinand Magellan in the early sixteenth century, and anybody who has tried Nigerian stews or Mozambican peri-peri knows the enthusiasm with which chilli peppers have been adopted by African cooks.

From their original use by the Carib population, popularity of fiery chilli peppers seems simultaneously to have developed in Africa and within the slave populations in the Caribbean and South America during the eighteenth and nineteenth century. At any rate, I have tried home-made hot pepper sauces from Tobago and the Bahamas which in appearance (deep saffron red-orange), preparation, consistency and taste are very close to central African peri-peri sauce. It is interesting to note that in the Caribbean some hot peppers are still known as 'Guinea' and 'Congo' peppers, suggesting that they may have been brought from Africa's Atlantic coast or used as condiments on the slavers' voyages.

With a handful of exceptions, British African cookery has ignored indigenous African cooking traditions. In southern Africa *stuiwe pap* (a very stiff form of *puthu* known, tellingly, by its Afrikaans name) is sometimes served with spicy tomato gravy as a side dish at barbeques, and irio is occasionally cooked and eaten by white East Africans. On the whole, however, white African cuisine in British colonies imported considerably more of its style and influence from the cookery cultures of India and Indonesia, and this book reflects that historical bias.

Zimbabwe, Zambia and Malawi

The first visitors to central Africa are thought to have been Arab merchants, who were trading with East Africa at around the time of the birth of Christ, and traced the trade routes from Sofala on the coast all the way inland to the Zambezi Valley escarpment and beyond well before the ninth century.

The Portuguese explored in the fifteenth and sixteenth centuries, sending columns of soldiers and traders inland from their coastal forts at Sofala and Moçambique. In fact, some of the oldest orange and lemon trees in central Africa are said to have been grown from seeds discarded by Portuguese soldiers, and were discovered by English settlers in Zimbabwe and Zambia in the 1890s.

Small numbers of whites, mostly British, but with a few Afrikaners and Portuguese travellers, explored Zimbabwe, Zambia and Malawi before 1890. Most of these early explorers were missionaries, hunters and traders. Jessie Lovemore was the daughter of the Reverend and Mrs Helm, pioneer missionaries and friends of the Ndebele king Lobengula; in 1874 the Helm family trekked from Swellendam in the Cape to the mission at Hope Fountain, in the centre of what is now the city of Bulawayo in Matabeleland, Zimbabwe. Mrs Lovemore was a baby at the time , but before her death in Bulawayo at the age of 87 she recorded a vivid description of cooking on the trek:

> 'After breakfast, midday dinner was prepared, clothes washed, and bread baked. The yeast we used for bread-making was 'sour dough'. This was a lump of dough taken from the kneaded bread and put into the bag of meal till the next baking, when it was soaked and mixed with flour and water to form leaven sponge the night before making the bread. Of course we usually had a piece given to us to start with, or we made it with hops.
>
> 'A bake-pot such as we used was a heavy cast-iron or wrought-iron flat pot, with a lid, on which one could heap coals. The procedure was to make a good fire and when there were enough hot embers, to put the pot containing bread or cake or meat on them and cover the lid with more. One usually had a fire going a little way off from which one could replenish the embers. Wood varies very much, some burns to ashes very quickly, while other makes good embers or hot coals.

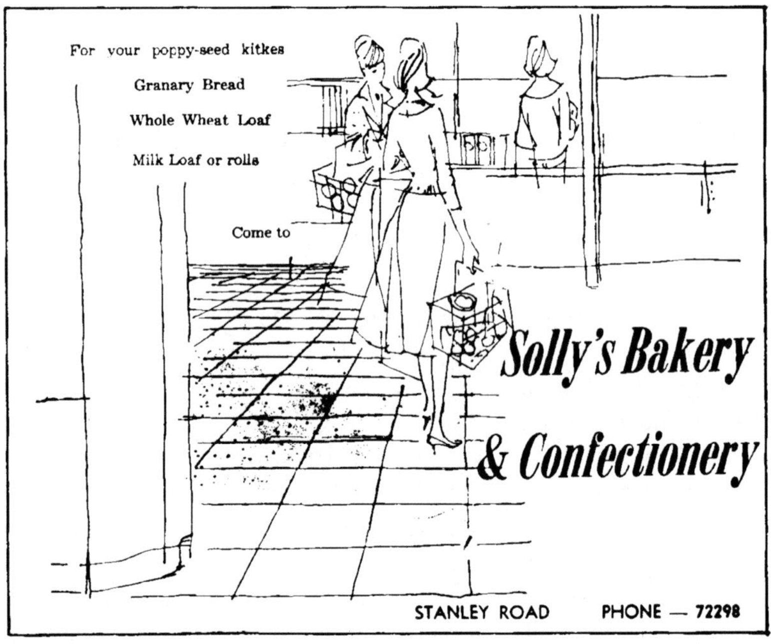

> 'We could not bring much butter, but used tail fat and dripping instead, the former being rendered out of sheep's tails. I doubt if ever

anything tasted as nice as a hot 'roaster-cookie' split open, with dripping or tail fat spread on it. 'Roaster-cookies' were made with dough ready risen to make into loaves. Some of it was flattened out and cut like big scones, and cooked on a grid-iron over hot coals.'

The earliest missionaries and ivory traders trekked with the usual dry supplies: mielie meal, rice, biltong, coffee, tea and sugar. They supplemented these with fresh game and, where they could be traded with locals, milk and eggs. Alfred Cross, who hunted with the hunter and explorer F. C. Selous in Matabeleland in the 1870s and 1880s, noted in his diary that Mrs Thomson, wife of the Rev. J. B. Thomson, one of the missionaries at Inyati and later at Hope Fountain, grew radishes and tomatoes in her garden at the mission. Mrs Thomson gave Alfred Cross jars of jam and chutney and a lot of tomatoes—Cross adding mournfully that he did not know how to cook them.

In fact, F. C. Selous appears to have been a reasonable camp cook. In 1871 he was travelling in Griqualand, and on Christmas Day he and his companions enjoyed '... a wonderful pudding of meal and eggs, flavoured with chocolate; we also made a sauce of meal, milk, honey and chocolate. Both pudding and sauce turned out a glorious success.'

> We lived on home-made bread, home-grown beef, pork, lamb and chicken; all our vegetables were grown on the farm. As children we would go to the compound and eat a delicious stew sitting around a fire and dipping the *sadza* (thick maize meal) into the communal pot of stew.
>
> *Memories of her childhood in colonial-era Rhodesia, by the writer Vera Elderkin*

The Union Jack was raised in what later became Cecil Square in Fort Salisbury, Rhodesia, on the 13th September 1890, by members of Cecil Rhodes' Pioneer Column. Organised settlement in the colonies of Southern Rhodesia, Northern Rhodesia and Nyasaland only began in earnest after the subjugation of the native tribes and landowners in a series of short, brutal wars and uprisings, culminating in the 1896 Matabele Rebellion in Southern Rhodesia. The first white settlers in Rhodesia consisted largely of middle-class, English-speaking immigrants, and until U.D.I. in 1965 they and their descendants continued to view white immigrants from other cultures and countries with some suspicion.

Pioneer life was tough: much of the food had to be imported from South Africa or from Portuguese East Africa, and early settlers lived largely on tinned meat with an occasional treat in the form of freshly-shot game.

The settler Ethel Tawse Jollie wrote in 1924, 'During the first fifteen years or so... no picture of Rhodesia is complete which does not include the bully-beef tin, the can of condensed milk and the native pumpkin and sweet potato,' and the philanthropist Kingsley Fairbridge, himself the son of a farmer who emigrated from the Cape to Rhodesia in 1896, confirmed that '...nearly everything we ate came out of tins—petits fours, champignons, condensed milk, Danish butter... bully-beef, plum-pudding, Canterbury cake, and so on.'

By 1895, when Alexander Davis published his directory to the town of Bulawayo in Matabeleland, built near the old capital of the Ndebele king Lobengula, the established businesses included millers, mineral water bottlers, bakers and butchers' shops. There were only four grocery stores, but the large number of hotels, restaurants and tea rooms suggests that many of the men living in Bulawayo (in 1895 the population was overwhelmingly male) habitually ate in commercial premises rather than employing a cook or cooking for themselves—indeed, Tattersall's Hotel advertised 'The largest Dining Room in Rhodesia', while the Sussex Hotel in Fort Street boasted 'two new bars' and a '*Table d'Hôte* daily'. (This is in contrast to, say, Nairobi in the much more elegant colony of British East Africa, which as late as 1912 had only three hotels.)

—SUNDAY LUNCH—
Smoked Beef Gherkins
Cream of Mushroom
Grilled Pilchards & Mustard Sauce
Roast Pork & Apple Sauce
or
Chicken Maryland
or
Bermuda Cold Buffet with Assorted Salads
or
Charcoal Grill (Steak, Chicken, Kebab)
or
Irish Stew
Fruit Salad & Cream
Cheese, Biscuits, Coffee
$2,75, Children under 10 $1,75.
Reservations 45049/45466
cp-62920-Y-10

For those who did cook, a 1909 advertisement for Haddon and Sly, the Bulawayo department store, tempted Rhodesian housewives with modern baking products ('no cook in the Old Country would be without Self-Raising Flour'), yeast cakes, 'Buttercup' brand tinned butter from New Zealand, and cans of beef dripping, lemon curd, treacle and castor sugar. In addition, just 20 years after the British South Africa Company annexed the territory, Haddon and Sly stocked angelica, pistachios, black Leicester mushrooms, truffles, olives and crystallised violets.

In fact, practically all the ornaments of a civilised (in other words, European) life could be purchased in the wilds of Matabeleland —at a price. The cost of provisions in early Rhodesia was astronomical, and white settlers were often unwilling to change their diets to include foods such as sorghum and maize which were grown locally, mostly on a subsistence basis. Without an organised farming industry and, more importantly, an effective distribution network, many fruit and vegetables had to be imported from South Africa. In the early days fresh milk and eggs were available in tiny quantities only from local black farmers or from those settlers who had the foresight to bring fowls and dairy cows... and who possessed the necessary expertise with livestock to keep them alive. In addition, although Rhodesia possessed railway links that by 1903 extended as far north as Victoria Falls, railway transit was prohibitively expensive and pushed up still further the cost of imported or transported goods.

> "As a child, my favourite dish was local rice (brown rice cooked with peanut butter) and chicken stew cooked with mild spices and tomatoes. This was a rarity which we usually got when a special visitor came."
>
> *Zimbabwean author Chenjerai Hove*

Sheila Macdonald recorded the details of a 1908 dinner menu, cooked to celebrate the return of her husband from the mine store he owned in Mazoe:

'Tomato Soup.

Oyster Patties (the oysters live in tins, but I shall disguise 'em).

Chicken and stuffing and bread sauce (when we are alone we have either stuffing or bread sauce, as bread is so expensive).

Plum Pudding.

No dessert because there isn't any.

No savoury because there aren't any eggs, and they are eight shillings a dozen to buy.'

Writing from Salisbury in 1907, Mrs Macdonald informed her mother that 'there is no scarcity of eggs or butter or milk now. But only a few years ago there was only tinned butter and milk to be had, and eggs were £1 a dozen. They are five shillings now, and this is the cheapest season of the year.' Five shillings in 1907 had the purchasing power of around £15 a century later: a pound in 1907 was worth about £60 today.

When Mrs Macdonald's husband first arrived in Rhodesia in the early 1900s he bought a pound of steak for his Sunday dinner and went into a trading store to buy some potatoes as a treat. He asked for sixpenny-worth of potatoes, and watched in amazement as the owner picked up a large potato, cut it in half, rolled the smaller half in brown paper and gave it to him. In 1891 the firm of Hopley and Papenfus conducted an auction in Salisbury to dispose of the surplus provisions brought by Lord Randolph Churchill's party. Butter was sold for eleven shillings a pound, while whole, tinned hams were knocked down for £2 each.

There was a contrast between the basic provisions—mielie meal, biltong, rusks, salt and coffee—which Afrikaans hunters and explorers

SMART and COPLEY LTD.

FAMILY CHEMIST

SINCE 1897

SHOP IN COMFORT IN OUR MODERNISED STORE FOR ALL YOUR MEDICINAL TOILET, SURGICAL or VETERINARY REQUIREMENTS OUR POSTAL SERVICE CATERS FOR OUR COUNTRY CUSTOMERS

PHOTOGRAPHERS

SEE OUR RANGE OF CAMERAS AND ACCESSORIES
YOUR FILMS DEVELOPED, PRINTED AND ENLARGED

QUALITY PRINTS PRODUCED

OPTICIANS

SIGHT TESTS BY QUALIFIED OPTICIAN
PRESCRIPTIONS DISPENSED

HEARING AIDS

SONOTONE THE WORLD'S FINEST HEARING AID STOCKED
TESTS, ADVICE AND REPAIRS BY TRAINED STAFF

P.O. Box 594 — Main Street, BULAWAYO — Phones 2220, 2221, 2222

took with them, and the distinctly more luxurious foodstuffs that their British equivalents transported through the wilderness. George Westbeech, an explorer in Barotseland in the Upper Zambezi Valley in what is now Zambia, kept a diary during much of the period he spent in this area. In January 1888 he looked after an ailing Swiss doctor, Dr Dardier, and fed him wine, jam, preserved grapes in syrup and preserved ginger, which suggests that Westbeech, at least, did not believe in Spartan rationing while in camp.

> I was born and brought up in Africa and I have been used to eating with our cook and gardener in their own houses at the bottom of the garden. They ate what we called *sadza* which was an extraordinarily thick maize porridge. It was served with meat stew. The meat was very gristly—I was surprised to learn that they preferred gristly meat—but the sadza was nice when you dipped it in the gravy!
>
> *Matthew Parris, journalist and former Member of Parliament*

Reliance on fresh game also had its hazards: in her book *Sally in Rhodesia*, describing life as a new settler in Rhodesia in the early 1900s, Sheila Macdonald related a disastrous dinner with neighbours, for which her husband shot a paauw, or kori bustard: a large and tasty game bird that looks rather like an athletic turkey. The full menu is described by Mrs Macdonald as follows:

'Consommé.
Salmi of Game.
Roast Paauw.
Trifle.
Cold Savoury.
Strawberries and Tinned Cream.'

When the roast bustard arrived at the table it stank and was so tough as to be impossible to carve. One of their guests asked to see the feathers from the bird and, on inspecting them, explained that Macdonald's husband had in fact shot a secretary bird—a ground-dwelling raptor that lives off snakes and carrion.

By the Second World War huge agricultural enterprises like the Mazoe Citrus Estates and Tanganda Tea Estates were beginning to change the face of central African commercial farming. This coincided with the explosion in European immigration from the United Kingdom after 1945 which at its peak in the late 1950s resulted in a European population of around 250,000 in the Federation of Rhodesia and Nyasaland. For many of the immigrants their new lives in the sun—with no food rationing, excellent wages, and the prospect of employing black staff to undertake the housework and garden chores—left them free to enjoy a middle-class existence in Bulawayo or Salisbury.

This life was in fact not so different from the ordered comforts of 1950s suburban England, but with the added inducements of a cook, lower income tax, and better weather. Even as early as the 1920s Ethel Tawse Jollie wrote, "[Rhodesian wives] are living a very different life from what they would at home. They belong to classes which never had much leisure to dispose of, and the standard they have almost unconsciously adopted is beyond their real needs or capacity."

Rhodesian food was characteristically hearty and based largely on 20th century English domestic cookery. However, many Rhodesian recipes seem also to have been influenced by Cape and East African cookery, and feature the spicing and flavouring typical of these cuisines. Comparatively few Cape Muslim or 'coloured' (a southern African term to denote mixed race) South Africans migrated to Rhodesia, so much of this style of cookery must have been introduced with the Afrikaans immigrants from South Africa. (In fact, although Rhodesians resisted the suggestion, their white population was largely of South African origin. Before the Second World War, more than half the settlers were South

African-born, and of the British-born population, around half had spent time living in South Africa before moving to Rhodesia).

Large numbers of Afrikaans farmers, mostly poor sharecroppers, emigrated from South Africa to Rhodesia from the 1890s onwards. As part of an effort to consolidate British South Africa Company claims to the area of Gazaland, near the border with Portuguese East Africa, the Company offered free farms to parties of settlers who trekked up from South Africa. This area, particularly around Melsetter and Enkeldoorn, was settled largely by Afrikaans-speaking farmers, mostly from the Orange Free State and Natal, who brought with them many of the Cape Dutch traditions of preserving and baking from south of the Zambezi.

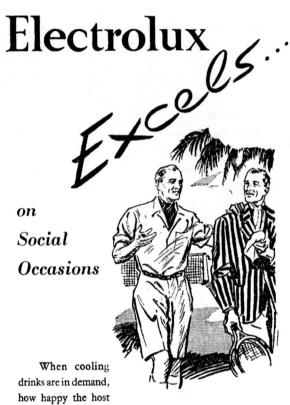

Kenya, Uganda and Tanzania

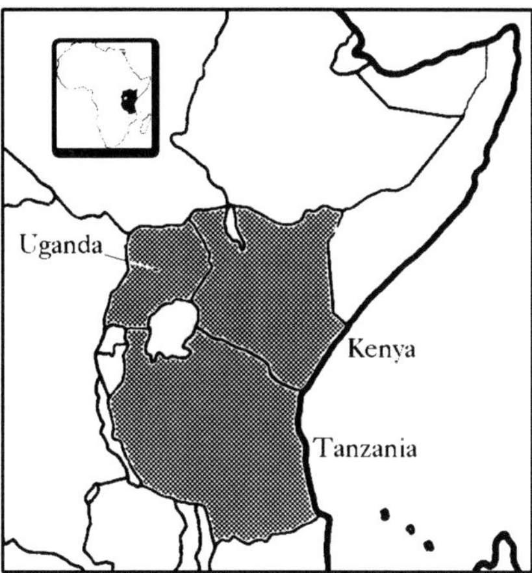

Kenya was the only area of East Africa to have been settled by significant numbers of white people intending to make the country their home. Uganda, Tanganyika and Zanzibar all had small white populations, but these were for the most part transient: businessmen, plantation managers and administrators instead of settlers. The legal status of the territories also affected the settlement policy since, as Protectorates rather than Colonies, Uganda, Tanganyika and Zanzibar did not encourage settlement by white people. Tanganyika, although twice the size, had just one-tenth of the white population of Southern Rhodesia.

Kenya came under British rule in 1895, although the Sultan of Zanzibar had granted some of the northern coast of his sultanate to the British East Africa Association eight years before, and settlement began in a desultory and unorganised fashion in the 1890s. In contrast to Rhodesia, where the majority of the country's early settlers came from South Africa, most Kenyan settlers were British-born. The first arrivals were middle-class and aristocratic: in industry and business in East Africa, the skilled blue-collar and white-collar roles that in Rhodesia and South Africa were filled by working-class whites were usually taken by Indians. As a result, the Kenyans demonstrated a degree of snobbishness

when it came to approving applications for settlement by whites. In 1906, the colonial authorities suggested that at least £1,000 was required as minimum capital to settle in Kenya—a sum that has the buying power of something like £70,000 a century later. In the same year, the imposition of a £50 deposit at Customs on arrival in Kenya indicates the determination of the government of the time to keep out penniless adventurers.

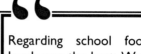

Regarding school food, Sunday lunch was the best. We knew it as *Dead Donkey*, but it was actually salted beef topside, with boiled potatoes and carrots.

The worst was on Tuesday—known as *Yacht Pond Slime* because of its resemblance to the algae growing on the school pond. I think it was some kind of veal stew. I used to always be the last to finish this meal, and regularly got into trouble for it. Whenever possible, I would spit the chunks of slime into my serviette and empty it out under the table where dogs were grateful recipients.

Dr Roger Leakey, Kenyan-born expert in terrestrial ecology and tropical agroforestry

However, there were some interesting and unexpected settlement plans that did not altogether fit the overall historical view of Kenya as the rich Englishman's playground. In 1903 the British Government approached the leaders of the Zionist movement to suggest that Kenyan land might be granted to Zionist Jews in order that they could set up their own homeland in the East African highlands. The Zionists politely refused the offer, and could not be swayed even by a further British concession: that the area could have a Jewish Governor.

Another wandering tribe, the Afrikaners, made a more substantial impact on the white population of East Africa when in 1908, with the agreement of Sir James Hayes Sadler, the Governor of Kenya, Jan Janse van Rensburg led a party of nearly fifty Afrikaans families, mostly poor sharecroppers and *hensoppers* ('hands-uppers': Boers who had surrendered to the British during the Anglo-Boer War) sailing to Mombasa on the German steamer S.S. *Windhuk*. The van Rensburg party was followed three years later by a further party of sixty families from Natal, led by C. J. Cloete. In a curious and sometimes uneasy convergence, these two officially-sanctioned groups joined the *bitter-einders* already in East Africa. These *bitter-einders* were Afrikaners who had not supported the truce that ended the Anglo-Boer War in 1902—and were prepared to fight to the bitter end, in other words—and who had emigrated in disgust to German East Africa after the war finished.

One Kenyan writer of British descent describes the East African Afrikaners as peasants, eating giraffe-meat sausages and stewed pigs' feet. Practically the entire Afrikaans community returned to South Africa between the beginning of the Mau Mau revolt in Kenya in the 1950s and Tanzanian independence in 1961 and, reflecting their status as a small, closed community divided from the English-speaking white Kenyans by language, class and religion, little or no Afrikaans cultural heritage remains in East Africa. However, it is interesting to see that in the classic book of Kenyan settler cookery, the *Kenya Cookery Book and Household Guide*, which has been published by the St Andrew's Church Women's Guild in Nairobi since 1928, there are a small number of dishes listed that are clearly of Afrikaans origin—green fig preserve, rusks, curried fish (actually pickled fish, a Cape recipe) and fish custard (in other words, fish bobotie)—while the 1925 *Uganda Cookery Book*, which was written in dual English/Luganda for the benefit of both cook and employer, contains a recipe for Cape Dutch frikkadels.

IMPERIAL HOTEL,
KAMPALA, UGANDA.

THE LARGEST AND MOST UP-TO-DATE HOTEL IN UGANDA.
Run on modern lines under European management.
Dinners and Dances specially catered for.
First Class Cuisine. Excellent Cellar.

BILLIARDS. TENNIS.

FOR TERMS APPLY TO THE MANAGER.
P.O. Box 88. 'Phone 65.

Besides the British and Afrikaans influences on Kenyan settler cooking, the third culture that informed the way East African colonists cooked was India. There were two sources: the first came from the Indians who settled, worked and traded in East Africa. Many shopkeepers in Kenya and Uganda came from Gujarat, where food tends to be strictly vegetarian and delicately spiced. The cashiers and book-keepers who worked for the colonial government were mostly from the Portuguese colony of Goa on the West Indian coast, south of Bombay; conservative, Christian, and used to the elaborately prepared rice, fish, pork and coconut dishes typical of Goan cuisine.

The second Indian influence came from the British themselves. From the 1920s onwards, charitable societies like the Kenya Association (1932) sprang up in East Africa to encourage Indian Army officers and their families to retire in the 'white highlands' of Kenya's Aberdare region. These settlers brought Anglo-Indian and Raj flavours and techniques with them, and in turn influenced Kenyan cookery—I am thinking particularly of the vast range of curried savouries, snacks and canapés, spiced sauces and chutneys that remain popular in Kenya even today.

Kenya's upper-class settlers treated black Kenyans with the same contempt that their English contemporaries displayed towards their own servants in England. In the 1930s the Kenya Association's guide to settlement couched a warning to prospective female settlers in terms typical of the time:

> "African domestic servants are still plentiful and cheap, although they need constant and patient supervision... Outside the larger towns where electricity is available, wood-burning stoves of the 'Dover' type and heavy charcoal irons are commonly used. All laundry is still done at home in most households and the farmer's wife must bake bread and make her household as self-supporting as possible."

Doctors and dieticians are emphatic on the value of fresh vegetables to good health.

Be sure that the vegetables and fruit you buy are the best value for money.

Shop at Maya Ram, the oldest and best-known greengrocer in the Municipal Market, Stewart Street, Nairobi.

Maya Ram for value and a fine selection of fresh flowers daily.

SHOP WHERE YOU SAVE

SHOP AT

MAYA RAM

Perhaps the most disappointing aspect of East African settler cookery is that in general it differed so little from middle-class British cooking of the 20th century: Henry Seaton, an East African civil servant in the early 1900s, describes a Kenyan dinner consisting of crayfish, braised duck with green peas, asparagus tips, followed by crystallised fruit and coffee, which could have been served in a hotel or upper-middle-class home in London or Paris. Having said that, there are a few specific recipes, even those of a purely British origin, that are very characteristic of East Africa. Even many of these British recipes are notable in having continued to be very popular in Kenya long after they had fallen out of fashion in the United Kingdom.

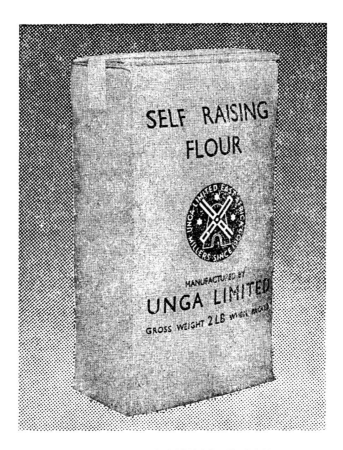

West Africa

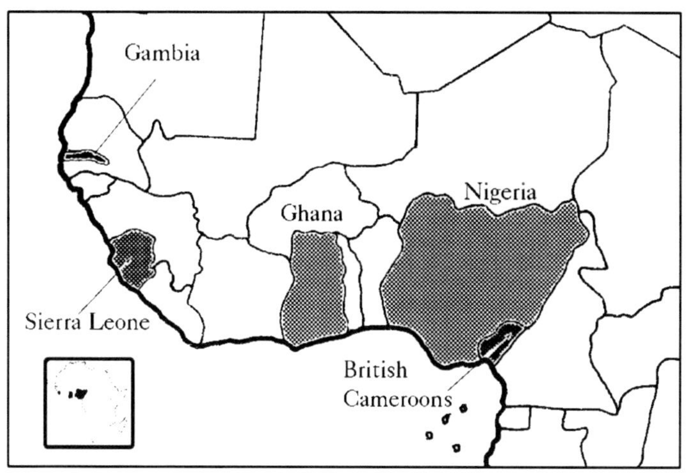

Because of its hot and humid climate, which was held to be dangerous for Europeans' health, and the ever-present threat of malaria, West Africa was never permanently settled by Europeans except for a handful of civil servants, traders and missionaries. (One poignant document in the Manuscripts section of the School of Oriental and African Studies Library in Bloomsbury is a little 12-page pamphlet containing lists of the names of white missionaries who died in Sierra Leone, the Gambia, the Gold Coast and Nigeria.)

> There is a big market being held today; go and buy two pigeons, one duck, twelve guinea-fowl's eggs, some wheat and a pineapple.
>
> *'Household Management'*
> *A Hausa Phrase Book, 1924*

Even their wives and children did not generally join male colonial officers, missionaries and traders in West Africa in any significant numbers until the years following the Second World War, and throughout the early part of the twentieth century preference was given to unmarried men under 35 years of age for government appointments in the region. Indeed, the official *British Colonial Handbook* warned against colonial civil servants taking "their wives out with them until they have themselves acquired experience of the local conditions". Official permission was, in any case, required before a man's wife was allowed to accompany him to West Africa; while children were strongly discouraged since "conditions are generally unsuitable for children, and are commonly believed to have an injurious effect on their development".

Because there were so few British women in West Africa, almost all cooking was carried out—in contrast with many of the other British African possessions—by native cooks, and most appear to have been extremely competent in reproducing their employers' favourite British recipes. Kitchens were usually located in the servants' compound well away from the main house, and most colonists employed a substantial number of domestic staff. In Kintampo in the Gold Coast (now Ghana) in 1916, Laura Boyle engaged for herself and her husband a cook, cook's mate, valet/houseboy, housemaid and a dozen men "who are hammock or garden boys as circumstances dictate".

Another intrepid wife who travelled to West Africa was Muriel Tew, who joined her husband (Mervyn Tew—later Chief Justice of Sierra

Leone) in Lagos shortly after their marriage in 1911. Nine years later Mrs Tew published a book on European-style cookery in West Africa: a slim, pocket-size volume bearing elaborate black-and-white advertisements for Poulton and Noel's tinned Oxford sausages and The London and Kano Trading Company. Mrs Tew's book suggests that settler cookery in British West Africa was almost entirely based on British Victorian cuisine. However, there are a couple of notable local recipes, such as instructions for the cooking of ground-nut soup and a recipe for pawpaw jam, which are absolutely typical of the era and of the locale.

The reliance on British cookery is confirmed by other works of the period such as Captain H. Osman Newland's splendid *Handbook to West Africa*. The Handbook was written for the benefit of newcomers to the region, and was designed to inform newcomers travelling out on the 'monkey-boat', as West African liners were called, precisely what to expect. Captain Newland's Handbook warned British visitors that there were only two dishes in West Africa that they might not recognise: palm-oil chop and ground-nut chop. (These indigenous dishes are both staples of modern West African cooking: palm-oil chop is a sumptuous dish of boiled eggs, beef, chicken and prawns cooked in palm oil, which gives the stew an alarming orange-red colour. Ground-nut chop has a similarly luxurious range of ingredients, but ground-nuts or peanuts

Wanted to . .

BUY, SELL, OR EXCHANGE

ANY KIND OF

WILD BEAST, BIRD & REPTILE

ALSO

CURIOS OF ANY KIND AND EVERY DESCRIPTION.

Also for EXPORT .

Any and all DESCRIPTIONS of

SPORTING AND PET DOGS, PIGEONS, &C., &C.,

Either FOREIGN or EUROPEAN.

CROSS,

WILD BEAST, BIRD & REPTILE MERCHANT,

LIVERPOOL.

Cablegrams: "CROSS, LIVERPOOL."

are added.)

British rulers in West Africa left many traditional rule structures in place, approved high standards of education for black people and—until the end of the nineteenth century, at any rate—encouraged black employees to rise to senior positions within the civil service and judiciary. As a result, this was one of the few regions of Africa under British rule in which black and white people sometimes worked together and, occasionally, socialised together under terms of (often uneasy) equality.

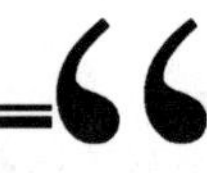

> Traditional English fare of turkey, pork, ham, stuffing, followed by Christmas pudding and mince pies... followed by ice cream and coffee for those who had any room left.
>
> *Joan Beech, describing Christmas dinner in the Gold Coast*

Mrs Tew sums up one of the challenges of colonial settler cooking, the limited repertoire of recipes that resulted from intermittent supplies and a restricted choice of local produce, in a single sentence. She gives a recipe for Fish Cakes, and next to it a recipe for Fish Croquettes, explaining that these are made exactly the same way as the fish cakes, and to the same recipe, but in a different shape, adding wistfully, "If you cannot get much variety in the way of food, it is sometimes a relief to see it served somewhat differently—served on a different dish even makes some change."

Mozambique and Angola

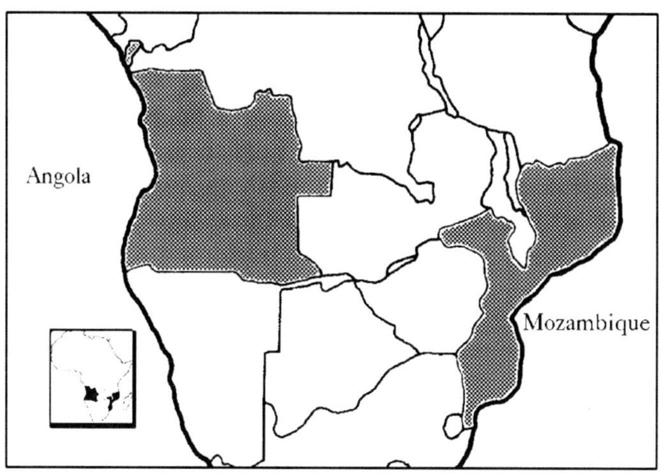

At first sight it seems odd to include recipes from two Portuguese colonies in a study of settler cookery in Britain's African possessions; after all, there are no recipes from the German-influenced South West Africa (now Namibia). However, the more I spoke to black and white Africans while researching this book, the more I was persuaded that Portuguese colonial cookery has had a notable impact overall on British settler cuisine across Africa, and that it was important to add a handful of recipes. It is not simply a question of antiquity: Portugal was, after all, the first European nation to explore Africa's coasts (Cape Verde, Lagos, Natal and Beira are all Portuguese names). Her colonies in Mozambique, Angola, Guinea and Cape Verde were in European possession

for nearly five hundred years, and all had a substantial British community—mostly traders and business people.

In fact, the 1900 Mozambique Company census shows that in districts such as Neves Ferreira and Chimoio, there were more English settlers than Portuguese. As well as the Beira Club, Beira, on the Mozambican coast, had its own English golf, sports and yacht clubs; a concert hall named after Queen Victoria; a Scottish pub; an English physician and a newspaper printed in English and Portuguese. A large number of Afrikaans settlers trekked north to Angola following the end of the Anglo-Boer War, although most of these settlers returned to South Africa or South-West Africa before the beginning of the Second World War.

The exotic
night spot
on the sea-front
promenade.
"ZAMBI" TEL. 5236
A LA CARTE MENU

There are very few countries in sub-Saharan Africa which did not have a population of Portuguese inhabitants during the colonial period, and for many settlers in English-speaking Africa—particularly South Africa and the Rhodesias—the cities of Lourenço Marques in Portuguese East Africa (now Maputo, the capital of Mozambique) and its neighbour Beira were the most glamorous seaside holiday destinations imaginable. The dispersal of Portuguese settlers in Angola and Mozambique during the 1960s and 1970s also had an impact on their countries of refuge. It is easy to forget the sheer numbers who lived there: in the 1960s Angola and Mozambique had between them well over a quarter of a million whites, many of them peasant farmers from rural Portugal who settled in Angola from the 1920s onwards. As calls for independence became more strident in Portuguese-speaking Africa, many of these whites emigrated—to Rhodesia, South Africa or back to Portugal or Madeira—and the Portuguese who stayed in Africa took their distinctive cuisine with them to other, neighbouring countries. However, today, thirty years after independence, the broad, shady boulevards of Maputo are lined with pavement cafés and restaurants that would not look out of place in any sophisticated seaside resort in Portugal.

My mother's family has lived for nearly a century in Kensington, one of the oldest suburbs in the South African city of Johannesburg. After Portugal's African colonies became independent in the mid-1970s, large numbers of white immigrants arrived in Johannesburg from Angola and Mozambique. Many settled in the southern district of Kensington and nearby suburbs like Orange Grove. As a result, you can walk through the tree-lined, sunny streets and pass dozens of Portuguese bakeries, fish shops, cafés and restaurants (shamelessly nostalgic, the wonderful Senhor Prego Restaurant, a Kensington institution located in a tin-roofed, colonial-era building on Broadway, used to boast on the exterior of its verandah of 'a taste of old L. M. [Lourenço Marques]'. Local newsagents stock Portuguese-language newspapers and magazines, and there is a whole network of Portuguese-owned businesses to be found there—everything from dressmakers to car repair firms—catering largely for a Portuguese South African customer base and often employing Portuguese-speaking black staff from Mozambique or Angola.

This pattern is repeated again and again across Africa, wherever Portuguese colonists have settled (some of the best peri-peri prawns I have eaten were in the tiny, intimate restaurant of the Mozambique Hotel in the little town of Manzini in the middle of the Kingdom of Swaziland). The favoured meat in Portuguese African cuisine is, without any doubt, chicken. However, there are some memorable fish

and seafood dishes available on the coast.

Portuguese baking is justly revered, and everyone in southern Africa is familiar with what South Africans call 'Portuguese rolls'—light, floury, white bread rolls—and *pasteis de natas*, the little flaky pastry tartlets filled with a rich egg custard which, dredged in powdered cinnamon, provide such a wonderful accompaniment to morning coffee in cities from Luanda to Cape Town.

and Commission Agents

(WHOLESALE AND RETAIL),

LISBON and BEIRA.

The Oldest Portuguese Establishment in the Town.

Wines, Liquors, Provisions, Boots and Shoes, Hardware, Guitars and Mandolins, Clothing, Etc.

Leather and other requisites for Shoemakers.

Bakery.

Portmanteaux, Etc.

ESTABLISHED 1891.

Portuguese Provisions and Wines.

A Large Assortment to select from, including Port Wines of the famous brands "Romariz" and "Companhia Vinicola."

BREAD MADE DAILY.

THE BEST IN THE TOWN.

Consignments received and realised to best advantage.

Tel. Address: "Milho, Beira."   Tel. Address: "Tigre, Lisbon."

Postal Addresses: P. O. Box 38, Beira, East Africa. Lisbon Office: Rua do Corpo Santo, 13, 1º.

South Africa, Botswana, Namibia, Swaziland and Lesotho

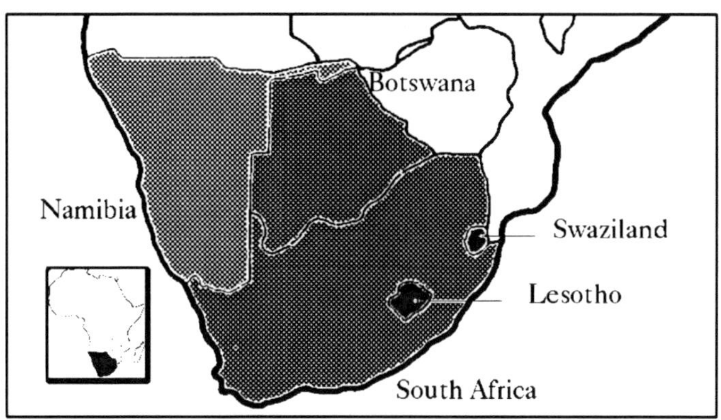

The food of South Africa—and 'Cape' cookery, in particular—is one of the most diverse cuisines in the world. South African traditional cookery demonstrates influences both clear and indirect from Africa, Malaya and Indonesia, India, France, the Netherlands, Arabia and Britain. In addition, there is a more recent body of recipes brought by nineteenth and twentieth-century immigrants to South Africa, and changed and adapted over the past century. In general, in fact, the cookery of southern Africa directly reflects the patterns of migration and immigration of its inhabitants.

> "In terms of a dish reflecting local national culture, I sometimes offer visitors *seswa*—local shredded meat—which can be made with beef, goat or game meat. Otherwise I am naturally proud of our Botswana beef."
>
> *Festus Mogae, former President of Botswana*

Ten thousand years ago the land was inhabited by hunter-gatherers. These people, the ancestors of the Khoikhoi and San or Bushman people, lived off game and wild plants, with fish and shellfish the primary sources of protein for those who lived by the sea. Today, the most accessible foodstuffs with a Khoikhoi and

San heritage are probably bush teas and preserves; rooibos, buchu and honeybush teas are available commercially and have a long history of use as medicines and beverages in both the pre- and post-colonial periods, while indigenous fruits such as the sycamore fig, marula and wild loquat are still preserved by drying or making into jam.

Beginning about 2,500 years ago, farmers and cattle-herders from the Great Lakes and Cameroon regions moved south in a series of migrations to what is now South Africa—almost all black South Africans are descended from these early settlers, who split over time into different, distinct national groups.

Five hundred years ago Portuguese and Dutch seafarers began to explore the southern African coast, and in 1652 Jan van Riebeeck set up a permanent supply station at the Cape of Good Hope, on the southernmost tip of Africa, to replenish Dutch East India Company vessels travelling between Batavia, Bengal and Europe. Gardens and farms were laid out, and a startlingly wide array of seeds and plants imported from Europe and the East—from sweet potatoes, pineapples, citrus trees and lettuce, to melons, cabbage, chillis, quinces and bananas.

Gradually the station grew in size and importance as Company officials were granted land around the region. During the seventeenth and eighteenth centuries the city of Cape Town expanded around the five-sided castle to become one of the most important strategic ports in the Dutch mercantile empire. Cape Town was a Dutch possession from 1652 to the early 1800s, and the primary influences which have broadly shaped South African

"Memories of different cultures include sitting on the back step eating sour porridge with my Zulu nanny, or shelling peas with her and eating half of them. She also illegally brewed delicious smelling *skokiaan* which she would not let me taste.

Prue Leith CBE, South African-born food writer, restaurateur, and patron of the Prue Leith Chef's Academy in Centurion, Pretoria, South Africa.

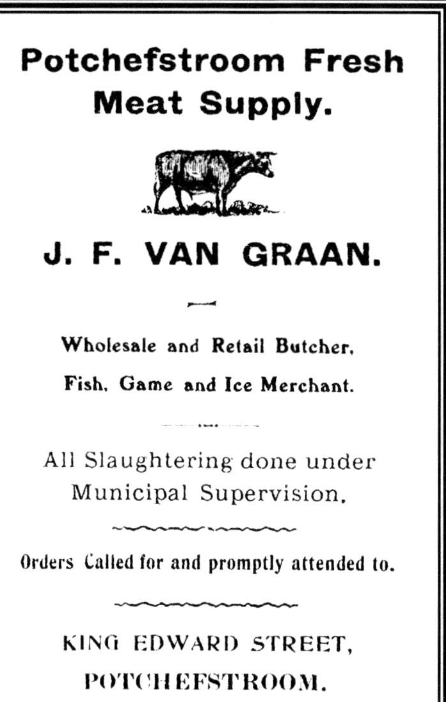

cuisine date from this period.

The two main influences on what is nowadays seen as traditional Cape cooking are Dutch domestic cookery, and the oriental cookery of Batavia, the Dutch East Indies colony (now Indonesia). Holland lends South African cuisine its magnificent preserves—an astonishing range of *konfyts*, jams, jellies and glacé fruit—and the rich dairy foods, buttery cakes, sweet tarts and biscuits that are still favourites. Dutch trekkers and frontiersmen also made popular some of the most enduring South African foods and dishes: biltong, rusks and mebos—foods designed to be eaten on trek, and (enduring in every sense) to be stored and carried with ease on horseback with little danger of deterioration over time.

From Java, Sumatra and the Dutch colonies in the East Indies came spiced dishes such as bobotie, frikkadels, kebobs, denningvleis and bredie. Many of these dishes still have their Malay names: denningvleis, for example, is a corruption of the Dutch/Malay hybrid *dendeng-vleis*, or dried buffalo meat; and the Afrikaans word for chutney, *blatjang*, is a Malay word meaning...well, it basically means chutney.

My strongest memories are of the wide variety of fruit—not so much in the shops but on the trees!

Dame Monica Mason, Director of the Royal Ballet, who left South Africa aged fourteen to join the Royal Ballet School

In addition, slaves from Bengal brought varieties of curry and spiced Indian foods to the Cape, some of which were adopted by the Malay slaves already in the colony (the Malay community, about 130,000-strong, is now generally known as Cape Muslim, and is traditionally centred around the beautiful Bo-Kaap district of Cape Town, on the slopes of Table Mountain). One could write a book on Cape curries alone: over the years, the traditions of India have become fused with those of Indonesia and Ceylon, so that many Malay curries are routinely made with Indian curry powder or curry paste (and in fact Cape Muslim cookery makes great use of ready-made, commercial curry powders and masalas). In addition, the unavailability of certain ingredients has led to substitutions in both Indian and Malay cuisines so that, for example, in South Africa roti flatbreads, whether made by Cape Muslim cooks or by Indian chefs in Durban tend to be made with plain, white flour (known as cake flour) instead of chapati flour.

By one o' clock we found our way back to the hotel to lunch, and had our first experience of a South African meal. We recognised then (our first experience was amply confirmed later on) that the diet in the colonies was not going to be as good as we were accustomed to in England.

Through South Africa with the British Association by J Stark Browne, 1905

NOW AVAILABLE
THE TASTY AND CRISP
Imported American
MATZOHS
100% Pure White Flour
BISCUITS
FOR TEA, COCKTAIL SNACKS, AND AFTER DINNER TITBITS
Manufactured by
THE WORLD FAMOUS
Horowitz & Margareten
of New York, and now available in 1lb. packets from all leading grocers.
Baked under the Most Sanitary Conditions, and carefully packed in Tightly-sealed Boxes . . . . to keep freshness IN, and to keep dust and moisture OUT.
Trade Enquiries:
B. S. & R. BEARE
(PTY.), LTD.,
P.O. BOX 25 BELGRAVIA, JOHANNESBURG.
Tel. Add.: "Beare."
C926I.

About 63,000 slaves were imported into the Cape between 1652 and 1807, when slave transports were officially abolished; most came from the East Indies, Madagascar and Bengal, although between 1808 and 1865 a further 5,000 slaves (known as 'prize Negroes') were seized from illegal slavers by the British and landed at Cape Town, where they were indentured for fourteen years before being freed.

The close contacts between indigenous people, settlers and slaves during much of the eighteenth century resulted not only in the birth of a new language—Afrikaans, or Cape Dutch—but also led to the assimilation into colonial cookery of recipes and cookery styles from outside the European tradition.

Two hundred families of French Huguenots—French Protestants—arrived in South Africa between 1670 and 1690, many in the farming district called Franschhoek (French Corner), 70km from Cape Town. The South African Huguenot Society estimates that around a quarter of all Afrikaners' genes descend from these 200 families, but despite the impact that the Huguenots made on the white population of southern Africa, within a couple of generations Huguenot families had stopped speaking French as a first language, and it is difficult to find any lasting gastronomic legacy beside the South African tradition of winemaking.

The first significant numbers of British settlers arrived in South Africa in 1820, and were settled at Grahamstown in the Eastern Cape. They were followed by steady numbers of immigrants, and the discovery of gold and diamonds in the 1870s and 1880s resulted in a flood of new arrivals from all over the world.

Ingredients

Visiting a market or supermarket in Africa is an invigorating experience. There is a longstanding belief held by many African people—in the face of all available evidence—that all the finest locally-produced fruits and vegetables are exported to Europe. As a tourist, perhaps the most refreshing aspect of shopping in Africa is the likelihood that you will end up buying ripe fruit or vegetables. That is, fruit actually picked at the point of ripeness, transported to the market or shop and offered for sale in the condition in which you would like to eat it: luscious, bursting with flavour, and with most of its nutritional content intact.

Walking around the fruit stands is a treat for me when I am in my grandmother's local Pick 'n' Pay in Johannesburg. The bananas are sun-ripened in plantations near the Mozambican border in Mpumalanga province; they are a startling, canary yellow, and all around them is the sugary, pear-drops smell of ripe banana. The Queen pineapples are grown in the tiny kingdom of Swaziland; they are small (you can cup one comfortably in one hand) golden orange in colour, with sharply serrated leaves. The watermelons are like cartoon fruit: the size of a fat two-year-old, striped green and white like giant humbugs, with perfumed, crisp, red flesh.

> In our garden at home we had a seemingly endless supply of paw-paw, bananas (the stumpy kind), guavas, avocado pear, mielies (white, not the yellow substitute branded corn on the cob), strawberries... No doubt they were seasonal, but viewed from a 40 or 50-year distance, the cornucopia always seemed full.
>
> *Rupert Pennant-Rea, Zimbabwe-born former Deputy Governor of the Bank of England and Editor,* The Economist

When we visited Livingstone, in southern Zambia, we arrived right in the middle of guava season; every market stall was piled with neat pyramids of creamy yellow guavas, some sliced open to reveal grainy crimson flesh, and everywhere their pungent, musky, tropical-fruit aroma. We escaped into a café for a pot of Tanganda tea in the English style— served strong, with lots of milk—and massive slices of chocolate cake, and the owner brought us, unbidden, cold coral-pink guava juice in tall glasses beaded with condensation.

Most of the ingredients that go into the recipes in this book are commonplace: you will find practically all in any half-reasonable supermarket. Unless otherwise specified, all recipes use medium-sized fruits or vegetables. However, it is worth looking at some of the ingredients in a little more detail.

Fruits and vegetables

Aubergine. Aubergines are known in most of Africa by their Indian name, brinjal, and are available in a far wider range of varieties, sizes and colours than in the United Kingdom. For home-grown brinjals I would always advise carrying out the traditional salting and rinsing to remove the bitter juices. However, this is increasingly unnecessary for the mild varieties on sale in supermarkets.

Avocado. While African farmers grow the rough-skinned Hass avocados for export, domestic consumers seem to prefer the smooth-skinned, green Fuerte-style avocado, and this is the variety that you will usually find on sale by the roadside in Africa. Not long ago I was in Borough Market in South London and saw a pile of massive Fuerte avocados almost the size of melons. "Those look familiar," I thought. Sure enough, they came from Swaziland, from one of the flat, hot lowveld farms in the south of the country. I bought two, and they were nutty, sweet and soft as butter.

> My aunt had two fabulous trees, apricot and fig, and many times I ate too many and had stomach ache.
>
> *Dame Monica Mason, Director of the Royal Ballet*

Citron. Also called the etrog, the citron is a large citrus fruit like a fat, warty, aromatic lemon, used most widely for its peel, which is usually candied. You will find it in South Asian grocery shops—my local Bengali greengrocer in Brick Lane always has citron when they are in season—and occasionally around the Jewish festival of Sukkoth, in late September/early October, when it is used in Jewish religious ceremonies.

Dates. Don't bother using fresh dates for any of the cooking recipes in this book. Either use dried, loose dates or, more economically, use the blocks of dried, compressed dates that most supermarkets stock in their baking sections.

Granadilla. Passion fruit, known in most of Africa by its Spanish name, which means 'little grenade'. Some granadillas are so sweet that they can be spooned up and eaten straight from the leathery rind, but generally they benefit from some sweetening. Granadillas make a great addition to fruit salads and smoothies, and are packed with Vitamin C.

> The best food in Durban was fruit—pawpaws, granadillas, mangos, avocado pears the equal of which I've never seen, and all grown in our own gardens.
>
> *Sylvester Stein, former editor of South Africa's* Drum *magazine*

Kale. A dark green, tough and fibrous form of cabbage, rather like winter greens, which requires extended cooking.

Lemon. For any recipe including lime, orange or lemon zest or peel, either buy unwaxed fruit or ensure that you scrub the fruit hard with hot water and a stiff brush before using the peel, in order to remove the layer of harmless wax with which producers coat their fruit. Freshly picked lemon and orange leaves are used to flavour both sweet and savoury dishes—often either bay leaves or lime leaves can be substituted.

Mango. I tend to use mangoes from Ivory Coast or central America fresh or in cooking. They are of reliable quality and are widely stocked throughout the year. However, for flavour and texture, look out for boxes of Pakistani or Indian mangoes in South Asian food stores—their rich, sweet flavour is incomparable. Also keep an eye out for the luscious, sun-dried mango slices now being exported from Burkina Faso in West Africa by a fruit-drying co-operative based there. In colonial kitchens stewed, unripe mangoes were one of the fruits often used as a substitute for apples in fruit pies.

Mielies. Mielies are simply maize—known in the United Kingdom in its most familiar form as corn-on-the-cob or sweetcorn. For many of the recipes in the book, corn-on-the-cob or even tinned sweetcorn can be used. However, my preference would always be to try to track down proper white maize cobs—sometimes available in Asian shops or African grocery stores.

Mushrooms. All the recipes that call for mushrooms work well with English field or button mushrooms; however, any edible mushroom with the exception of the truffle would be appropriate.

Naartjie. A small, highly aromatic, tight-skinned mandarin orange. There are a variety of mandarins, tangerines and clementines, and, to be honest, I use any miniature orange with a tight skin in a recipe that calls for a naartjie. The skin should never be thrown away—dried, it forms an important flavouring in many traditional South African Cape recipes.

> We would go down to the tobacco barns, where they cooked the maize cobs in the hot ashes scraped out of the flues that were used to cure the tobacco.
>
> *Memories of her childhood in Rhodesia, by the writer Vera Elderkin*

Pawpaw. I cannot see the attraction of pawpaw. Its flesh is bland and soapy, and requires plenty of seasoning in the form of ginger or other spices to pep it up. I have successfully made mock apple pie after a colonial West African recipe, using under-ripe pawpaws spiced with cloves and cinnamon. In Mozambique, paw-paw roots are an important traditional medicine for diseases of the reproductive system, and the jet-black seeds, which contain chloroform, are crushed and swallowed as a remedy for worms.

Pineapple. I use medium-sized pineapples from Ivory Coast, but any medium-sized pineapple will give a good result. To test whether a pineapple is ripe, try pulling out the centre leaves of its crown, which should come out easily, but by far the most reliable method is simply to sniff the base and see if it has the sweet, unmistakeable smell of ripe pineapple.

Potato. In most of the recipes in the book I have specified whether waxy or floury potatoes should be used, and clearly you will get a better result with the appropriate potato. However, using the wrong sort is unlikely to be a disaster, and you can get away with using a multi-purpose variety like Maris Piper.

Squash. There are a bewildering variety of squashes in use across Africa. They range from pattypan squashes, like a tiny lemon-yellow flying saucer, whose skin is tender enough to eat, to the almost spherical lagenaria gourds from west Africa, two feet across, whose rind is used to make storage containers. Most squash, pumpkin and butternut keep for a long time in a cool cupboard, and are a great standby for quick soups.

Tamarind. The tamarind is a beautiful tree; tall, with fringed, wispy leaves. Its seeds are contained in long, brown pods that look as though they have been stitched from brown suede. The seeds come encased in a caramel-coloured pulp that tastes like sour dates, and which adds a fruity, astringent undertone to many Malay and Indian dishes. You can buy the pulp in jars, already blended and ready to add to your curry. Alternatively, look out for blocks of Thai tamarind pulp sold in oriental and Indian grocery shops; to prepare these, break off a chunk and soak it in boiling water before straining out the seeds and tough fibres. Use the same approach to fresh tamarind, scraping out the pulp and soaking it in hot water before straining it.

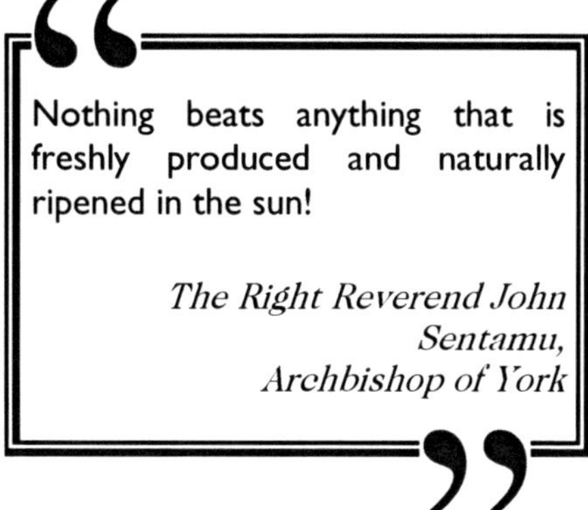

Nothing beats anything that is freshly produced and naturally ripened in the sun!
The Right Reverend John Sentamu, Archbishop of York

GOOD HOLIDAY
in Mozambique
AC
FILTRO
FÁBRICA DE TABACOS ULTRAMARINA
CIGARROS
TIPO AMERICANO
LUANDA
ANGOLA
CIGARROS
ZORRO
TABACO SEMI-CLARO
DEPÓSITO DE VENDA ■ AV: MANUEL DE ARRIAGA 957, TEL. 6892, C.P. 2443
LOURENÇO MARQUES

Herbs and spices

In the seventeenth century Jan van Riebeeck was charged with building a fort and gardens near the beachfront in what is now central Cape Town. The purpose of the settlement was to grow fresh fruit and vegetables to supply the vessels of the Dutch East India Company—the Cape formed a convenient restocking point on the five-month voyage between Indonesia and Europe—which by the 1650s was one of the main suppliers of aromatic spices to European cooks, perfumers and apothecaries. African cuisines still make great use of spices and flavourings, and some are listed below.

Allspice. The unripe berry of a Central American tree; a member of the Myrtaceae family, which includes myrtle, clove, eucalyptus and guava. Allspice is used whole and ground, and lends its warm, clove-like flavour to meat stews and milk puddings. Although it is grown mostly in the Caribbean, there are also plantations in Réunion in the Indian Ocean.

Star anise. Tasting and smelling strongly of aniseed, this star-shaped seed pod comes from a far Eastern shrub. Its use in Africa tends to be restricted to dishes of Indian or Malay origin.

Aniseed. Almost identical to fennel seed, but with a sweeter, more intense flavour, aniseed is one of the traditional flavourings for rusks; I was told by an Afrikaans cook that aniseed was used as a flavouring agent because its strong aroma meant that ants and other insects were less likely to be attracted to the rusks.

Bay leaf. Fresh bay leaves give a sweet, warm, spicy flavour to curries, stews, pickled fish and milk puddings. Dried bay leaves are slightly mustier—always use fresh leaves if available. Keep a look out for West Indian bay leaf—the leaf of the allspice tree—which is sometimes available fresh or dried from West Indian bakers or grocery stores. These are intensely scented, with a citrus-y, clove-like flavour, and are brilliant for use in sweet puddings and bobotie.

GLASBAKE
HEAT-RESISTING OVENWARE
Made in U.S.A.

Foods cooked in Glasbake ovenware retain their full flavour. You can serve appetizing meals in the same dishes that you used for cooking, too ! Only Glasbake has the exclusive "Heat Quick" bottom — cleans easily — is guaranteed for 2 years against Heat Breakage.

Use Glasbake for storing foods in your 'frig—designed to take the least possible space.

You can
COOK
SERVE
STORE
foods in
GLASBAKE

FOR TOP-OF-STOVE WARE ALWAYS ASK FOR Range-tec

Black pepper. Used whole and ground, as well as being an important constituent of Malay and Indian masalas.

Cardamom. Both black and green cardamom are used in African cookery, particularly Indian and Malay dishes from southern and East Africa. Black cardamom usually has a strong, smoky smell which disappears entirely during cooking—the smell is due to the traditional drying technique over a wood fire. Green cardamom is the best seed to use for sweet purposes such as biscuits and cakes.

Chilli. Chilli peppers originate from Central and South America, and only reached Africa in the early sixteenth century. In most of Africa the preference is for very hot chillis, like the peri-peri or birds-eye. However, most of these peppers are very fiery indeed to palates unused to them. I recommend using Cayenne and Serrano peppers—the large (typically about 10cm long), comparatively mild, scarlet or dark green hot peppers available in most supermarkets—with the seeds removed. Leaving the seeds in will give a more fiery taste to the recipe, and using a stronger chilli such as Thai birds-eye or Scotch bonnet will obviously have the same result. African curries often have a distinctive 'burnt' taste that comes from the custom of frying chopped chilli with curry leaves in ghee or oil until brown, before adding mustard seeds and other spices.

Cinnamon. Whole quills (rolls of dried bark the size of a short pencil) and ground cinnamon are used in African colonial cookery in curries as well as in milk puddings, cakes and biscuits. Cinnamon also forms one of the ingredients of the traditional Boer remedy *rooilavental*, used to counteract wind and heartburn.

Cloves. The dried, unripe buds of a tree from the *Myrtaceae* family from Indonesia. Cloves were a prized, imported spice in east Africa from at least 1200 onwards, when they were mentioned in Swahili literature from the island of Pate. The Dutch jealously guarded their plantations in the North Moluccan islands, but after their monopoly of the spice trade ended in the early nineteenth century the trees were introduced to other suitable growing regions—cloves are known to have been planted in Zanzibar in 1818 by Sultan Seyyid Said, brought from the French possession of Réunion—and today the world's largest producer is the island of Pemba, near Zanzibar, off the Tanzanian coast. Cloves are used in stews and curries as well as puddings and preserves.

Coriander. A favourite, versatile herb. The leaves are widely used to garnish and flavour curries and chutneys, and is also extensively used in Portuguese recipes from Mozambique and Angola. The seeds are used in curries and masalas and also give a warm, spicy flavour to fruit compotes, cakes and biscuits.

Cumin. Cumin is used in stews and curries of Arab, Malay and Indian origin, and is also popular as a savoury flavouring in Mozambican and Angolan cuisine.

Curry leaves, also known as curry *patta*. These are fresh, soft leaves from the South Indian bush *Murraya koenigii*, and are widely used in Natal Indian cuisine. Just throw half a dozen into the oil when you fry onions for curry: they lend a distinctive aromatic, woody flavour.

> “Curries were perhaps the most distinctive food we ate. Indeed, strange though it may seem, I tend to think of curry as the closest to a national Rhodesian dish there is.”
>
> *Zimbabwe-born artist Trevor Southey*

Curry powder. Many cooks from South Asia and Europe turn up their noses at the use of curry powder—a finely powdered blend of spices and chilli—preferring to use freshly-prepared spices to flavour their curries. However, in Africa many Indian and Malay cooks continue to use proprietary curry powders (brands like Cartwrights or Rajah) as one of the main sources of flavour for traditional South Asian and Indonesian dishes, or buy powders ready-blended from masala stalls in the famous spice section of the Indian market in Durban or the spice market in Mombasa.

Fennel. A beautiful plant with delicate, feathery leaves scented with aniseed. The seeds are used in curries and stews, and also extensively used in traditional Boer and Malay medicine as a digestive tonic.

Fenugreek. Fenugreek is a popular spice in Africa. You can even buy fresh fenugreek greens in many South African and Kenyan supermarkets, and they add depth of flavour to any savoury dish of Indian origin. The spice is formed of the tiny, yellow legumes, strongly flavoured with an unmistakeable ‘curry’ taste, used whole or ground.

NEW

BERKELEY HOTEL

THE HOTEL WITH ATMOSPHERE

MUSIC DAILY DURING COCKTAIL HOURS
5.15 to 7.15 p.m.

• FOR THE EXACTING CLIENTELE

IN THE HEART OF THE CITY

Cor. Bree and von Weilligh Streets
(Two minutes from Park Railway Station)
Johannesburg

Exclusive accommodation. Excellent cuisine. Hot and cold running water in all rooms. Tariff from 21/- per day, inclusive

Under the personal supervision of Mr. C. Nathan

Telephone 22-1533 (three lines)

NEW BERKELEY HOTEL

(PTY.) LTD.

Ginger. Originating from China but grown in and imported widely from India, ginger is used in Africa to add heat and flavour to a range of foods. These include stews, curries, sweet biscuits and puddings. Ginger is also an important flavouring for preserves, and flavours one of the most popular traditional soft drinks when used in ginger beer. Fresh ginger should be peeled before use and chopped finely or pounded to a paste.

Mace and nutmeg. The nutmeg tree is native to the Banda Islands in the Moluccas, in the Dutch East Indies. For nearly 200 years the Dutch East India Company held a monopoly in trade of nutmeg and mace, until the British and French smuggled plants out of the Banda Islands in around 1800, and successfully transplanted them in their own colonial possessions. Nutmeg was a familiar spice along the east African coast long before then, however. In a 1936 letter to the London periodical *East Africa and Rhodesia*, a correspondent notes that nutmeg is recorded in Kenyan Swahili wedding songs of the 1700s as one of the spices added to coffee, along with honey, cloves and *mumiani*—a magical paste said to have been made from dried human blood.

> "Chicken and curry always had this other ethnic flavour which you smelt as you passed the doors of little Indian restaurants.
>
> *Zimbabwean writer Chenjerai Hove*"

Nutmeg is the kernel of a small tropical fruit that looks a little like an apricot. Inside the fruit is a startlingly bright, scarlet covering or arillus, surrounding a small brown nut. The nut is nutmeg; the arillus is dried, turns brown and becomes the spice mace, usually bought as a powder or as semi-rigid 'blades'. You should buy nutmeg whole and grate it as needed on a fine-toothed grater. If you are able to find nuts with their husk still intact, they will last much better than shelled nuts. In African colonial cookery nutmeg is used in some stews and curries, and is an indispensable ingredient in Dutch milk puddings like melktert.

Masala. A masala is a blend of roasted, powdered spices used to flavour curries in the Indian and Malay traditions; it also refers to the spicy paste with which meats and fish are marinated and flavoured before cooking.

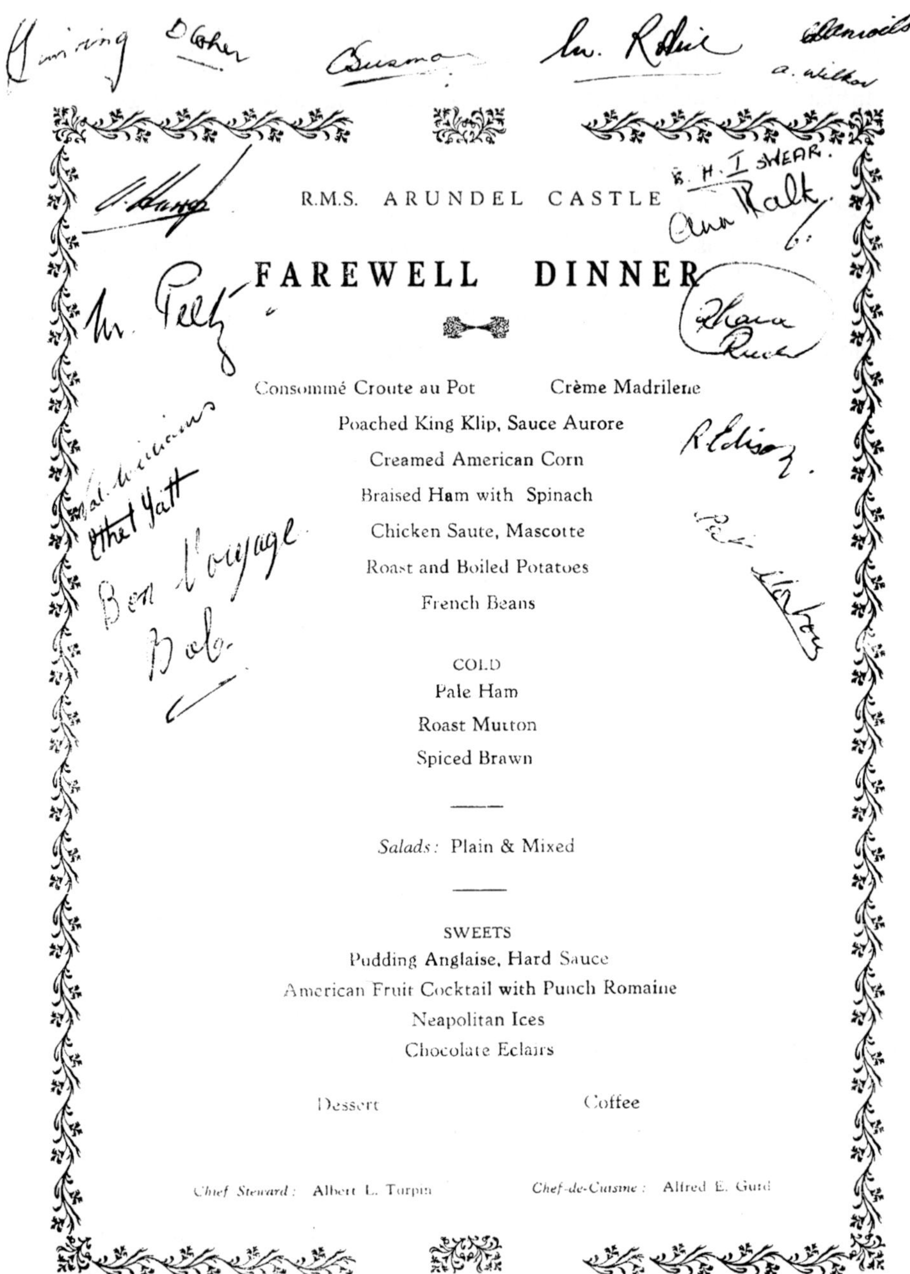

R.M.S. ARUNDEL CASTLE

FAREWELL DINNER

Consommé Croute au Pot — Crème Madrilene

Poached King Klip, Sauce Aurore

Creamed American Corn

Braised Ham with Spinach

Chicken Saute, Mascotte

Roast and Boiled Potatoes

French Beans

COLD

Pale Ham

Roast Mutton

Spiced Brawn

Salads: Plain & Mixed

SWEETS

Pudding Anglaise, Hard Sauce

American Fruit Cocktail with Punch Romaine

Neapolitan Ices

Chocolate Eclairs

Dessert — Coffee

Chief Steward: Albert L. Turpin — *Chef-de-Cuisine:* Alfred E. Gurd

TOURIST CLASS — THURSDAY, 9th JUNE, 1955

Orange flower water. This fragrant water is distilled from the blossom of orange or Seville orange trees. It used to be very popular as a flavouring in the distinctive ethnic cuisine of the Sephardic Jewish community of Zambia and Zimbabwe, and is also extensively used in Mozambican cookery to flavour jams, sweets and syrups.

Rosewater. Rosewater is distilled from rose petals, and has a strong, perfumed flavour. Try to find Indian or Lebanese rosewaters, since they have a stronger and more long-lasting flavour than the English-produced rosewaters available in supermarkets. Rosewater is used in Malay and Indian cookery to flavour drinks and sweets. It gives saboera biscuits their characteristic, floral aroma, and is also used in some old recipes for Dutch milk puddings.

Sorrel. Cape sorrel (*Oxalis pes-caprae*) grows wild in the Cape, and is related to the sorrel grown in Europe; early sailors and colonists alike followed the lead of the local Khoikhoi people in using the plant as a herb, and its high vitamin C content was useful remedy for scurvy. Sorrel is tricky to find in supermarkets, but is increasingly common in farmers' markets.

Turmeric. I once made the mistake of buying a couple of chrome yellow, dried turmeric roots and trying to grind them into powder for a curry. The root is as hard as iron, and whirled round the grinder for several minutes with barely a scratch, while I had to buy a fresh set of blades for the grinder. Ground turmeric is clearly the sensible option; just be careful with the amount of turmeric you add to recipes, since too much can leave a residual bitterness.

Worcestershire sauce. Not really a spice, but an enlivener of African settler cookery for over 100 years—the explorer George Westbeech used it to season roasted elephant's trunk in Barotseland in the 1880s. In fact, in the first English language book of Africa colonial cookery, Mrs Barnes' *Colonial Household Guide* of 1890, African settlers are described as being "fond of pickles, hotchpotch, chutney, and other such condiments".

Laura Boyle describes her shock at seeing, in the hut of a single colonial officer in Ejura in the Gold Coast in 1916, a tablecloth left on the table *all day*. The table is described as bearing a bottle of Worcestershire sauce and ashtrays bearing advertisements for brands of

Scotch whisky. The combination of the Worcestershire sauce, whisky ashtrays and tablecloth left on the table after breakfast seems to have informed Mrs Boyle's view that single male colonial officers in general lacked sensitive temperaments.

Meat, fish, game and poultry

Because of the lack of refrigeration until the recent historical era, meat and poultry in Africa were usually eaten by colonists very soon after slaughtering. Some meats could be dried and preserved in the form of biltong or tassal, or kept in a brine bath or 'pickle'. This limited the range of meat recipes; in the colonial repertoire there are large numbers of stews, casseroles, bredies and curries in which the meat is cooked slowly at a comparatively low temperature in order to soften it, and give it the tenderness that in Europe would have come from extended hanging. Indigenous cooks often either preserved meat by smoking, or used appropriate cooking techniques to tenderise freshly-slaughtered meat.

Supreme Meat Market

121 Abercorn Street : Tel. 62032

September Special Offer

ON GOOD, MIDDLE-GRADE

BEEF

BEEF MINCE per kg	55c
BEEF RIBS, per kg	60c
NECK BEEF, per kg	65c
BRISKET, per kg	65c
PORTERHOUSE, per kg	85c
TOPSIDE, per kg	90c
AITCH-BONE, per kg	90c
SILVERSIDE, per kg	90c
T-BONE, per kg	90c
TENDERISED STEAK, per kg	90c
RUMP STEAK, per kg	$1,50

Lamb, mutton and goat.

Lamb usually refers to the meat from a sheep under a year old; at its best, it is delicately-flavoured and beautifully tender: at its worst it can be bland and fatty. Mutton is the preferred meat in most of Africa; it comes from an older sheep (or, very often, from a goat) and has considerably more flavour, more fat and a tougher texture; the strong flavour means that it is the perfect foil for the intense spicing of colonial African stews. Hogget, sometimes called winter lamb, comes from a sheep between a year and two years old; it is not too fatty but has a good flavour, and is an excellent compromise.

Goat is a lean meat, rather like venison, and can often be fibrous and strongly-flavoured, while kid is tender and delicious.

Pork. Although Africa has a number of indigenous pigs—the best known probably being the warthog, whose meat actually tastes more like veal or mutton than farmed pork—pork as a meat is not greatly used in Africa, and commercial breeding across the continent is on a comparatively small scale compared with sheep or beef cattle. This is partly because of the strong Muslim influence in North and East Africa, and also because pigs are particularly susceptible to many African parasites and livestock diseases. However, the Portuguese influence in Goa and subsequently in Mozambique and Angola has led to pork remaining a popular dish in post-colonial Portuguese-speaking Africa.

Beef. In many areas of Africa, herding people moving south and east over the last two thousand years brought with them the humped, long-horned zebu, ndama and nguni cattle. These breeds are resistant to tsetse fly and were valued not only for their milk and beef, but also treated as a form of wealth. Beef remains an immensely popular and often socially prestigious meat across Africa.

Chicken. The universal meat of Africa—wherever one buys a stew or curry from a café, pavement vendor or chop-house, it is invariably chicken. Many of the recipes in this book can be cooked perfectly satisfactorily with fresh or frozen chicken pieces from the supermarket. It is evident, however, that the better the quality of the chicken, the better the resulting dish. While I would not recommend using an expensive, corn-fed chicken for a simple curry, if you treat yourself to a whole, fresh, free-range bird occasionally, this will give you and your guests a depth of flavour and texture that is a world away from the bland taste and watery texture of intensively-farmed chickens from the supermarket.

> “If we wanted to offer a foreign visitor a cooked dish from my tribe, Buganda, we would prepare chicken, fried in onions and fresh tomatoes, and smoked mushrooms, with a spoonful of curry powder served with steamed bananas or boiled rice. Side dishes included *nakati ne ntula* (bitter leaves and bitter tomatoes and aubergine) fried in onions, and fresh tomatoes, boiled sweet potatoes and boiled pumpkin.
>
> *The Right Reverend John Sentamu, Archbishop of York, remembering his childhood in Uganda*”

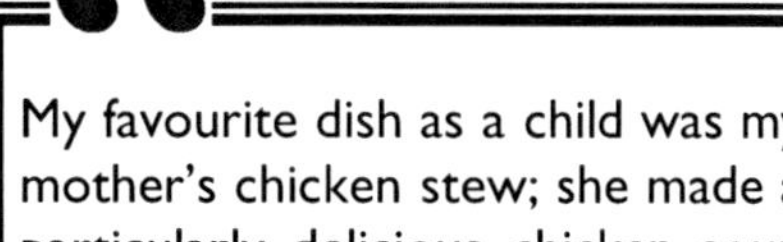

> My favourite dish as a child was my mother's chicken stew; she made a particularly delicious chicken soup which was a cure for everything!
>
> *Joel Joffe (the Lord Joffe CBE), one of Nelson Mandela's defence lawyers at the 1963-64 Rivonia Trial*

Game. Many types of game are eaten in Africa—usually antelope such as impala or kudu, and game birds like francolin, guinea fowl and pigeon. Outside Africa, recipes for buck and antelope can be used interchangeably with deer venison, while farmed rabbit, guinea fowl and pheasant are easily available from supermarkets and butchers. Early settlers were not hampered by modern views on game conservation: the early Zimbabwean pioneer Jack Carruthers wrote airily of using lion fat for frying and cooking, and described its sweetness. Older writers such as C. Louis Leipoldt give recipes for exotic meats such as giraffe, zebra (which he judged the tastiest of all game meat) and fried locusts (said to be similar to whitebait), and one or two of the more interesting recipes are adapted for use in this book for interest's sake.

In contrast to the fashion in Britain for 'high' or well-hung game during most of the nineteenth and twentieth centuries, game in colonial Africa tended to be hung for at most a day or two, and was considered unfit for cooking after three days. Meat that was required for use over a number of days was dried into biltong rather than being cooked and eaten fresh each day.

> Sadza with fried fish always came from Malawi or some far away places like Zambia or Mozambique.
>
> *Zimbabwean author Chenjerai Hove, remembering favourite dishes from his youth*

Fish. Until the production of ice in commercial quantities allowed the import of fresh fish from the coast into the towns and villages of Africa's interior, the only fish readily available was either tinned, smoked for preservation—like the famous red herring, which is still smoked in Scotland for export to West Africa—or locally-caught freshwater fish like bream, trout or barbel. The fish recipes in this book are suitable for any white ocean fish like hoki, coley, pollack and hake.

Shellfish. Africa's coastline has a wealth of shellfish—from the fat lobsters and crayfish fished on the Atlantic coast to the famous 'L.M. (Lourenço Marques) prawns' from the warm Indian Ocean waters off Mozambique. Some African shellfish can be found in British supermarkets—for example, Waitrose recently began buying its tiger prawns from a fishery in Madagascar—others, like Cape abalone, cannot, and a substitute must be sought.

Dry goods

Rice. The fashion in urban Africa is for parboiled rice, often the South African Tastic brand, which is said never to stick. I am not entirely sure why it should be so popular: if rinsed and cooked properly, rice should not stick, and parboiled rice takes longer to cook than ordinary long-grain rice. I use Indian basmati rice. It is a long-grain rice with a distinct, instantly-recognisable, nutty aroma, and can be served with everything from curry to fish-cakes. In southern Africa, rice is often served accompanied by other starchy side dishes like mashed potato or mashed butternut; similarly, it is not unusual to be offered two different potato accompaniments, perhaps fried potatoes and mashed potatoes, at the same meal.

Mielie meal. Mielie meal (ground white maize) is different from the more common Italian polenta (Italian ground maize). Mielie meal is whiter than the golden polenta and tends to be slightly more coarsely ground. If possible, use a good brand of African mielie meal such as Iwisa or Impala, both of which are widely available in specialist grocery shops. Mielie meal also makes an interesting addition to breadcrumbs when frying croquettes or fishcakes, and gives an attractive, speckled appearance to the fried food. If adding it to a bread, cake or pudding recipe it should usually be cooked beforehand, but some old recipe books fail to mention this!

> Today what I boast of and actually cook myself in the mornings is plain mielie meal.
>
> *Sylvester Stein, former editor of* Drum *magazine*

Eggs. At home, I use large, Class A, free-range hens' eggs. Some farmers' markets and department store food halls carry ostrich eggs, and farmers' markets are also very good for duck eggs (infinitely superior to hens' eggs for baking purposes, I am told).

Flour. Where flour is specified, it is ordinary plain white flour. A couple of recipes call for wholemeal flour, and I would always recommend stone-ground, wholemeal flour, which in South Africa used to be called Boer meal. Some pudding recipes use the old-fashioned technique of mixing vinegar and bicarbonate of soda as a rising agent. Use malt, white wine or cider vinegar; and you must remember that, as soon as the two have been mixed, the pudding should be baked as quickly as possible.

Nuts. These recipes predate the widespread occurrence of nut sensitivities and allergies. Some of the recipes contain nuts and common sense dictates that you cook these only for people who have told you that they do not have an allergy or sensitivity to nuts.

Equipment

The challenges that settler cooks in Africa faced will be apparent to anyone who has ever camped or even attempted the meanest barbecue on holiday. The primary difficulties lie in obtaining supplies of foodstuffs miles from the nearest trading store, and often in unfamiliar and foreign surroundings; the storage of fresh food in a hot climate; and dealing with unexpected attempts by insects and hungry animals determined to steal food.

The acquisition of familiar food itself could be tricky, even for representatives of imperial rule: in northern Nigeria before the Second World War, one colonial housewife was visited by the butcher in a remote outpost. She asked her translator to obtain from the butcher one-and-a-half pounds of veal cutlets, but neither the translator nor the butcher had ever heard of veal. Eventually she asked what meat the butcher had available, and her translator's face brightened. "Oomp," he explained. Oomp turned out to be hump. Not camel, but the fleshy bump on the shoulders of a zebu ox.

Other obstacles were storage and transport, and early travellers overcame some of the challenges by carrying dry goods whenever possible: dehydrated foods are lighter to carry, and are less susceptible to rot and decay. Two well-known African veld foods are rusks and biltong: rusks are a sort of dehydrated bread or scone, while biltong is similar to American jerky—spiced, dried beef or game meat. Both were developed by early South African settlers as a way of preserving and transporting foods.

Early buildings were almost universally constructed of mud, mud-brick or wattle and daub (known as pole and daga in southern Africa), and were far cooler than the later, corrugated iron buildings. Until corrugated iron replaced grass thatch as a roofing material, a wise settler built his kitchen standing some way from the main house. Everybody expected a kitchen to burn down occasionally, and the phlegmatic colonists tended just to shrug their shoulders and build another. One of the frequent comments made about colonial African food is that it was usually lukewarm—because it had to be carried from a kitchen located some distance away.

Sheila Macdonald left an endearing description of her kitchen in Salisbury in 1907:

> "There is a stove in it, and the fuel is wood only. Sometimes the wood is dry and burns well and brightly, more often it is quite green, and smokes and splutters in the most distressing way. As well as the stove there is a small wooden table on which reposes a large enamel basin for washing up purposes. Above the stove is a row of nails on which hang two large saucepans, one small ditto, one frying pan and a meat mincing machine, while on the floor in the corner is a breadmaking machine, the latter a most ingenious contrivance, for you turn a handle and behold your bread is kneaded...
>
> "That's absolutely all there is in my kitchen."

> "As a child I did like *tzimmes*, which was a Yiddish/Russian stew of silverside beef and veg. Also mabela meal, the chocolate-coloured 'kaffir corn' or 'guinea corn' for breakfast."
>
> *Sylvester Stein, former editor of* Drum *magazine, describing his childhood in Durban, South Africa*

The earliest settler kitchens employed clay ovens. Usually these were outside, and were made simply by knocking a hole in an abandoned ant-hill and scraping out most of the internal earthen structure, leaving a large natural oven with ventilation chimneys already constructed above it. A fire was lit in the oven and, after burning for an hour or so, the coals scraped out, the chimney blocked with grass and the residual heat used to bake bread or roast meat. The oven 'door' would be blocked with stones or plastered up with wet clay to keep in the heat; at Inyati Mission in Zimbabwe during the Matabele Rebellion in 1893, the troops laagered there horrified the missionaries by pulling up gravestones to use as oven doors.

Others used cast-iron three-legged bake-pots with a flat lid (the South African potjie, or Dutch oven), and even today bread is often made in camp by scraping the coals carefully off a fire and placing the baking pan on the newly-uncovered, hot ground; the cook then inverts a saucepan over the bread and heaps coals on the flat base. Gold miners routinely used prospecting pans to bake bread and roast meat—scraping the coals out of a fire lit in a hole, placing the bread or meat in the hole in a pan covered with a second, inverted pan, and then heaping live coals over the top.

Later arrivals enjoyed cast-iron, wood-burning Dover stoves, imported at great expense from Britain and, from 1932, made in South Africa. These solid-fuel stoves were used for everything from baking and frying to heating the irons on laundry day. From the early- to mid-20th century onwards these were gradually replaced by gas and electric stoves, but it was a slow process of change, and as late as the 1970s many households, particularly in rural areas, were producing food prepared on solid-fuel or oil-fired stoves that British cooks would have regarded as horrifyingly old-fashioned. In East Africa those settlers who had not yet scratched together the funds for a cast-iron stove typically enjoyed food cooked in old petrol cans, cut in half, with live coals heaped over and around them.

Freshness of food was a problem. In his account of a journey through southern Africa in 1905 the British scientist J. Stark Browne wrote of a picnic at Livingstone, not far from Victoria Falls in Northern Rhodesia:

> "I have already alluded to the way in which food dried up in this hot, arid country; the greatest care had to be taken when picnicking, if everything eatable was not to be spoilt. On this occasion the bread became in a few minutes like unburned toast; the butter in the dishes turned to oil and had to be put on the bread with spoons; the finest of dust peppered the jam; the cakes grew solid and hard; eating was hardly an epicurean delight, and seemed to add to our thirst.'

Until the widespread introduction of paraffin, gas and, later, electric refrigerators, meat and dairy products were kept wholesome through the use of a cool box. Until the 1930s, many urban African households relied on a zinc-lined ice-box, which relied on a large block of ice, delivered once or twice a week by the ice-man, to keep the contents cold.

Other models used the principle of the evaporation of water to keep their contents at a low temperature: when water evaporates from a surface, it takes some of the heat away from the surface, whose temperature drops. One well-known East African design was a wooden box the size of a tea chest, with pierced, zinc sides. The sides were covered with sacking or flannel flaps and a mount on the top of the box held a pierced vessel filled with water which slowly dripped onto the sacking to keep it damp. So long as the sacking was moist, the evaporation kept the food inside the box cold and fresh. An added refinement described in 1950s Nyasaland was to construct hollow sides made of chicken wire within which pieces of charcoal were solidly packed (the proximity of charcoal was believed to keep meat fresh and sweet), and over which water was ladled at intervals.

This cool box was often kept hanging by a chain from a tree, out of the reach of jackals and hyenas, or from one of the struts supporting the thatched roof of the kitchen. Often not even a cool box could keep meat fresh, and in summer it was usual to cook the Sunday joint as soon as it arrived on Saturday morning, before putting it in the meat-safe overnight and re-heating it on Sunday.

Similarly, milk was often boiled up as soon as it was delivered, to sterilise it, as still happens today in India. This meant that fresh cream was a luxury, usually available only to settlers with their own dairy cows, and evaporated or sweetened, condensed milk (and, in the twentieth century, powdered milk) was widely used as a substitute. Maizena water (a suspension of corn starch in water) or a milk substitute made by soaking oatmeal in cold water overnight was also used—the oatmeal liquor had the advantage that it could also be added to tea, coffee and cocoa as well as cakes and puddings.

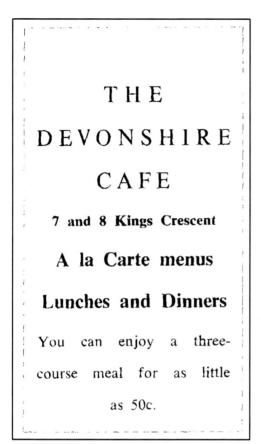

Water was boiled and then passed through an earthenware water filter holding two to four gallons of water, which resembled a large china barrel with a tap at the base. Boiled water could also be hung in a canvas water bag, which kept the contents refreshingly cool through evaporation, and these were particularly favoured by railway travellers, who dangled these bags outside the carriage windows.

All discarded containers were pressed into use in the kitchen. The ubiquitous water vessel across Africa was an old petrol can, its top cut off and a wooden handle nailed across it. Petrol tins were delivered in strong, wooden cases—two four-gallon tins to a case—and the cases, too, were recycled for use in furniture, forming anything from a dressing table to a kitchen cabinet. Cocoa tins were used for steaming cylindrical loaves of Boston Bread, studded with chunks of sweet brown dates; whisky bottles were turned into jam jars and drinking glasses by wrapping a red-hot wire around the bottle just below the shoulder and snapping off the neck. Bottles substituted as rolling pins, and glass tumblers as biscuit-cutters, while the edge of the lid of a tin of golden syrup could be rolled across a sheet of pastry instead of a pastry cutter.

With typical settler ingenuity, one Rhodesian colonist suggested using a paintbrush instead of a knife to butter bread, and another was caught filtering melted butter through a sock in order to strain out hundreds of black ants which had invaded the open tin of butter.

Keeping ants away was a constant battle, and most colonial kitchens contained dozens of saucers and bowls containing water, in which bottles, jars and plates containing foodstuffs could stand so that the ants could not reach the food. Even bedsteads stood with each foot in a rusty tin of water, often with a drop or two of paraffin or petrol floating on the water as an added barrier against insects.

Before their departure from Britain, many settlers and colonial servants stocked up by visiting the Army and Navy Store in Victoria, which started life as a co-operative society founded by a group of army and navy officers; the Civil Service Stores in the Strand; or Fortnum and Mason's famous equipment department on the fourth floor of the shop in Piccadilly. These stores offered every appurtenance of a civilised lifestyle: the 1907 Army and Navy Co-operative Society catalogue has nearly 1300 pages (beginning with Household Blend Tea and ending with Pediment Barometers) and weighs eight pounds.

Together with provision suppliers such as Lazenby's of Wigmore Street in London and MacSymon's Stores in Liverpool, which was the acknowledged expert in the export of groceries to West Africa, these companies would continue to serve their overseas customers by mail order until the decline of empire drove them to close their export departments or, in the case of the Army and Navy Stores, to abandon their co-operative foundation and their orientation towards the requirements of the colonial services, and seek new customers. Some, like the Civil Service Stores and MacSymons, were unable to survive and closed down altogether.

COLCOM:

the name for quality pork sausages

Only Rhodesia's finest pork goes into the making of Colcom Pork Sausages, the melt in the mouth mealtime treat. The only pork sausages approved by the Central Africa Standards Association, Colcom Pork Sausages are the best your money can buy. Ask for Colcom by name.

COLCOM

COLCOM FINE FOODS

Provisions

Appendix B of the 1900 *Handbook to British East Africa and Uganda* by John B. Purvis, a British clergyman and the Director of Technical Instruction in Uganda in the late nineteenth century, gave emigrants taking up a post in East Africa the following guidelines regarding provisions. The first inventory is for the 1,400km (about 900 miles) from Mombasa on the Indian Ocean coast to the Toro kingdom in Western Uganda; the second is the list of provisions needed for one man for a year at a government station. The tinned and dry goods listed would of course have been supplemented through trading with local suppliers, shooting game and growing a small amount of fruit and vegetables. The total cost of these provisions translates, at twenty-first century prices, to around £1,600.

Suggested provisions for the road from Mombasa to Toro in Western Uganda

21lbs. Huntley & Palmer's assorted traveller biscuits, in 2lb. tins
4lbs. Huntley & Palmer's Osborne (or to taste), in 2lb tins
26lbs. Moir's jam or marmalade, in 1lb. tins
6lbs. Danish butter (deduct from jam if taken in 1lb. tins)
9lbs. Lazenby's potted meats in small tins
5lbs. Demerara sugar in 2lb. tins
10lbs. tongue (Armour brand), in 2lb. tins
4lbs. sardines, in small tins (¼lb.)
4 lbs. tea (at 1s. 8d.), in 1lb. canisters
2lbs. coffee (ground Mocha), in 1lb. canisters
2 lbs. cocoa (Van Houten's), in 4lb. tins
1lb. Liebig, in 2oz. jars
2lbs. desiccated soup (Edward's), in small tins
3lbs. pea soup with mint (Symington's), in small tins
1lb. meat essence (Brand's), in small tins
4 lbs. oxtail soup in 1lb tins
6lbs. corn flour (Brown & Polson's), in ½lb. tins
2lbs. Bermuda arrowroot, in ½lb. tins
10lbs. condensed milk, in 1lb. tins
2lb. pepper
1lb. mustard

2lbs. salt (table) in a bottle
2lbs. chocolate Menier, in tin
2 pints champagne
6lbs. Ozokerit candles
1lb. curry powder (in tin)
3lbs. Primrose soap (cut in small pieces)
2lbs. marrow fat, in 1lb tins
2 bottles sauce—Worcester or other kind
4lbs. apple rings or dried pears, in 2lb. tins
Tiny bottles of essence (1oz.), lemon, vanilla, almond, clove
6 lbs. preserved potatoes
1 bottle lime juice,
1lb. dubbin, in 2 tins
3 4oz. bottles saccharine in tabloids, at Burroughs & Welcome

Provisions needed for a year at a *boma* or administrative station

60lbs. assorted biscuits, in 2lb. tins
24 lbs. jam and marmalade (Moir), in 1lb. tins
20lbs. tea, in 3lb. tins
10lbs. coffee (unground Mocha and Mysore) in 1lb. tins
6lbs. cocoa (Van Houten's), in 2lb. tins
4lbs. curry powder, in small bottles
2lbs. desiccated soup (Edward's), in 2lb. tins
1lb. Liebig, in 2oz. packets
20lbs. Ozokerit candles (some for torch, others plain)
10lbs. corn flour (Brown & Polson's), in 1lb. packets
6lbs. Bermuda arrowroot
8lbs. salt, in bottles
1lb. pepper, in ½1b. tins
2lbs. mustard, in ½1b. tins
6 lbs. Primrose soap
2 lbs. custard powder (Bird's), in small tins
1lb. blacking
1lb. Keating's bug powder, in small tins
2lbs. raisins (muscatels), in bottle
Essences, few small oz. bottles

6lbs. sardines, in ½lb. tins
6lbs. Lazenby's potted meats, in small tins
1lb. dubbin, in tins

For travellers to West Africa, Alan Field suggested in 1906 that for two weeks on the river, an officer should take the following:

One	7-lb tin ship's biscuits
Six	lbs flour
Three	tins roast beef
One	tin spiced beef
One	tin lamb and peas
Two	tins tongue
One	tin turkey
Six	tins vegetables
Four	tins sausages
Six	tins sardines
Three	tins bacon
Two	lbs sago
Two	lbs rice
Twelve	small bottles Bovril
Six	squares desiccated soup
One	pound tea
Twelve	tins 'Milkmaid' brand milk
One	tin figs
Four	tins Plasmon cocoa
One	tin cheese
Two	tins jam

Field also proposed that travellers carry with them twelve pints of dry champagne and a bottle of cognac.

xiv.

Culture and etiquette

In contrast to the experience in India, where early interaction between Indian and white people was often on an equal social basis, and where the British were quick to adopt many aspects of Indian cuisine (the first Indian restaurant in London opened in London in 1773, and today Britain has over 8,000 Indian and Bangladeshi restaurants), white settlers in British Africa were determined to maintain a set of rigid social codes that helped to underline the cultural distance between them and the African people they ruled.

Maintaining a Western-style diet rich in protein, wheat, sugar and dairy products must have been a constant struggle for settlers, who faced difficulties in growing familiar crops in unfamiliar surroundings and climatic conditions, and raising livestock—bred for centuries in Europe—in areas of Africa subject to extremes of weather and a range of newly-discovered African parasites that infested colonists' Hereford cattle, Aylesbury ducks and Gloucester Spot pigs with enthusiasm and voracity.

So why did they do it at all?

In a process of colonisation founded on the premise that white people were intrinsically superior to black people, diet and the range of cultural activities that attached to eating formed an important means of expressing settlers' ethnic and cultural identities. European identity was demonstrated not only by the clothes a settler wore or the exploitation of land he or she claimed and occupied (usually through coercion), but also through the solidarity expressed with other Europeans in the form of shared behaviour and social interaction—which often took place around the consumption of food and which in some cases (for example, the 1930s

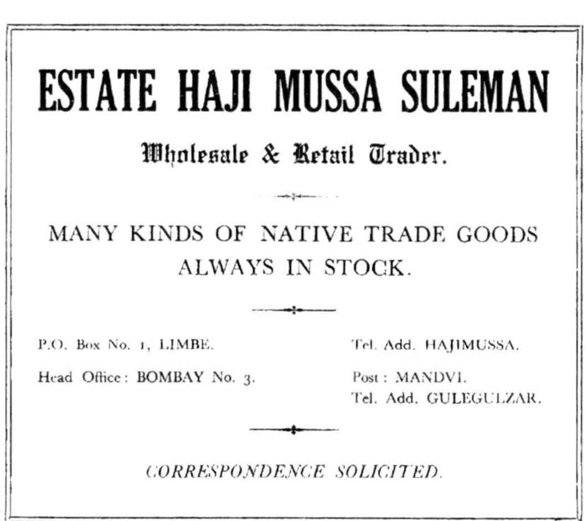
ESTATE HAJI MUSSA SULEMAN
Wholesale & Retail Trader.
MANY KINDS OF NATIVE TRADE GOODS ALWAYS IN STOCK.
P.O. Box No. 1, LIMBE.
Tel. Add. HAJIMUSSA.
Head Office: BOMBAY No. 3.
Post: MANDVI.
Tel. Add. GULEGULZAR.
CORRESPONDENCE SOLICITED.

Nigerian dinner party described later in this chapter) was ritualistic in its sense of ceremony.

For a colonist to reject this expression of community—for example, by adopting the way black people dressed or ate—was to 'go native'; to reject the values of his or her fellow Europeans and to abandon whiteness; and Victorian colonists like Percy Clark, who was one of the first white people to settle the Old Drift area near what is now Livingstone in Zambia, wrote witheringly of settlers, traders and hunters who committed such solecisms as sitting down to eat with "natives".

For many British people in Africa, the only interactions they experienced with black people took place with servants in the kitchen or the garden. Cookery books were composed in the vernacular (*The Uganda Cookery Book, Containing 142 Recipes in English and Luganda*, is an example published in Kampala in 1925), and pidgin languages like kiSettler (based on Swahili and used in Kenya and Uganda) and chiLapalapa (based on Ndebele and used in colonial-era Zimbabwe) developed as tools for communication between servants and employers.

Until comparatively recently, British settlers' social behaviour continued to obey many of the rules and strictures of an earlier age. For example, in Victorian Britain it used to be the universal custom for new arrivals to a neighbourhood to leave visiting cards at the houses of their neighbours as a sort of introduction. There were a bewildering number of social rules surrounding the leaving of cards: for example, on leaving an area, one would leave a card with one corner turned up and the initials P.P.C.—standing for *pour prendre congé* (to take one's leave)—pencilled in the opposite corner. On moving in, one's neighbours would first call between tea and dinner to leave cards, but would not take refreshment on this initial visit.

In the United Kingdom, this habit was in abeyance by 1918 and declined in popularity until it was finished off by the Second World War. In colonial communities in India and Africa, however, it remained customary right up to the outbreak of war. Margaret Trowell accompanied her husband, a Government medical officer, to East Africa in the 1930s, and remembered that as a new arrival she and her husband had to call to leave cards and sign the visitors' book when visiting a new station, no matter how remote.

As late as 1947, a new arrival in King Williams Town in the Eastern Cape of South Africa, received a late afternoon visit from two elderly neighbours; the women refused refreshment and apologised profusely for not being able to leave visiting cards. Una Hurst was astonished at these two "very kind old ladies, still clinging to past tradition that had died out in England long ago."

Major Robert Foran, the Assistant District Superintendent of the British East African Police in the early 20th century, was disciplined by his superior for not having left cards in Mombasa on his arrival there. (Foran had his revenge: he immediately sent his servant to every colonist's house and made the lady of the house sign to acknowledge receipt of his card. As a consequence he was 'cut' by Mombasa society and ostracised. Foran's response was to celebrate the money that he would save by not having to stand people drinks at the Mombasa Club—and he tipped Sefu, his servant, a hundred rupees accordingly.)

> "Full English Christmas dinner at the height of summer, warm sherry on the lawn, turkey and Christmas pud lying like lead in the tum; Dad sweltering under a Father Christmas outfit as he dispensed presents from under a cotton-wool-studded apple tree. The best bit was recovering in a hammock under the pergola, with a box of sugared almonds and a book."
>
> *Prue Leith CBE, South African-born food writer, restaurateur, and patron of the Prue Leith Chef's Academy, Restaurant and Chef's Studio in Centurion, Pretoria, South Africa.*

In Fort Jameson, in the wilds of Northern Rhodesia, on the occasion of the Governor's first visit in the early 1920s, the District Commissioner and his wife decided to share the banqueting over three nights, one after the other, to ensure that nobody from the tiny British community should be left out. This was unusual, however: usually nobody below the rank of Post Office employee attended such functions. Also in Northern Rhodesia, in 1903 a correspondent in the service of the British South Africa Company based at Mpika in Northern Rhodesia described in the *Journal of the Royal African Society* a Christmas dinner five days' journey away for which "all the Boma men were clean-shaved for the occasion, we wore dress clothes and hardly recognised ourselves, let alone each other."

In many communities black tie and formal dresses were worn for dinner as a matter of course and, as the description of the Northern Rhodesian Christmas dinner indicates, even in half-wild bachelor establishments in the bush it was often expected that men would change for dinner. Meals were often staid and formalised affairs—only 15 years ago, my elderly cousin and her husband would sit down for dinner at their pecan farm in rural kwaZulu-Natal at eight o'clock sharp, summoned by a bell rung by the maid. Their meal followed an unvarying pattern: soup, meat and two veg, and a hot pudding, even when the temperature outside was in the eighties.

Henry Stabb, who travelled through Botswana and Zimbabwe in the 1870s, discerned a similar pattern to the life of the small community of British traders carrying on business with the Tswana and Ndebele people in Shoshong and Bulawayo. Following coffee and 'a morning smoke' at daybreak, traders and their guests ate a breakfast of boiled meat with pumpkin or rice at around 9am. Lunch, at 1pm, consisted of a cup of tea and biscuits, bread and cheese or preserved meat; and dinner at sundown was usually identical to breakfast. Stabb noted the scarcity of fresh vegetables, which he ascribed to the lack of water.

In northern Nigeria in the 1930s, dinner-parties were conducted along highly formal lines. In one account, they appear to have been made bearable only by the serving of lavish amounts of alcohol, which began at eight-fifteen with whisky, and continued until the party sat down for dinner nearly two hours later. Many guests changed to pink gin as an aperitif just before dinner was ready, at which point the hostess rose and led the female guests upstairs to powder their noses—proceeding in strict order of their husbands' seniority—while the men knocked back a final drink. The women then entered the dining room in precisely the same hierarchical order, and sat at the table, waiting for the men to come in off the verandah, while consommé cooled in the soup-plates in front of them.

Check List for Successful Parties . . . !

☐ 

100% Vegetable Fat

☐ 

OIL

For Salads and Frying

☐ **NEW ERA SOAP**

For Washing

☐ 

Antiseptic Toilet Soap

☐ **Embassy Floor & Stoep Polish**

EPIC OIL MILLS LTD.

28 LOVEDAY STREET (SOUTH)

JOHANNESBURG

GUARANTEE Epic OF PURITY

Upper-class English-speaking colonial homes in Africa enjoyed vast numbers of domestic servants who (outside South Africa and the Rhodesias, where black women were trained and employed—often under the influence of mission schools—as servants from the early twentieth century onwards) were almost always men. The 1935 *Colonial Office Handbook* suggested that the number of staff required by Colonial Office employees in African colonies ranged upwards from two (a cook and 'small boy'), the minimum required in the Gold Coast. In Northern Rhodesia, the *Handbook* suggested that a married couple would need to employ six to eight staff, including a wash-boy, kitchen-boy, garden-boy and a couple of children, employed to retrieve tennis and golf balls.

> Do not flog your boys, if you can possibly avoid it, and preferably not the cook. He might poison you.
>
> *"VERB. SAP." on going to West Africa 1906*

Where staff waited at table, the custom until the Second World War was to follow the Victorian style of waiting known as 'butler service', where a servant would present a dish filled with food and the guest would help himself or herself. On the occasions when roast meat was served, the master of the house would carve the meat straight onto each guest's plate, with the servant placing the plate in front of the guest and offering vegetables and accompaniments. In Afrikaans-speaking homes service was less formal but usually defined by sex; traditionally, the women of the house would dish up individual plates of food and serve the men

> You would go out to dinner at one or the other of the neighbouring bungalows and see something vaguely familiar, like a flower painted coffee set or some etched wine glasses, and after giving the object a hard look, would remark, 'Funny! We have some just like that in our bungalow'
>
> *Joan Beech, remembering post-war dinner parties in the Gold Coast*

before serving their own meals. This is paralleled in some Muslim Malay and Indian homes where very often the men and women would eat separately, and in some traditional communities this remains customary.

(On a related note, my great-grandmother worked before the First World War as a governess-cum-schoolmistress on a farm in South Africa owned by a rural Afrikaans-speaking family. She told how the entire family, plus various illegitimate children of black farm workers fathered by the patriarch, sat down for dinner on her first evening at the farm. Following the meal, a maid brought a damp *doek* or napkin and the patriarch carefully wiped the gravy from his mouth, moustache and beard before handing the doek to his eldest son. The eldest son carefully cleaned off his moustache, beard, face and hands with the *doek* before handing it to the second son, who did the same, and my great-grandmother watched in fascination as the napkin was handed from man to man in strict order of precedence, becoming dirtier and less appealing as it circulated. Finally, after the youngest son had wiped his face, he passed the *doek* to the farmer's elderly mother, who cleaned her hands and face before passing it to the farmer's wife. The farmer's wife dabbed at her face with it and passed the limp, damp, greasy, grey rag to my great-grandmother, who took it gingerly and immediately passed it to the farmer's eldest daughter

without using it.

She was vexed to overhear one of the farmer's daughters quietly observing in Afrikaans to her sister that the new schoolteacher hadn't wiped her face, and wondering if all the dirty English had such poor personal hygiene.)

In many expatriate communities (often called bomas after the Swahili word *boma*, meaning fort) that grew up around civil service and trading outposts, it was the accepted custom for servants to lend the household china and serving dishes to one another for dinner parties. One officer's wife remembered that in Uganda guests became used to seeing their own cherished crockery appearing on a neighbour's dinner table, but she pointed out that that the wife of a senior civil servant could become ominously tight-lipped while taking a portion of vegetables from her own favourite silverware in the house of one of her husband's junior subordinates.

Visitors to Africa often comment on the hospitality extended to visitors as a matter of course. The generosity and warmth with which guests are received is a relic of the time when to deny hospitality to any traveller through Africa might have resulted in his or her death: by starvation, lack of water or attacks from wild animals. However, many settlers, far from being prosperous, lived life close to a subsistence level and, for the first years at least, at a dramatically lower level of luxury than that which they had enjoyed before arriving in their new home.

For example, 'poor whites' who entered East Africa intending settlement were transported to the government camp site outside Nairobi, where up to fifty families lived in squalor in tents, awaiting land grants from the colonial government. Farther south, the Hulley family arrived to farm in Rhodesia from the Transvaal in 1896, and forty years later Zillah Carey (née Hulley) remembered the settlers' diet of stamped maize, meat, wild honey and vegetables, while her baby sister was fed on sugared goats' milk and maizena water (made by soaking stamped maize in water).

> "The summer treat when the leaves were green was sadza with green pumpkin leaves (*mubowora*). The greens were prepared in the traditional way, with a small amount of milk cream to make the soup. Very delicious."
>
> *Zimbabwean author Chenjerai Hove*

My great-grandmother was descended from a wealthy family whose sons for generations had served in India, Ceylon and St Helena as servants of the East India Company. Her father decided instead to explore Africa, and so he, his wife and children lived in poverty in the little town of Ladysmith in Natal, where he was a sporadically successful farmer and part-time police officer.

Kind-hearted Cousin May, the wife of an Indian Army general, spent her leisure time collecting clothes from the family in England for her impecunious African relatives. At regular intervals she would ship to Ladysmith tin steamer trunks filled with garments entirely unsuitable for life on a dusty farm in sub-tropical Africa: silk dresses; top hats; taffeta ball-gowns; muffs, tippets and spats, with boxes of Floris scent and Charbonnel et Walker violet creams tucked among them. My great-grandmother's mother caused a temporary sensation in town by sweeping into church one Sunday in a Worth dress, leaving a trail of Cousin May's expensive *eau de toilette* in the air behind her; and it was a general rule in Ladysmith that if one should see on the road a Zulu woman wearing an apron sewn from crimson organza or lilac silk, she would without doubt be from the Marshall's farm.

Soups, snacks, starters and savouries

A selection of first courses and last courses—savouries were often served as the final item on a menu, and in colonial Africa the custom seems to have lasted longer than in Britain. Many of the dishes in this section make a tasty and simple light lunch: just add a handful of peppery watercress or sweet lamb's lettuce leaves.

Chilled lime and avocado soup

Mozambique

Avocados are grown throughout Mozambique, and are sold in great heaps by the side of the road when in season. This is a favourite soup; the lime and chilli helps to temper the blandness of the avocado.

2 medium-sized avocados, perfectly ripe
1 litre cold vegetable stock
The juice and grated zest of a lime
½ teaspoon peri-peri sauce or Tabasco
Salt and freshly-ground black pepper to taste

Halve the avocados, remove the stones and scoop out all of the ripe flesh. Reserve about a tablespoonful of flesh and chop it into small cubes; roll them in lime juice and set them aside. Blend the avocado flesh with the lime juice and peri-peri sauce until perfectly smooth, then add half of the vegetable stock and blend for another minute. Mix in the remaining stock, add salt and pepper to taste, and chill until served.

On serving, garnish with the reserved avocado cubes.

Sorrel soup

South Africa

When the first seafarers began to explore the Cape they were delighted to find a sorrel plant, *Oxalis pes-caprae*, growing wild. Cape sorrel is a pretty little weed, with abundant, lemon-yellow flowers and an astringent, lemony flavour very similar to the sorrel cultivated in Europe; its high vitamin C content helped to counteract scurvy and other negative effects of a sailor's diet. It is also used by indigenous people of southern Africa as a natural medicine, and makes a fine summer soup. Sorrel is uncommon in British supermarkets, but you will occasionally see it for sale in bunches at food fairs and farmers' markets.

1 litre fresh vegetable stock
1 large handful of sorrel leaves
150ml double cream
Salt and freshly-ground black pepper to taste

Rinse the sorrel leaves thoroughly. In a food processor or blender, blend the leaves with 500ml of stock. Place in a saucepan and add the remaining stock and boil for one minute. Remove from the heat and allow to cool slightly before adding the double cream. Allow to heat gently and add salt and pepper to taste.

Peanut soup

Kenya

An immensely popular soup from Kenya—a recipe even appears in the United Nation Food and Agriculture Organisation cook-book. Soups and stews using peanuts (and similar legumes like the cowpea) are common in indigenous African cooking, and it is pleasing to find a recipe that 'jumped the fence', so to speak, and also became popular with colonists. It seems likely that these stews or thick soups were made first of all with the nut from a different species: the Bambara Groundnut (*Vigna subterranea*), which—unlike the peanut, which comes from South America—is native to sub-Saharan Africa.

250g unsalted, roasted peanuts, without skins (or 250g unsalted, crunchy peanut butter)
1 large onion
1 stick celery
600ml chicken or vegetable stock
600ml milk
1 tablespoon butter
1 tablespoon plain flour
2 tablespoons single cream
Salt and freshly-ground black pepper to taste

If using whole peanuts, chop them roughly and grind to a rough paste with a pestle and mortar, rolling pin or in a food processor. Coarsely chop the onion and celery, and put in a pan with the milk.

Add the peanut butter or ground peanuts. Bring to the boil before turning the heat down low and cooking for an hour, just about simmering, but stirring regularly to ensure that the milk does not burn. Leave the mixture to cool before blending thoroughly in an electric blender or food processor. If you do not have a blender, you can rub the mixture through a wire sieve with a wooden spoon. In a large saucepan melt the butter, and then add the flour. Cook this mixture gently for a minute or so on the bottom of the pan, stirring it with a wooden spoon or wire balloon whisk, before pouring in the stock, stirring constantly. Bring to the boil, still stirring, and add the milk mixture. Allow to boil before reducing the heat; add the cream just before serving, and season to taste after adding the cream.

Ground nut soup

Nigeria

Another recipe for ground-nut soup, this time a silky, Edwardian version from West Africa.

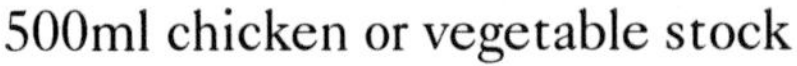

500ml chicken or vegetable stock
125g whole roasted, unsalted peanuts or 125g crunchy peanut butter
2 spring onions, finely chopped
1 tsp Worcestershire sauce
Salt and freshly-ground black pepper to taste

If using whole peanuts, chop them roughly and grind to a rough paste with a pestle and mortar, rolling pin or in a food processor. Place the peanut butter or ground peanuts in a bowl; add 150ml cold water and mix to a paste. Bring the stock to the boil, then add the peanut paste, Worcestershire sauce and chopped onions and simmer for ten minutes. Add salt and pepper to taste.

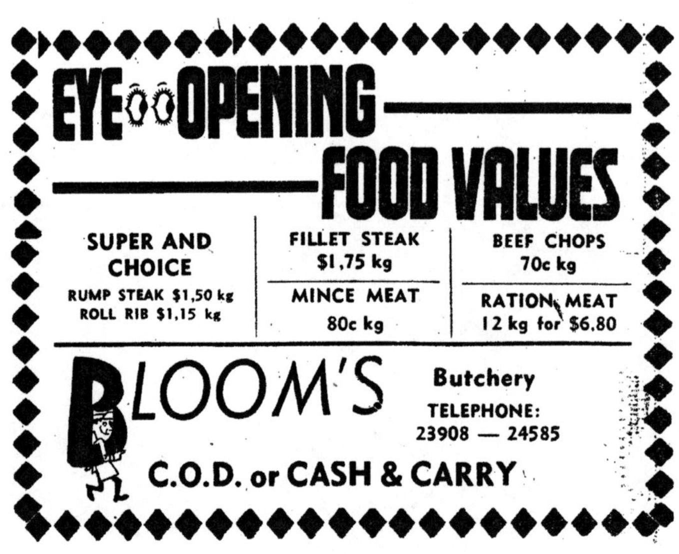

Butternut and apple soup

South Africa

Many English supermarkets stock South African butternut squashes: these are excellent quality and will happily keep for weeks in a corner of the kitchen. This recipe may be made with almost any sweet squash, such as pumpkin.

2 medium butternuts
1 medium cooking apple
2 medium onions
50g butter
1 teaspoon medium curry powder
½ teaspoon of ground nutmeg
750 ml vegetable stock
500 ml milk
Salt and freshly-ground black pepper to taste

Peel, seed and dice the butternuts. Peel, core and chop the apple. Peel the onions and chop roughly. Fry the onions until golden, using a large, heavy-bottomed saucepan. Add the curry powder and fry the mixture for a further 30 seconds, stirring continuously. Add the butternut and apple and cook for a further 2 minutes, before adding the nutmeg and cooking for another minute or so. Carefully pour in the stock, then the milk, and simmer until the butternut is soft (about 15 minutes). Leave the soup to cool slightly before puréeing or blending until smooth: if you do not have a blender or food processor you can press the soup through a sieve.

Caldo verde (green kale soup)

Mozambique

This traditional Portuguese soup is offered in just about every Mozambican restaurant in Africa. It makes a hearty, warming winter supper. You can use curly or regular kale for the soup: just make sure that it is cut as thinly as possible—a couple of millimetres wide, no more.

3 tablespoons olive oil
1 large onion
2 cloves garlic
300g Portuguese *chouriço* sausage (spicy Spanish *chorizo* makes an excellent substitute)
6 waxy potatoes
2 litres water
500g kale
Salt and freshly-ground black pepper to taste

Peel and dice the sausage and potatoes into 1cm cubes, dice the onion and finely chop the garlic. Heat the olive oil in a very large, heavy-bottomed pan, and cook the onions on gentle heat until soft but not brown. Add the garlic and sausage and cook for a further four minutes. Add the potatoes and cook for a further minute, then pour in the water and bring to the boil, before turning down the heat and simmering the soup for ten minutes. In the meantime, thoroughly wash the kale to remove every trace of grit, and cut the leaves into very narrow strips, or juliennes, the width of a matchstick, discarding the tough leaf stems. Add them to the soup and bring again to the boil, before turning down the heat and simmering for a further ten minutes before serving.

Mulligatawny soup

South Africa

This recipe helps to demonstrate the Cape's long connection to India through the East India Company, which established and maintained trade routes between London and India via Ceylon, Mauritius, St Helena and the Cape of Good Hope. The name mulligatawny is a corruption of the Tamil description *milagu tani*, or 'pepper water'. This version is based on one of Hildagonda Duckitt's foolproof recipes from her 1891 work *Traditional South African Cookery.*

1 chicken, weighing about 1kg
3 litres water
1 tablespoon medium curry paste
2 teaspoons medium curry powder
2 medium onions
1 tablespoon butter
1 tablespoon soft brown sugar
30g fresh or block tamarind or 1 tablespoon prepared tamarind paste
1 teaspoon salt
1 tablespoon mango or apricot chutney

'Cut the fowl into small pieces, as for chicken curry. If an old one, let it boil gently for four or five hours, with two or three quarts [about 3 litres] of water. If you have a neck of mutton, or any other meat that will make some stock, you may add a little to this. The next day remove the fat and strain the soup, putting back any nice pieces of fowl. A few slices of ham may also be added to make a good stock. Brown the onions, mix all the ingredients, add to the soup, and let it boil for a couple of hours.'

There is little to add to Mrs Duckitt's admirably clear instructions except that, if using fresh tamarind, you will need to soak the paste in a cup full of boiling water for ten minutes, stir thoroughly and then pass the liquid through a sieve to get rid of the seeds and fibres. Also, after browning the onions, mix in the ingredients in the pan and allow to cook for a minute in order to avoid the 'raw' taste of uncooked curry spices.

Orange and tomato soup

Zimbabwe

It seems a shame not to use fresh tomatoes for this soup, especially in summer, although at a pinch tinned Italian tomatoes will make a reasonable substitution. This summery soup always makes me think of the orange groves around the Mazowe Valley in northern Zimbabwe and the startling, intense perfume that suffuses the air for miles around when the orange trees are flowering.

1 large onion, roughly chopped
30g butter
1 clove of garlic, crushed
1 litre vegetable stock
1.5kg fresh tomatoes (or two tins of tinned tomatoes)
1 teaspoon chopped oregano or thyme
A bay leaf
Salt and freshly-ground black pepper to taste
1 large orange

In a saucepan lightly fry the onion and garlic in butter until golden, then carefully add half the vegetable stock. Skin and de-seed the tomatoes, then chop them roughly and add to the stock and onions, and simmer for half an hour. Remove from heat, fish out the bay leaf, and leave the soup to cool before purééing or blending until smooth: if you do not have a blender or food processor you can press the soup through a sieve. Use a sieve to remove the zest from the orange (scrub the rind well with hot water beforehand to remove any wax on the skin) and then juice the orange. Add zest and

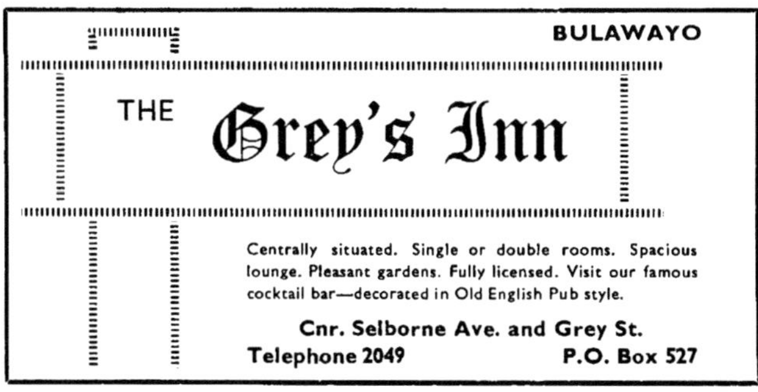

juice to the soup, and then top up with the remaining stock before reheating the soup.

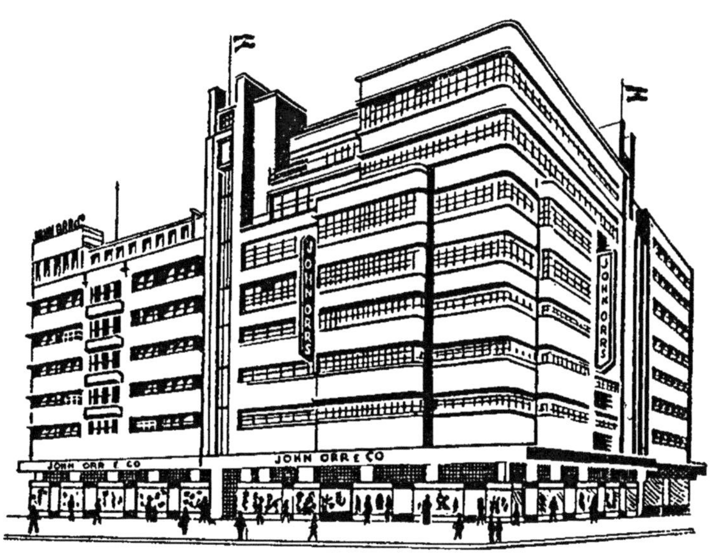

The JOHN ORR Store in Johannesburg

One of a chain established in some of the principal cities in South Africa that has developed from the parent store founded in Kimberley a few years after the discovery of diamonds there in the seventies of last century.

Very conscious of its reputation built up through upwards of 70 years it holds firmly to its policy of selling only goods of dependable quality and giving complete satisfaction to customers through its friendly, well-trained personnel.

As a retail organisation the name JOHN ORR is held in high regard by thousands of shoppers in every centre where it operates. The Johannesburg Store provides comprehensive ranges of merchandise from all parts of the world to meet the requirements of those needing stylish apparel and things of beauty to adorn the home.

Situated in the central shopping area, bounded by Pritchard, von Brandis and Kerk Streets customers find the Management and staff never failing in their efforts to provide the utmost in shopping service.

Visitors are cordially invited to make a leisurely inspection of this up-to-date store.

JOHN ORR & CO
JOHANNESBURG

Green mielie soup

South Africa

This recipe is based on C. Louis Leipoldt's; it can be made with fresh corn-on-the cob, but it really is better made with proper, fresh mielies, which can be bought in some African and Caribbean shops and markets.

Four mielie cobs
1 litre cold water
500ml white wine
500ml vegetable stock
A bouquet garni
½ teaspoon ground nutmeg
1 teaspoon soft brown sugar
Salt and freshly-ground black pepper to taste

Mix together the water and wine and add the nutmeg, pepper and bouquet garni; bring the mixture to the boil in a saucepan. Cut the mielies from the cobs and add them to the pan, boiling them for 20 minutes or until tender. Remove the bouquet garni; liquidise the contents of the pan, add the vegetable stock and add salt to taste, and cook for a further 10 minutes. Stir in the sugar just before serving.

Sugar Bean Soup

South Africa

Sugar beans are small, white haricot beans grown across southern Africa. Ordinary white haricot beans are fine for this traditional Cape dish, which has its parallel in the Zulu bean stew *mbaqanga*.

250g dry white haricot beans
500g of the cheapest lamb or winter lamb (mutton) that you can find—shank or neck will be perfect
2 litre water
4 grated carrots
1 grated onion
1 large tomato, peeled and chopped
3 whole allspice
1 bay leaf
Salt and freshly-ground black pepper to taste

Rinse the beans under the tap in a colander and turn out into a bowl. Cover with cold water and leave to soak for at least three hours—preferably overnight. When soaked, drain the beans and place them in a large saucepan with the meat and 2 litres of water. Bring to the boil and then turn down the heat and simmer for 45 minutes. Add the remaining ingredients and simmer for a further 30 minutes. You will need to top up the liquid as it evaporates.

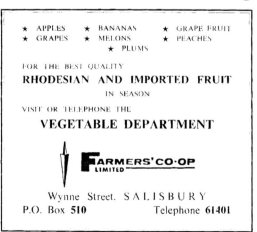

Kebobs

South Africa

A very traditional Cape Muslim dish, kebobs are a sort of spiced Scotch egg. They make great picnic or party food, or a tasty snack for supper, served with a green salad.

6 hard-boiled eggs, chilled in the fridge

Coating

500g minced beef
20g melted butter
1 clove garlic
1 teaspoon green chilli
1 teaspoon freshly-ground black pepper
½ teaspoon ground nutmeg
1 teaspoon ground cumin
½ teaspoon salt
1 onion, grated
1 beaten egg
Oil for deep-frying

To hard-boil the eggs, place them in a pan of cold water, bring them to a gentle boil, and cook for a total of 12 minutes from the time you first switched the heat on. After 12 minutes run cold water into the pan and leave the eggs to cool before refrigerating them.

Crush the garlic, seed and finely chop the green chilli, then mix together all the ingredients for the meat coating. Take the eggs and carefully fold a little of the meat mixture around them, making sure that the egg is totally covered. When all the eggs are coated, either deep fry the kebobs for five minutes, or you can shallow-fry them, turning them constantly, for about eight to ten minutes or until thoroughly browned. Traditionally, when kebobs are shallow-fried the cook will add two or three bay leaves to the oil to flavour it.

For a Satisfying Lunch

try the Nairobi and Nakuru Station restaurants. Table d'hote and a la carte menus. Fully licensed. Easy parking, friendly atmosphere. Open daily including Sundays.

NAIROBI 7 a.m. - 8 p.m.
NAKURU 9.30 a.m. - 10 p.m.

Pasteis de bacalhau

Mozambique

You see these golden salt cod fritters on sale all over Mozambique and Angola, and every Portuguese bakery in Johannesburg offers its own version. You can find salt cod in many African and Caribbean food stores: choose the fattest, whitest piece you can find.

450g dry salt cod
225g floury potatoes
2 eggs
1 onion
2 cloves garlic
1 handful parsley
1 handful chives
Freshly-ground black pepper to taste

Cover the salt cod with cold water and soak for 12 hours. Change the water at regular intervals to get rid of the excess salt. Drain and pat dry, then poach in boiling water for six minutes. Drain the fish, remove the skin, and flake the flesh into pieces; remove any remaining bones. Peel the potatoes and boil until well done, then drain and leave to cool. When cool, push the potatoes through a sieve or mouli into a large mixing bowl. Very finely chop the garlic and onion, and add to the flaked fish; then break up the fish and onion, grinding them together to a rough paste in a food processor or food mill, or even using a large pestle and mortar—if you have the patience and the muscle power. Add to the potatoes in the mixing bowl.

Chop the chives and parsley and add to the fish and potato mixture, and roughly mix all together with a wooden spoon. Then add the beaten eggs and a good seasoning of black pepper, and mix the whole combination together with your hands until it forms a fairly stiff paste. Form the paste into balls the size of a gold ball and deep fry them in hot oil until deep golden in colour. You can serve these hot or cold: they keep well in the fridge, and are excellent for picnics.

Indian toast

Kenya

Toasts used to be very popular in colonial Africa: 'first toasts', which were canapés, and 'second toasts', which were 'savouries'—the last hot course, served before cheese and fruit at a formal dinner in the British tradition. The savoury was a small, protein-rich, highly-seasoned dish, one final opportunity for the cook to show his or her competence, and it is a shame that one simply does not see savouries on most menus any more. You will find that many of these traditional savouries make great dishes for a light supper: just add salad and perhaps some warm bread.

This is a spiced, scrambled egg recipe, adapted from the original which almost certainly came to Kenya from India with the officers and civil servants who retired there.

Four slices of fresh, hot toast
30g unsalted butter
3 eggs
1 teaspoon curry powder
1 teaspoon mango chutney
3 chopped anchovies
1 tablespoon fresh breadcrumbs
1 tablespoon finely chopped spring onion or chives
Paprika for garnishing
Salt and freshly-ground black pepper to taste

Melt the butter on a low heat in a small saucepan. Add the beaten eggs and breadcrumbs, and stir constantly until the eggs begin to thicken. Add the curry powder, onion, chutney and anchovies and keep stirring until the eggs thicken a little more and all the ingredients are mixed; however, cooking until the egg becomes solid will spoil the dish. Halve the toast slices and divide them between two plates, and heap the egg mixture on the toast. Dust with paprika.

Boiled ostrich egg

South Africa

Ostrich eggs typically contain the equivalent mass of about 20-24 hens' eggs. They are much more watery, however, and for this reason many cooks advise leaving the yolk and white to stand overnight to settle so that some of the excess liquid can be poured off before cooking. One unusual use for ostrich eggs in Kenya and South Africa was as an ingredient in farm soap; when mixed with fat and caustic soda (extracted from wood ash), they were said to make a soft, gentle soap that was ideal for shampooing.

1 ostrich egg

Place the ostrich egg in a large pan and cover with cold water. Bring to the boil and, once boiling, cook for 1¼ hours, topping up the water if necessary. At the end of cooking, cover the egg with cold water and leave to cool. Remove the egg-shell and cut into slices; serve with salt and pepper and tartare sauce.

Hot smoked salmon on toast

Kenya

This is perfect for using up the odds and ends of smoked salmon that fishmongers and supermarkets sell off labelled 'trimmings'. Often the pieces need checking over to make sure that there are no bones or indigestible skin attached.

1 cup of smoked salmon trimmings, roughly chopped
4 slices fresh, hot, toast
30g unsalted butter
2 spring onions
1 teaspoon Worcestershire sauce
Squeeze of lemon juice
Freshly-ground black pepper

Halve the toast slices and divide them between two plates. Melt the butter in the saucepan on a medium heat. Finely chop the spring onions, green part included, and add to the melted butter. Add the chopped, smoked salmon and stir until the fish is heated through and has begun to lose its translucent appearance. Add the Worcestershire sauce, lemon juice and a generous helping of black pepper to taste, and pile on top of the toast.

Kedgeree

Kenya

Kedgeree was a breakfast favourite and is one of the many recipes illustrating the links between British Africa and British India. Based on the Indian dish *kitchri* (spiced rice cooked with pulses) Raj cooks added fish, and the Anglicised dish was transported to the Cape and Kenya. Kedgeree makes a great, quick family supper dish.

4 hard-boiled eggs, chopped
200g flaked, cooked, lightly smoked haddock (this can be poached or even microwaved until cooked through)
175g uncooked, long-grain white rice
500ml water
125ml single cream
½ teaspoon mild curry powder
½ teaspoon salt, or to taste
1 tablespoon chopped fresh parsley for garnish

Cook the rice in 500ml water until cooked and tender. Drain, and add all the remaining ingredients except the parsley. Lightly mix all the ingredients together, and return to a low heat, gently stirring occasionally until the dish is piping hot. Sprinkle with parsley and serve.

Ostrich egg cheese omelette

South Africa

Approximately 55ml of ostrich egg is equivalent to a normal hen's egg. The quantities below will make the equivalent of one 3-egg omelette, and you will usually be able to achieve at least five of these omelettes from a normal ostrich egg. Cheese omelettes are a good way to use an ostrich egg: the texture and flavour of the egg both benefit from being cooked with a strong, hard cheese such as Cheddar. Do not add salt until just before serving, or the egg will become very tough.

1 ostrich egg
2 tablespoons single cream
1 tablespoon chopped chives
Salt and freshly-ground black pepper to taste
1 tablespoon butter
30g mature Cheddar cheese per omelette

Make a small hole in both ends of the egg-shell and shake the contents into a bowl or jar. Allow to stand overnight in the refrigerator, and before cooking, pour off the top couple of inches of clear, watery liquid which will have risen to the top.

Beat the egg thoroughly with the chives, cream and seasoning. Heat a pan until very hot, then add the butter. When melted and sizzling, pour in 175ml of the egg mixture, and tilt the pan to cover all the base of the pan. Sprinkle the cheese over the egg mixture and draw the edges toward the centre of the pan exactly as for an ordinary omelette, but do not overcook—leave the centre creamy and slightly liquid with melted cheese. Sprinkle a pinch of salt or to taste over the omelette immediately before serving (do not add salt to the raw egg, otherwise the omelette becomes tough).

Scotch woodcock

Kenya

There are dozens of recipes for Scotch Woodcock, all based on a Victorian original, and sharing the same simple mixture of scrambled egg and anchovy; the creamy, scrambled egg benefiting from the sudden, contrasting and concentrated hit of flavour that comes from the anchovy.

Two slices hot buttered toast
1 teaspoon unsalted butter
2 tablespoons double cream
2 eggs
4 anchovy fillets
Cayenne pepper

Mash the anchovy fillets on a plate with a fork until semi-pureed—do see if you can find the fillets that are flavoured with garlic and herbs, since they add an interesting depth of taste to the dish. Add a couple of drops of the oil in which the anchovies are packed if the fish seems too dry to break down easily. Spread the anchovy puree over the toast slices. Put the butter in a pan over a low heat and add the beaten eggs and cream. Stir gently with a balloon whisk until the mixture thickens and the eggs begin to scramble—do not on any account let them become dry, they should be hot through but still wobbly and semi-liquid. Pour the eggs over the toast and dust with cayenne pepper.

Scotch toast

Kenya

Smoked haddock is one of the most satisfying fish around: comparatively inexpensive and easy to cook, with obvious bones and a rich flavour that goes well with eggs, curry and cheese.

4 slices hot toast
500g smoked haddock fillet
30g butter
½ teaspoon curry powder
Juice of ½ lemon

Cook the haddock fillet—you can either microwave it for 5 minutes on full power and leave to stand for two minutes, or poach it in simmering, salted water for 8-10 minutes. Flake the flesh and remove the bones. Add the rest of the ingredients and stir well to mix. Spread the mixture on toast and flash under a hot grill until the surface is just coloured. This mixture can also be used to fill an omelette or served as a garnish on scrambled eggs.

Chopped or *gehackte* herring

South Africa

The use of Marie biscuits—semi-sweet, plain biscuits—in chopped herring is typical of South African Jewish cuisine. You can substitute kitke crumbs (South African Jews tend to use the Lithuanian term *kitke* for challah—semi-sweet, plaited bread).

6 rollmop herring fillets
5 hard-boiled eggs
1 small onion
2 green apples—Golden Delicious or similar
1 teaspoon lemon juice
10 Marie biscuits
60g sugar
50ml cider vinegar
1 teaspoon freshly ground black pepper
¼ teaspoon ground nutmeg
2 teaspoons finely chopped parsley

Rinse the herrings and pat them dry. Remove any remaining skin and pull out all visible bones before finely chopping the flesh. Place the herring in a mixing bowl. Peel, core and grate the apples, and toss in a teaspoon of lemon juice to prevent the apple from turning brown; finely grate the onion and squeeze out the juice; crush the Marie biscuits with a rolling pin; coarsely grate three of the eggs, then add apple, onion, Marie biscuits, egg, parsley, pepper and nutmeg to the fish, and stir with a wooden spoon to mix. Add vinegar and sugar to taste, and, once flavoured to the satisfaction of your palate, turn out onto a flat dish and mould into a circular shape. Finally, grate the remaining two hard-boiled eggs over the top of the chopped herring.

Beef biltong

South Africa

There is probably no other South African food which possesses for settlers and expatriates alike quite the same emotional power as biltong. This is partly due to the difficulty of obtaining it outside South Africa: most countries have regulations which make it difficult or impossible to import uncooked, dried meat—which is all that biltong is. There is a story of the Boer War soldier and politician Deneys Reitz, who served in the British Army during the First World War. While in the trenches, Reitz received a parcel of biltong from home. He kept cutting off strips of meat and chewing away until he overheard a British officer remarking sourly, 'What a hog that man is for tobacco.'

'Biltong' means 'buttock-tongue', and literally signifies the strip or tongue of meat that is carved from the back or thigh of the ox. Traditionally, beef biltong is spiced with coriander, pepper and fennel seed. You can enjoy it cut into small slices—which is the type of dried beef usually known as tassal. Another way to try it is to whiz a couple of small pieces in a food processor until they are reduced to a powder, and then add the powder to butter and spread it on fresh bread.

Very few countries have a modern tradition of making some sort of biltong, jerky or tassal, but there are a number of manufacturers in the United Kingdom, United States and Australia making biltong for commercial sale, and any number making it for home consumption, particularly since an enterprising South African started to sell home drying kits worldwide.

H. G. Issels wrote a humorous booklet about his trek through Matabeleland in 1894, and of the Boer squatters living on the Transvaal side of the Limpopo River, awaiting the opportunity to enter Rhodesia. He spoke to a couple who made a living by shooting game and selling the meat, hides and horns. The meat was turned into biltong, and Issels commented on the sticks of biltong hanging from the fowl roosts, covered in chicken droppings. 'Yes,' said the husband, 'that is correct, but once a year, before we go to Pretoria, we give it a good wash in the river.'

A strip of beef from the inner back or thigh, measuring 50cm long and about 15cm across.
15g salt
50ml malt vinegar

Curing mixture

250g salt
250g soft brown sugar
50g peppercorns
50g coriander seeds
20g fennel seeds

Trim off any remaining tendon, but leave some of the fat, and try to trim the beef into a rough oval in profile. Coarsely crush the spices and add to the salt and sugar, and place the mixture in an airtight container. Moisten the meat all over with vinegar, then take 15g salt and rub it well into the surface of the meat, covering the entire surface. Leave for one hour, then rub in a handful of the spiced mixture, and hang the meat vertically in a draught where flies and animals cannot get at it, and where it is out of direct sunlight. Rub the meat with a fresh handful of the spiced mixture every day for seven days. After seven days the outside should be quite tough and hard: the biltong can then be hung up somewhere cool and dry, out of the reach of flies and animals, to finish drying.

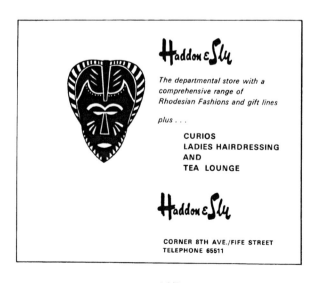

Tassal

South Africa

This is the old-fashioned, impromptu fashion of curing meat—also known as the camp method. You will find that it gives a much tougher and chewier product than biltong, and is probably an older recipe; the name comes from the Portuguese word *tassalho*, which means dried or preserved meat. Hildagonda Duckitt's recipe for tassal states simply:

Take any meat, beef, venison, springbok etc. Cut the meat in long strips about three inches thick, sprinkle slightly with salt, pepper, a little coriander seed (bruised) and vinegar; leave for a day, then hang to dry; if wanted, just soak a little and grill on the coals.

Pickled fish

South Africa

Judging by its spicing, this much-loved Cape dish probably originated in Java or Indonesia; there is a similar recipe still in use in Sri Lanka, probably brought there by the Dutch. The preservative qualities of the vinegar, sugar and salt mean that the fish will remain perfectly wholesome for a week or more—in fact, you must leave it for at least 24 hours before eating in any case, to allow the flavours to diffuse through the layers. In the old days, every house had a cool larder in which to leave dishes like this.

Nowadays, when houses are kept at a warmer temperature all year round, it is best to refrigerate the fish after preparing it. The recipe calls for four tablespoons of curry powder or curry paste—about a quarter of a cup—which at first sight appears unpalatable. However, if you make sure that you use a mild curry powder the amount should be fine: it also plays an important part in thickening the pickle.

1.5kg firm white fish
½ tablespoon salt
3 onions
1 clove garlic, crushed
1 lemon or lime leaf
1 bay leaf
1 coarsely chopped, mild red chilli
4 tablespoons mild curry powder or mild curry paste
1 teaspoon turmeric
1 tablespoon soft brown sugar
10 peppercorns
5 allspice
A 2.5cm piece of root ginger
0.75 litre approx white wine vinegar or malt vinegar
2 tablespoons vegetable oil

Wash the fish and cut into slices about 2.5cm thick and shallow-fry until cooked. You will probably need to undertake this in batches. Do not dust with flour or breadcrumbs before cooking. Sprinkle the cooked pieces with salt and leave on one side. In the meantime, slice the onions thinly into rings and gently fry in the bottom of a large saucepan until translucent and just starting to brown.

Add all the other ingredients except the vinegar and fry for thirty seconds. Then pour in about 0.5 litre vinegar and bring to the boil before turning down the heat and boiling gently for a further five minutes: this is your pickle solution.

In a dish or casserole arrange layers of the fish, interspersed with layers of the spiced onion pickle. When the dish is full you should still have some pickle left over. Top it up with the remaining vinegar and boil for five minutes, and then pour, hot, over the fish. Leave to cool and, once cold, cover securely and leave in the refrigerator for 24 hours before eating. Pickled fish is traditionally served with bread and butter. I tend to use filleted fish for pickled fish, but in fact it is traditionally made unfilleted—you will find that the vinegar dissolves the small bones and softens the large ones.

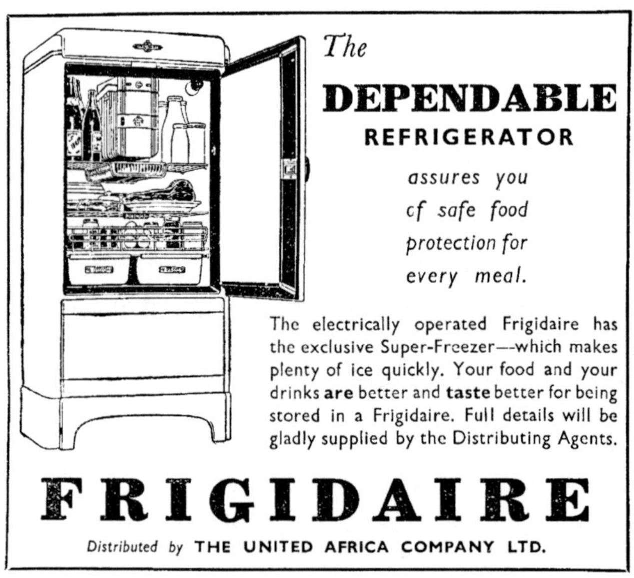

Bulawayo savoury

Zimbabwe

This comes from Zimbabwe's first cookery book: the *Bulawayo Cookery Book and Household Guide*, compiled by Mrs N. H. Chataway in 1909 in aid of the building fund for the new English church in Bulawayo. The recipe was contributed by Mrs Chataway herself, and makes a delightful canapé (further north, in Malawi, canapés were known by settlers as Patsy-go-lows, from the chiNyanja expression *patsokolo*, meaning 'before'.)

3 slices of fresh white bread
2 teaspoons soft butter
The white of a fresh egg
2 teaspoons lemon juice
2 tablespoons whipping cream
Pinch of salt
2 tablespoons finely diced, cooked meat: chicken or ham, or try chorizo sausage
3 green and 3 black stoned olives
Ground paprika

Finely chop or mince the olives. Whip the egg white with a pinch of salt until it forms stiff peaks. Whip the cream until it forms soft peaks, then fold together the egg white and cream, and fold in the lemon juice—this is called a white mayonnaise by Mrs Chataway. Lightly butter the slices of bread and spread them with the white mayonnaise, then, using a biscuit-cutter, carefully cut out rounds of approximately 4cm diameter. Cover each round with the diced meat and sprinkle with the minced olives, then garnish with paprika.

Main courses

A range of hot dishes suitable for everything from an informal family lunch to a formal dinner.

Aubergine casserole with cheese

Zimbabwe

This aubergine dish is a family favourite from 1960s Rhodesia, but the combination of Mediterranean flavours is typical of Italy or the South of France. I serve it in winter with mashed potatoes—a very southern African combination!

Mediterranean emigrants made up an important minority of the white population of the Federation of Rhodesia and Nyasaland. One of their most striking memorials in Zimbabwe is St Barbara's Church at Kariba, on the border between Zimbabwe and Zambia. This little open-air church was built by Italian workmen employed on the vast Kariba Dam project in the 1950s, and is dedicated to the memory of the men who died during the construction project.

Aubergines are called by their Indian name, brinjals, in southern Africa, and grow readily throughout the continent. African shops and markets are as likely to offer white or speckled brinjals as purple, but with British supermarkets' mania for consistency of appearance it seems unlikely you will see white brinjals unless you grow them or search out different varieties in farmers' markets and ethnic food shops. Whatever sort of brinjal you choose, you will find that this is an interesting way to use them, and makes a substantial, hearty, vegetarian dish. Try serving it with rice, or with herbed mashed potatoes, drizzled with basil or truffle oil.

3 large aubergines or brinjals
1 tin chopped, peeled tomatoes
½ teaspoon mustard powder
25g butter
450g soft cream cheese
100g freshly-grated Parmesan cheese
A handful of fresh thyme
250ml vegetable stock
Salt and freshly-ground black pepper to taste
One handful fresh breadcrumbs
Olive oil for frying

Preheat your oven to 190°C. Wash the aubergines, remove the stalks and cut into inch-thick rounds. (The traditional way to remove the bitter juice is to sprinkle them with salt and leave them on a dish for an hour—this drains much of the juice from the flesh of the aubergines. However, with mild, supermarket aubergines this procedure is unnecessary.) Thoroughly rinse the aubergines and wipe them dry with a clean cloth or kitchen towel.

Fry the slices of aubergine until lightly browned on each side—about 4 minutes or so. Mix together the finely-chopped thyme with the cream cheese and the Parmesan cheese: you should use freshly-grated Parmesan cheese for this dish, not the powder that comes in a cardboard tub. Butter a casserole dish, and arrange a layer of aubergine slices in the bottom of the dish, then spread a layer of cream cheese mixture over the aubergines. Repeat until all the aubergines and cheese are used, making sure that you finish with a layer of aubergines. Mix the tomatoes with the vegetable stock and mustard powder, and season with plenty of freshly-ground black pepper and salt. Pour carefully into the casserole over the layers of aubergine and cheese, and sprinkle the breadcrumbs over the top. Bake at 190°C for 30 minutes.

Fish frikkadels

South Africa

Frikkadels are like spiced rissoles, and are a favourite Cape dish. This takes a couple of minutes to make in a food processor, and a quick and economical version of this dish can be made with 500g of tinned tuna.

2 slices stale white bread, crusts removed
1 cup water
500g cooked firm white fish, flaked
1 garlic clove, crushed
1 onion, grated
1 firm, ripe tomato, skinned and grated or finely chopped
1 egg
1 teaspoon salt
½ teaspoon freshly-ground black pepper
½ teaspoon ground nutmeg
1 tablespoon fresh chopped parsley
400ml sunflower oil

Soak bread in a cup of water for 5 minutes, then squeeze out all the moisture. Add with all remaining ingredients, except oil, to the minced fish, and mix well. Form the mixture into walnut-sized patties and shallow-fry in medium-hot oil for about five minutes on each side, or until lightly browned. Serve hot with rice, blatjang and tomato salad.

Zambezi fish bobotie

Zimbabwe

Apart from prawns and sea fish air-freighted at vast expense from the Cape or Mozambique, the most common fresh fish consumed in colonial Rhodesia was freshwater bream, fished in large quantities from the Zambezi River and Lake Kariba, as well as from numerous smaller lakes and dams. Bobotie is a traditional meat dish from the Cape in South Africa, in which savoury custard is poured over curried meat. This fish version is said to have been popularised in the late nineteenth century by Mr Cronjé, who owned the Alphen wine estate in the Cape.

Freshwater bream is not by any means a taste sensation; it has a coarse, dry flesh, so you will find that cooking it in this way keeps it moist and lends it flavour. Any cheap sea or freshwater fish is ideal for this dish.

1kg cooked white fish fillet
1 thick slice of white bread
2 medium eggs
2 teaspoons brown sugar
2 medium onions
1 cup of milk
2 tablespoons medium curry powder
2 tablespoons cider or white wine vinegar
Olive oil for frying
Salt and freshly-ground black pepper to taste
6 fresh lime or bay leaves (optional)

Preheat your oven to 180°C. Flake the fish, breaking it up and removing any remaining bones. Cut the crust off the bread, soak it in the milk and squeeze dry; reserve the milk. Fry the chopped onions in a little oil until golden; add the curry powder and cook for a further 30 seconds, then pour in the vinegar, sugar, add a couple of pinches of salt and some black pepper, and allow the mixture to boil for a minute.

Remove from the heat and add the flaked fish and bread, and stir thoroughly. Stir in one of the eggs, lightly beaten, and turn the mixture out into a buttered baking dish, smoothing the top level with a palette knife or spatula. Beat the remaining egg and milk together, and season with salt and pepper before pouring over the fish mixture.

Traditionally, Cape cooks decorate bobotie with rolled lemon leaves; for a similar effect, you can roll up fresh lime or bay leaves into cylindrical 'cigars', and poke them into the mixture so that a little of the leaf roll protrudes above the surface of the egg custard. Set the baking dish on a baking sheet or shallow pan, and fill the pan with cold water to the depth of about an inch up the sides of the dish (this will stop the custard from curdling), and bake at 180°C for about 50 minutes, or until the egg custard is set and golden. Serve with rice.

Lobster Thermidor

South Africa

This lobster dish from the French classical repertoire may seem like an odd choice to find in a book on African colonial cookery; however, it was the signature dish of the old Thrupps restaurant in Pritchard Street in central Johannesburg, and is remembered with affection by many Joburgers. The highly-flavoured sauce makes this an excellent way to use cooked supermarket lobster, which is sometimes lacking in flavour. When you feel in need of some tender, loving care, this is perfect for a romantic dinner for two.

1 cold cooked lobster
1 tablespoon butter
1 tablespoon plain flour
60ml warm milk
1 teaspoon mustard powder
1 bay leaf
A pinch of salt
A pinch of chilli powder or dash of Tabasco sauce
75g chopped button mushrooms, lightly fried in a little butter until cooked
1 tablespoon grated fresh Parmesan cheese

Slice the lobster in two lengthways using a heavy knife or sharp chopper. Remove the lobster meat from the body, tail and claws and chop into pea-sized pieces. Scrape the remaining deposits from the inside of the lobster half-shells and clean under running water; dry them, wrap in cling film and store in the refrigerator (these will form the serving dishes for the lobster).

Make a roux by stirring together the butter and flour over a medium heat until the butter sizzles and forms a paste, then remove the pan from the heat and gradually whisk in the warm milk, stirring constantly to break up the lumps. Add the bay leaf and return to the heat, stirring constantly, and cook gently until the milk boils and thickens to form a smooth white sauce. Remove the bay leaf and add the mushrooms, chilli powder, mustard and salt and pepper to taste, and stir in the lobster meat. At this stage you can refrigerate the mixture for up to 24 hours, or serve it immediately. If you refrigerate it, you need to gently but thoroughly heat it over a low to medium heat before proceeding with the next step.

Divide the mixture between the two half-shells and sprinkle with Parmesan cheese. Flash the shells under a hot grill or place on the top shelf of a hot oven until the cheese is brown and bubbling. Serve with French bread and a simple green side salad.

Hake and slap chips

South Africa

You may not know that fish and chips are almost as universal in southern Africa as they are in the United Kingdom. In fact, the dish became popular in South Africa in the early twentieth century as a result of large-scale immigration from Britain. In particular, it is a dish that was associated with the East End of London and the Jewish communities living there. In Africa flaky, white hake tends to be used, and the chips are fat and soft—known as *slap* chips.

150g self-raising flour
½ teaspoon salt
½ teaspoon baking powder
200ml lager or water
1.5kg floury or general-purpose potatoes—Maris Piper or King Edward are my first choice
800g skinned fillet of hake cut into four pieces
2 litres sunflower oil
Salt and malt vinegar to taste

Reserve two tablespoons of flour and place the rest of the flour in a mixing bowl. Add the salt and baking powder and make a well in the middle, then gradually pour in the beer or water, whisking well to mix into a batter. When the batter is smooth, cover it and chill in the fridge. Peel the potatoes and cut them into slices about 1.5cm-2cm thick, then rinse under cold water and leave to soak in a bowl of fresh cold water.

When you are ready to cook the fish and chips, drain the chips and pat them dry with kitchen towel or a clean tea towel. Heat the oil in a chip pan to 190° and fry the chips for about 12 minutes or until golden brown and soft inside. You will probably need to fry the chips in a couple of batches. When the chips are cooked, rub the fish fillets with the remaining flour. Stir the batter and dip two of the fillets into the batter, ensuring that they are completely coated, before lowering them carefully into the hot oil. Cook for about 4-5 minutes, or until golden brown.

Repeat with the final two pieces of fish. Serve with lemon wedges, salt and malt vinegar.

Bean curry

South Africa

A tasty vegetarian curry made in the Durban style. You can throw the ingredients together in less than 15 minutes—and very successfully, too—with tinned haricot beans and canned tomatoes, and then just leave it to simmer. You can adapt this recipe using any dried or tinned pulses. If you can get hold of a bunch of fenugreek leaves from an Indian food shop, chop them and add them to the curry just before serving.

300g dried haricot beans, soaked in cold water for 8 hours or overnight, or 500g tinned haricot beans

3 onions, finely chopped
2 cloves garlic, crushed
1 red chilli, chopped and seeded
2 peeled and chopped tomatoes, or a tin of chopped tomatoes
1 teaspoon ground turmeric
1 teaspoon mild curry powder
1 teaspoon garam masala
A piece of ginger root 2.5cm long, peeled and chopped
1 teaspoon salt
½ teaspoon freshly-ground black pepper
1 handful coriander leaves, chopped
1 handful fenugreek leaves if available
2 teaspoon oil or ghee

We have a large Indian population in the province, the largest settlement of Indians outside of India, so any curried dishes are associated with them. These were just normal dishes as I grew up.

Zulu politician Dr Mangosuthu Buthelezi describes a favourite dish from his childhood

If using dried beans, pick them over before soaking to remove any small stones, then soak them overnight or for at least 8 hours

before draining; reserve the liquid. If using tinned beans, drain them and rinse them under running water. Pound together the salt, ginger, pepper, garlic and chilli into a paste and stir in the turmeric and curry powder. Cook the onions until golden, and add the curry paste. Cook for a further minute, stirring all the time, and then add the tomatoes. Cook for another minute before adding the beans, and add enough of the soaking water or fresh water to just cover the beans. Simmer over a medium heat, stirring occasionally, for 30 minutes or until the beans are soft and the liquid has reduced to form a sauce, and stir in the garam masala and chopped coriander (and fenugreek, if you can find it) just before serving.

Banana curry

Uganda

An unusual vegetarian curry from the 1920s: excellent made using large Caribbean plantains, but it also works very well with floury, slightly under-ripe bananas.

50g desiccated coconut
275ml milk
1 tablespoon mild curry powder
25g butter or ghee
6 or seven bananas
1 teaspoon Vietnamese *nam pla* fish sauce, or traditional anchovy sauce
1 teaspoon Worcestershire sauce
Salt and freshly-ground black pepper to taste

One hour before cooking, soak the coconut in milk. Peel and slice the bananas. Melt the butter or ghee in a frying pan, and add the curry powder, letting it sizzle for a minute or two. Add the bananas and fry until lightly browned all over. Add the anchovy sauce or nam pla fish sauce, Worcestershire sauce and milk and coconut, and season to taste with salt and pepper. Simmer for 15 minutes or so, and stir a beaten egg into the sauce just before serving, to thicken it.

I remember visiting my Indian and English friends and being treated to vegetable curry and rice; chapatti and *mandazi* (doughnuts) and *kabalagala* (banana pancakes); and cucumber or banana sandwiches (in the absence of cucumbers!)

The Right Reverend John Sentamu, Archbishop of York, remembering meals in colonial-era Uganda

Mauritian fish stew

Mauritius

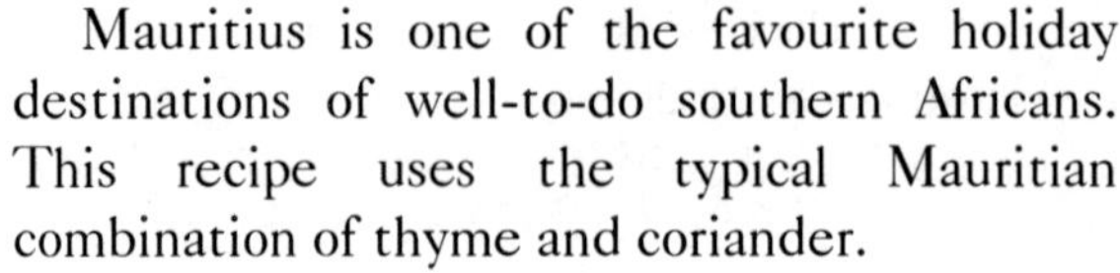

Mauritius is one of the favourite holiday destinations of well-to-do southern Africans. This recipe uses the typical Mauritian combination of thyme and coriander.

1kg firm white fish
2 onions
500g peeled, chopped tomatoes
2 tablespoons vegetable oil
A 2.5cm piece of root ginger
400ml hot water
2 cloves of garlic
1 tablespoon lemon or lime juice
1 bay leaf
1 tablespoon finely chopped thyme
2 tablespoons finely chopped coriander
A handful of curry leaves
Salt and freshly-ground black pepper to taste
A tablespoon of mixed, finely-chopped thyme and coriander to garnish

Cut the fish into cubes about 3cm square, and gently brown them in oil. Do not overcook them, or they will start to break up. Remove the fish and set on one side to cool. Finely chop the onions and garlic, peel and finely chop the ginger, and cook gently over medium heat until the onions become translucent. At that point add the lime or lemon juice, thyme, coriander, bay leaf and curry leaves and cook for a further two minutes. Carefully add the tomatoes and 400ml hot water, turn down the heat and simmer very gently for about 20 minutes.

After 20 minutes, taste the sauce and adjust the seasoning, then add the fish and allow to simmer for a further ten minutes. Sprinkle with the reserved coriander and thyme just before serving, accompanied by crusty bread, saffron rice and salad.

Gesmoorde vis (Smothered fish)

South Africa

Gesmoorde vis is a traditional Cape Dutch dish which has been widely adopted by English-speaking southern Africans. The addition of chilli is a typical Malay or Cape Muslim refinement. This particular recipe is reproduced by courtesy of Adelaine Hain, an anti-apartheid activist and mother of the British former cabinet minister Peter Hain. Mrs Hain usually uses cod loin or a chunky piece of haddock fillet, and varies the amount of chilli ("nice and hot for the family, not so hot for some guests.")

> "I still have a yen for *braai* with *stuiwepap*, I love my mother's recipe for *Gesmoorde Vis* (which should be made with snoek but she has to use cod) and I drink rooibos tea!"
>
> *Peter Hain, MP, born in Kenya to South African parents*

2 tablespoons light olive oil or vegetable oil for frying
1 large onion, coarsely diced
1 large potato, peeled and diced
1 small, hot green chilli
1 clove of garlic, crushed
400g peeled or chopped tinned tomatoes
450g cod, haddock or hake fillet
Salt and freshly-ground black pepper to taste

De-seed and finely chop the chilli. Skin the fish and remove any remaining bones, before cutting it into pieces about 5cm square. Heat the oil and gently fry the onion for a few minutes; add the potato cubes, stir to coat with oil, turn down the heat and continue to cook very gently for another five minutes until just softening (about five minutes). Add the crushed garlic and cook for another minute or two. Add the tomatoes and chilli, cover the pan and simmer for another five minutes. At this stage add the fish, season with salt and pepper and continue to simmer for about 10 minutes or until the fish is cooked. Mrs Hain notes "If you use a hob-to-oven dish you can put it into the oven on very low heat until you are ready to serve—leaving it in the oven like this improves the taste to my mind!"

Fish breyani

South Africa

This spicy rice and fish dish is the perfect one-pot meal for an old friends' dinner. The breyani can be made before guests arrive, and will happily keep hot for ages while you get stuck into the sherry and catch up on news.

1 kg firm white fish, cut into pieces about 5cm square
130g cooked or tinned brown lentils
6 potatoes, peeled and cut into 2.5cm cubes
500ml cold water
500g basmati rice
4 tablespoons sunflower oil
250ml hot water
50g butter or ghee
3 sticks cinnamon or cassia
5 crushed cardamom pods
5 cloves
5 whole allspice
1 handful chopped coriander leaves and stalks
1 tomato, peeled and chopped
3 bay leaves
300ml plain yoghurt
Salt to taste

Marinade

6 cloves garlic, crushed
1 teaspoon salt
2 green chillis, seeded and chopped
1 teaspoon ground turmeric
1 teaspoon ground cumin

Beat together the marinade ingredients with a pestle and mortar. Rub it over the fish, turning and mixing thoroughly in order to cover all the fish. Leave to marinade in the refrigerator for at least 30 minutes, and then fry the fish in a tablespoon of hot oil until firm and light golden in colour. Set the fish on one side to cool.

Place the rice in a sieve and rinse it until the water runs clear. Heat a tablespoon of oil in a deep frying pan over high heat and add the rice. Stir well to coat the rice with hot oil, and then add 500ml cold, salted water. Bring to the boil and boil for 10 minutes. Remove from the stove, drain and leave to cool.

Heat the remaining oil in a pan and fry the potatoes until browned. Remove them with a slotted spoon and set them aside to cool. Add the chopped onions to any remaining oil and fry them until golden brown. Remove about half the onions with a slotted spoon and set them aside. To the remaining onions, add the cinnamon, crushed cardamom pods, cloves, whole allspice, tomato, plain yoghurt, chopped coriander and salt, and simmer for 10 minutes on medium-low heat, stirring occasionally.

Now it is time to build up the layers of the breyani, ready for cooking. In a large saucepan, cover the base of the saucepan with a single layer of cooked potatoes. On top of the potatoes sprinkle half the reserved rice. Next put in the pieces of fish, and spoon the sauce over them. Sprinkle the lentils over the fish and sauce, and then cover the lentils with the remaining rice. Dot the top with specks of butter or ghee and the bay leaves, and spread the reserved onions over all before sprinkling the hot water over the top. Close the saucepan, making sure that it is sealed tightly—traditionally this is done with flour-and-water dough. I use a sheet of aluminium foil, shiny side down, laid over the top of the saucepan, the lid on top of it, and then crimp the edges of the foil down over the sides of the saucepan for a close seal.

Cook the saucepan on high heat for five minutes, then turn down the heat to its lowest setting and simmer it for 30 minutes, without opening the lid.

Mozambique prawns

Mozambique

A delightful recipe—one does not often find seafood cooked in beer—that has become a modern standard in southern Africa. You can use cooked or uncooked prawns for this dish—if using cooked prawns, reduce the cooking time by 5 minutes. This dish is very attractive, with the pink prawns and green parsley in a saffron sauce, but make sure that you use a good-quality, pure lager—Becks is my favourite—for cooking it.

1kg shelled prawns
25g unsalted butter
1 tbsp olive oil
1 pinch saffron strands
2 cloves garlic, finely chopped
2 tablespoons chopped parsley
1 tablespoon peri-peri sauce
150ml lager
Juice of 1 lemon

Place the saffron in a glass bowl and pour onto it 40ml boiling water. Leave to steep for 15 minutes. In a large, shallow pan heat the oil and butter until sizzling hot, then add the garlic and fry for 30 seconds. Add the parsley, saffron water and peri-peri sauce, pour in the lager, and cook for about a minute. Add the prawns and lemon juice, turn down the heat and cook on medium heat for about 15 minutes (only 7-10 minutes if using cooked prawns) or until the prawns are pink and firm. Serve with rice and green salad.

Zanzibar fish stew

Tanzania

I used to own a shop, and one morning a woman came inside, transfixed by a beaded ostrich egg hanging in the window. 'My mother had one of those hanging up when I was a child!' she explained. 'Ah, then you must be from Kenya or Uganda,' I suggested. In fact she was from the island of Zanzibar, on the coast of Tanzania, where families also hang up these eggs as a good luck and fertility charm. We began talking about cultures and cookery, and she described the fish dish she makes for her British-born children when she wants to cook Zanzibari. This is perfect served with a leafy green salad or with saffron rice.

1 kg uncooked flaky fish—salmon, hoki or haddock are ideal
1 tin coconut milk (or one carton coconut cream plus one cup warm water)
1 cup warm water
2 anchovies or 1 teaspoon Vietnamese fish sauce
2 bay leaves
5 peppercorns
5 allspice
5 cloves
30g butter
Salt and freshly-ground black pepper to taste

Put the butter, spices, bay leaves, anchovies and water into a saucepan. Add either one tin of coconut milk or, if using coconut cream, one carton of coconut cream and 1 cup of warm water. Bring to a gentle simmer and leave to simmer at a low heat for 20 minutes, stirring occasionally. Cut the fish into fairly large chunks and add them to the sauce, stirring well to coat the fish, and leave to simmer in a covered pan for a further 15 minutes, turning the pieces halfway through cooking. Check the seasoning and add a little salt if required before serving.

L.M. prawns

Mozambique

L.M. stands, of course, for Lourenço Marques, the colonial-era name for the beautiful city of Maputo in Mozambique. L.M. prawns are huge, meaty specimens up to seven or eight inches in length, fished off the Indian Ocean coast in the rich, sub-tropical waters that lie between Mozambique and Madagascar; the king prawns available in British supermarkets are sad little things in comparison. Enjoyed with a cold Laurentina beer in one of the dozens of restaurants or cafes that line the broad boulevards running down to the Indian Ocean, they are one of the highlights of a visit to Maputo.

1 bowl peri-peri marinade sauce (see page 258)
Fresh king prawns or tiger prawns—for a starter dish allow three per person; for a main course allow six or more large prawns per person

Rinse the prawns in fresh water; twist off the heads, shell them, removing the legs, and carefully remove the vein running down the back before rinsing again and patting dry with kitchen towel. Leave the shell on the tail. Put the prawns in a shallow dish and pour half the marinade over them, turning them to ensure that every bit of flesh is covered. Reserve the rest of the marinade. Cover the dish with cling film and refrigerate for 3 hours, turning the prawns every hour. Either thread the prawns on skewers or arrange on a grill pan, and grill under a hot grill for about four to six minutes per side, turning once. Serve hot with green salad and plain rice or French fries, and the reserved marinade sauce for dipping.

This dish can also be made with pre-cooked prawns, in which case they should just be thoroughly heated through, about two or three minutes each side—any more and they will be horribly tough.

Shrimp omelette

Mozambique

When in Johannesburg, one of our first lunchtime dates is always at the excellent Belém Café at Park Meadows Shopping Centre in Kensington. I always have the same thing—I crave it when I am not in South Africa, and I am delighted to say that the Belém version never fails to satisfy: shrimp omelette. This is unusual in so much as it is made with little pinkish-grey shrimps identical to the ones that you find in British waters. You could probably make it with prawns, but a lot of the speed and easy charm of the dish is lost; it becomes watery and the egg needs to be cooked for longer in order to ensure that the prawns are safely warmed through.

3 medium eggs
1 tablespoon olive oil
75g cooked shrimps
1 ripe tomato, finely chopped
1 spring onion, finely chopped
Salt and freshly-ground black pepper to taste

Heat an omelette pan and, while it is heating, whisk three eggs. When the pan is hot, pour in the oil and leave for a moment. When you can smell the oil, pour in the eggs and scatter the shrimps, tomato and onion over. Make the omelette as normal, seasoning at the very end of cooking (if you add salt too early the eggs will toughen). The Belém Café serves this omelette with golden French fries, a green salad, a soft Portuguese white bread roll and a small pot of peri-peri sauce to drizzle over the omelette.

An unqualified Success!
Poirette
CHOCOLATES AND SWEETS
always best sellers!
MONTGOMERY • MACARTHUR • MAIS-OUI
CHOCOLATES.
TOFFEES • CARAMELS • BON-BONS.

Zambezi chicken

Mozambique

Zambezi Chicken is now pretty much a fixture on Portuguese restaurant menus, in Africa and overseas. The method of preparation—an elaborate, spicy masala cooked with coconut milk—indicates that it probably originated in Goa and was transported to Mozambique as part of the vast export of slaves, cultures, produce and recipes that took place during the colonial period. Don't be alarmed by what appears to be an intimidating list of ingredients: I have added a cheat's version at the bottom of the recipe!

1.5kg chicken, jointed or cut into portions
1 tablespoon olive oil
3 onions
2 cloves garlic
2 tablespoons roughly chopped coriander
1 tablespoon chopped parsley
1 tablespoon tamarind paste (optional)
200ml coconut milk
200ml water
1 teaspoon medium curry powder
1 teaspoon salt
3 cardamom pods
1 peri-peri chilli pepper, seeded and chopped

Masala

200g desiccated coconut
1 tablespoon cumin seeds
Five individual threads of saffron
A 2.5cm piece of cinnamon stick or tablespoon of ground cinnamon
5 cloves or 1 teaspoon of ground cloves
1 tablespoon ground nutmeg
1 tablespoon coriander seeds

First, prepare the masala: heat your oven to 200°C. Mix all the masala ingredients together and spread thinly over a dry baking tray. Roast in the oven until the coconut is toasted to a light golden colour. Tip the spices into a bowl, and once fully cooled grind in a food processor into a powder . You can use a pestle and mortar, but be prepared for at least 15 minutes' hard work.

Finely chop the onions and garlic, and fry in the oil over a medium heat until translucent. Add the chicken and continue to sauté, turning often, until the chicken is lightly browned all over. Add the masala mixture and all the remaining ingredients except the chopped parsley and coriander, and simmer for 25 minutes, stirring occasionally, and adding more water if the sauce evaporates. At the end of 25 minutes add the coriander and parsley, and cook for a further five minutes.

The cheat's version:

Instead of making the masala from scratch, simply mix 4 tablespoons of any commercially-made garam masala and 200g of desiccated coconut in a bowl.

Malay chicken curry

South Africa

Malay curries have a characteristic sweetness and aroma that comes from the use of typically Indonesian spices such as allspice and cloves. It is interesting to look at early books of southern African interest such as the *South African Gold Fields Emigrant's Guide* of 1880, and see that, well over a century ago, the distinctiveness of Malay curries was recognised: the *Emigrant's Guide* reveals that Victorian passengers on Union Steam Ship vessels had a choice between 'Curry and Rice' and 'Malay Curry and Rice'. This recipe is adapted from the best and simplest recipe I know for this classic Cape Muslim dish, by Faldela Williams.

1.5kg chicken portions
2 onions, cut into rings
1 tablespoon oil
4 cloves garlic, crushed
A 2.5cm piece of ginger, peeled and chopped
1 teaspoon ground turmeric
2 teaspoons ground cumin
2 teaspoons ground coriander
2 cardamom pods, gently crushed
5 whole cloves
2 whole allspice
1 red chilli, seeded and chopped
1 teaspoon soft brown sugar
Salt and freshly-ground black pepper to taste
400g chopped tomatoes
4 waxy potatoes, peeled and cut into quarters

Gently fry the onions and chicken in oil until the onions are golden. Add the garlic, ginger, chilli and spices, and stir well to coat the chicken and onions. Add half a cup of cold water, stir again and cover the pan; leave to simmer for about 20 minutes. Add the tomatoes, sugar and another half cup of water, stir the curry and leave to simmer for another

10 minutes. At the end of that time, add the potatoes and another half cup of water, and leave to cook for about 15 minutes, or until the potatoes are thoroughly cooked through.

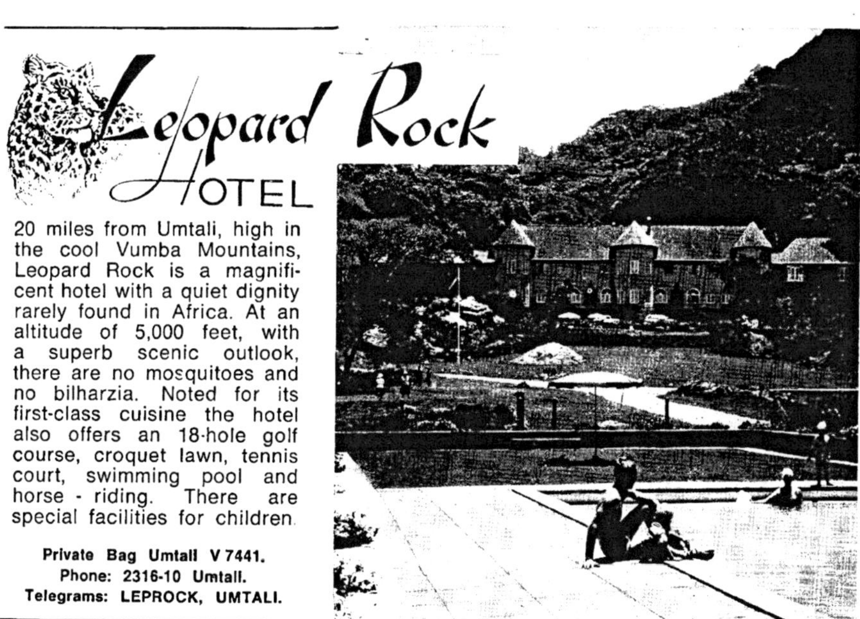

Chicken in cashew sauce

Mozambique

Mozambique is one of the world's largest producers of cashew nuts, and they find their way into all sorts of recipes. This is also good made with raw peanuts: just toast them in a hot frying pan for a minute and then rub the skins off with a tea towel before grinding. This dish is closely related to the Congolese, Angolan and West African recipes for meat, fowl and seafood served in a sauce made from peanuts or groundnuts. There is a also a famous Brazilian-African peanut sauce called *vatapa*, which tastes rather like a spicy satay sauce and is often served with chicken or fish.

2kg chicken, jointed or cut into portions
1 red peri-peri or bird's eye chilli (for a milder dish, use half a large, red cayenne chilli)
1 large onion
Juice of a lime
1 cup un-roasted, unsalted cashew nuts
3 tomatoes
2 tablespoons chopped coriander leaves
2 tablespoons olive oil
Salt and freshly-ground black pepper to taste

Chop the onion finely, and mix with the lime juice, 1 tablespoon olive oil, finely-chopped chilli and a good grinding of black pepper. Pour over the chicken pieces and leave to marinade for at least one hour, turning once. Heat 1 tablespoon olive oil in a deep pan and fry the chicken until lightly browned. Add 450ml cold water and cook for ten minutes. Grind the cashews: you won't be able to grind them totally smooth, but the paste should be of a similar texture to crunchy peanut butter—you can use a food processor or a large pestle and mortar, or even a rolling pin. Peel the tomatoes and chop very finely, then mix the tomatoes and cashews together and add to the chicken, along with 400ml water. Bring to the boil and then turn down the heat and simmer for 20 minutes, stirring occasionally. Just before serving, sprinkle the chopped coriander into the sauce.

The Thorn Tree

The branches of the thorn-tree at
noontime beckon to the passer-by
— HAIKU POEM

Even coffee tastes better in the open air geniality of Nairobi's most popular coffee house. **Not** just at noontime either

THE NEW STANLEY — A HILTON HOTEL

Pullau chicken

South Africa

Another Indian recipe from Durban, giving a dry, fragrant curry.

1.5kg of chicken pieces—legs and wings are perfect for this dish
1 large onion, chopped fine
2 cloves garlic, crushed
A piece of ginger root 2.5cm long, peeled and finely chopped
1 teaspoon poppy seeds
2 teaspoons cloves
1 teaspoon ground allspice
1 2.5cm piece of cinnamon stick or 1 teaspoon ground cinnamon
2 tablespoons plain yoghurt
3 tablespoons oil or ghee
½ teaspoon black pepper
1 teaspoon medium curry powder
Salt to taste
1 tablespoon lemon juice or tamarind paste

Heat the oil in a large, thick-bottomed saucepan over a medium heat, add all the ingredients except the yoghurt and lemon juice or tamarind and fry for five minutes, stirring constantly. After five minutes, turn the heat down as low as possible and cover the pan, leaving the chicken to cook slowly for about 20 minutes. Stir the content occasionally to prevent them from burning. At the end of 20 minutes add the yoghurt and lemon or tamarind and cook for a further minute before serving.

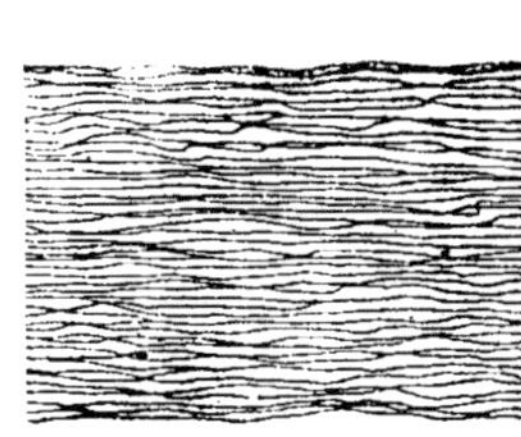

The White Horse Cellar
Estab. 1742
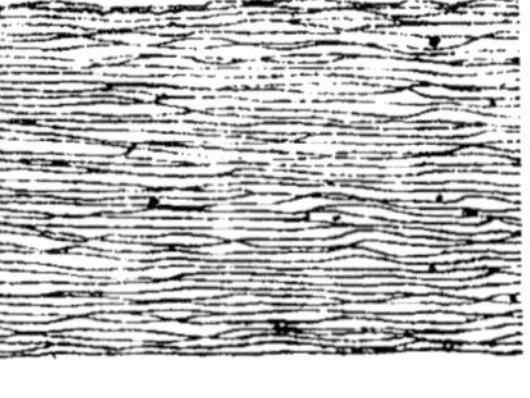

Chicken casserole with cumin

Angola

Arab traders from Yemen and Oman introduced cumin—a bitter-fragrant seed better known as a curry spice—to East Africa a thousand years ago or more. Its use in central Africa for flavouring stews and curries meant that it entered the Portuguese colonial cooking repertoire very early, and remains popular in Angola and Mozambique as a flavouring. Here it is used to flavour a rich tomato gravy in this typical Angolan casserole.

1 chicken of approx 2kg, cut into portions
6 large tomatoes, skinned and chopped
3 medium onions, finely chopped
2 cloves garlic, crushed or chopped
2 teaspoons freshly-ground cumin seed
1 teaspoon freshly-ground black pepper
½ teaspoon salt or to taste
1 tablespoon olive oil

In a deep pan or casserole fry the onions and garlic over medium heat until soft but not brown. Add the chilli pepper, followed by the tomatoes and cumin. Gently simmer for 30 minutes. Add the chicken and bring the stew to the boil, then turn down and simmer for 30 minutes, adding a little water if the tomato gravy becomes too dry.

Peri-Peri Chicken

Mozambique

A favourite dish in Mozambique.

1 bowl peri-peri marinade sauce (see recipe on page 258)

Allow 300g chicken per person approx (I usually buy a whole chicken and quarter it, but you can buy chicken quarters or portions from the supermarket or your butcher.)

Put the chicken in a shallow dish and pour half the marinade over, turning the chicken to ensure that every bit of meat is covered. Reserve the rest of the marinade. Cover the dish with cling film and refrigerate for at least an hour, turning the chicken occasionally. Arrange on a grill pan, and grill under a hot grill for about ten minutes each side, turning once. Serve hot with green salad and rice or hot, golden chips, and use the reserved marinade sauce for dipping. Grilling is definitely second-best for this dish—my preference would always be to cook it over a barbeque on a warm summer afternoon.

This recipe can be used for almost any meat or fish: try it with lamb or pork chops, or with trout or hoki fillets.

Ashanti chicken

Ghana

One of the classic dishes of West African settler cuisine, Ashanti Chicken is an elaborate dish, similar to *ballotine de poulet* in the French culinary repertoire, but with the playful conceit that the stuffed, boned chicken is carefully moulded back into the shape of a roast chicken around the forcemeat filling. The widest-known recipe is probably a version given by Marie Louise Pickering in her 1936 book *Tropical Cookery*; Mrs Pickering was the wife of the general manager of the Marlu Gold Mining Areas in the Gold Coast—now Ghana—and Marlu itself is named after her. Mrs Pickering's recipe calls for a pound of sausage-meat, which makes for rather a rich, stodgy filling: this is a lighter version.

To bone the chicken you will need a very sharp knife, and a trussing needle (or thick embroidery or upholstery needle) and cotton string or thick cotton thread to sew it back up again. If you don't feel confident boning a whole bird, many traditional butchers will be happy to do it for you.

1 roasting chicken of about 1.75kg
200g finely chopped streaky bacon
200g sausage-meat or minced pork
200g minced or finely chopped chicken or veal
3 hard boiled eggs
1 onion, finely chopped
1 large tomato, peeled and finely chopped
1 teaspoon freshly-ground black pepper
1 teaspoon salt or to taste
½ teaspoon ground nutmeg
3 tablespoons sunflower or olive oil for basting

If you are boning the bird yourself, cut along the backbone (if the bird is trussed for roasting, it sits upside down, with the backbone underneath) and work in both directions away from the incision using the point of the knife, filleting the meat away from the bones, and making sure not to cut through the skin: it is a slow, laborious process, and your knife must be razor-sharp. When you come to the joints of the wings and drumsticks, follow the bones with the point of the knife as far as you can go before cutting round the joint from the outside of the chicken—you will need to close the holes before stuffing the chicken by tying string tightly around them.

> I was speechless when I thought of how many hours he must have laboured away to produce this culinary masterpiece— completely skinning two chickens, removing all the bones, mincing up and cooking all the flesh and then stuffing it back into one of the skins into the shape of a real roast chicken. Or perhaps both chickens were cooked first and then taken apart. I was so stunned at the result that I never did find out how it was done, but managed to convey to Kwasi my unbounded admiration for his efforts.
>
> *Joan Beech, describing the Gold Coast delicacy, 'Ashanti Chicken'*

When the chicken is boned, gently remove as much of the flesh from the skin as possible, being careful not to tear the skin or cut through it. Coarsely chop the meat and make a forcemeat mixture by combining it with the minced chicken or veal, pork or sausage-meat, bacon, onion and tomato, and season it well with salt, pepper and nutmeg. With the breast side downwards, gently half-fill the chicken skin with the forcemeat mixture, then lay the peeled hard-boiled eggs along the middle of the chicken as a sort of stuffing, and continue filling the skin. Don't forget to tie string around the apertures left at the ends of the legs and wings. When full, you will need to spend a couple of minutes pushing the stuffing round to give the appearance and proportions of a proper roast chicken. Finally sew up the opening and arrange the chicken in a roasting tin with the seam downwards; lightly oil the chicken, dust it with a little flour and pour in a couple of tablespoons of olive or sunflower oil for basting.

To roast the chicken, preheat your oven to 190°C; the chicken will need to cook for about 2 hours. Baste regularly. Before serving, drive a skewer right into the middle of the chicken and then lay the skewer quickly against your wrist to test the temperature: if the skewer is hot, the chicken is cooked through. If the skewer is simply warm, the chicken will need to cook for longer—you can lay a piece of aluminium foil over the breast and the ends of the drumsticks to prevent them from burning. To serve, simply cut into slices at an angle.

Chicken pie

South Africa

A favourite from the Cape.

2 kg chicken, cut into portions
500g shortcrust pastry
2 onions
½ tsp ground allspice
½ tsp ground mace
50g butter
Salt and freshly-ground black pepper to taste
Juice of a lemon
100g chopped ham
2 hard-boiled eggs
The yolk of one raw egg
100ml white wine
1 tablespoon uncooked vermicelli
1 bay leaf

Preheat your oven to 180°. Put the white wine and bay leaf into a saucepan and add a pint of water. Add the chicken pieces and vermicelli, bring to the boil and simmer, uncovered, for 30 minutes, stirring occasionally. Remove from heat and take out the chicken pieces with a slotted spoon. Fish out the bay leaf and discard; whisk the lemon juice and egg yolk in a jug, and stir them into the remaining stock along with the butter, allspice and mace. Add salt and pepper to taste.

In the base of a deep pie dish arrange the chicken together with the chopped ham and boiled eggs cut into slices. Pour the sauce over, and cover with a shortcrust pastry crust rolled out quite thick and with a couple of holes for the steam to escape. Brush the crust with milk and bake for 40 minutes or until golden brown. Hilda Duckitt suggests rolling together a little butter and plain flour, forming the paste into balls and putting them in the bottom of the pie dish to thicken the gravy as they dissolve—an admirable idea.

Guinea Fowl Casserole

Tanzania

The farmed guinea fowl we buy in supermarkets and butchers in the United Kingdom are almost always young, tender and delicious. However, settlers in Africa very often stewed their guinea fowl—when shooting for the pot one was as likely to knock over an elderly, tough fowl as a young one, and indeed the expression 'shooting for the pot' infers that whatever was shot was most likely to be stewed or casseroled rather than roasted.

1 kg guinea fowl
3 onions, finely chopped
3 carrots, scraped and sliced into discs
1 clove garlic, roughly chopped
2 bay leaves
2 sprigs rosemary
Salt and freshly-ground black pepper to taste
Cold water
1 tablespoon butter
1 tablespoon plain flour
60ml double cream
2 tablespoons finely chopped parsley

Heat your oven to 180°C. Your guinea fowl will probably come trussed, with giblets inside: remove the giblets from the bird's internal cavity and rinse the fowl before putting it in a deep casserole dish. Add the chopped onions and carrots, and the fresh herbs, and lightly season with salt and pepper. Pour on cold water to cover the bird, place the casserole on the stove and bring the water to the boil. As soon as the water boils, cover the casserole with a tight lid—it is a good idea to lay a sheet of foil shiny-side down over the top of the casserole to seal in the steam, turn down the foil around the edge of the casserole, and then put the lid on over the foil. Place the casserole in the oven and cook for 1 hour.

Remove the casserole and pour off 300ml of the cooking liquid through a sieve into a jug; there should still be an inch or two of liquid left in the bottom of the casserole. Turn the oven temperature down to 100°C, put the lid tightly back on the casserole and replace it in the oven. Warm a pan, and melt the butter. When it is beginning to sizzle, stir in the plain flour and cook for a couple of minutes, stirring every few moments. Slowly but steadily pour in the cooking liquid, stirring constantly as you do so, and keep stirring as the sauce heats through and begins to thicken. Bring to the boil, then remove from heat and add the cream and parsley, and season to taste with salt and freshly-ground black pepper to taste and pepper.

> "I didn't like guinea fowl much, perhaps because I used to accompany my male cousins when they went on their shooting trips. We were always warned to watch out for the shot in the meat and to try not to crack a tooth by munching on it.
>
> *Dame Monica Mason,*
> *Director of the Royal Ballet*"

Carve the guinea fowl into portions for serving, and pour a little of the sauce over each portion, leaving the rest on the table for guests to help themselves.

Grilled guinea fowl with orange

Zimbabwe

Guinea fowl are found all over central and Southern Africa, and their slightly dry flesh, very similar to pheasant, benefits greatly from some sort of marinade. Farmed guinea fowl are widely available from supermarkets, and are much more tender and succulent than the wild variety. This recipe is perfect for barbeques: somehow the smokiness imparted by cooking over coals goes beautifully with the semi-caramel taste of the marmalade. However, it can also be grilled under a gas or electric grill.

Juice and zest of 2 large oranges
1 teaspoon crushed peppercorns
2 tablespoons olive oil
1 tablespoon dark orange marmalade
½ teaspoon sea salt
1 tablespoon brandy
1 teaspoon soy sauce or balsamic vinegar
1 anchovy pounded to a paste in a pestle and mortar
2 small guinea fowl, cut into quarters

Thoroughly mix the orange juice and zest, salt and peppercorns, marmalade, brandy and anchovy, and then add the olive oil; beat the marinade with a fork or whisk to thoroughly amalgamate the liquids, and then pour over the guinea fowl, turning the pieces and ensuring that the marinade coats every inch of the meat. Leave the birds to marinade for at least 4 hours—overnight for preference. When ready to cook them, turn them one last time to coat them with marinade again. You can oven cook them at 190° for 20 minutes, or grill them starting with the 'inside' side upwards, cooking for ten minutes and then turning once and cooking for another ten minutes, or barbeque them for ten to fifteen minutes each side.

Serve Yourself and SAVE
at
PAREKHS
63 LOBENGULA STREET

Some of our Regular Low Prices . . .

★ JIK, 500 ml, inc Sales Tax 25c
★ SURF, Family Size, inc. S/Tax . 99c
★ COLGATE (With FREE Razor Blades) LARGE SIZE, inc. Sales Tax 55c
★ CHOICE, Bath Size, inc. Sales Tax 25c
★ BUTTERCUP MARGARINE, 250 g, inc. S/Tax . 25c
★ HOLSUM, 500 g, inc. Sales Tax 49c
★ SWAT Insect Killer Spray, Large, inc. S/Tax . 75c

Listen to PAREKHS POP SHOW, TONIGHT at 8.15 — Radio Mtwakazi. FM 98,87 mHz, and be a Winner !

SERVE YOURSELF and SAVE at
PAREKHS

CUT-DOWN PRICES AT
MATSHOBANA
BUTCHERY and GROCERY

We offer:

★ NECK BEEF at, per kg 75c
★ BOLO at, per kg 80c
★ ROLL BEEF at, per kg $1,20
★ SUPER RUMP STEAK at, per kg ... $1,80
★ BONE STEAK at, per kg $1,20

Deliveries anywhere in Town. Try us for Quick Service.
TELEPHONE 60334

Braised pigeons with cherries

Zambia

Cape pigeons are found all over Zimbabwe and Zambia; they are smaller than English wood pigeons, but plump, with a wonderful flavour. You never see them for sale, so the only way to taste them is to know someone with a shotgun. The flesh, like English wood pigeons', is rather dry, so Cape pigeons benefit from being cooked with liquid, and braising them with cherries is a great way to enjoy them. If you can find little crimson morello or bitter cherries, so much the better. You can make this recipe very successfully using wood pigeons—and some supermarkets stock bottled bitter cherries from Poland and Germany, which are perfect used instead of fresh cherries.

2 pigeons, cleaned and trussed
1 onion
1 lemon
1 tablespoon butter
2 glasses red wine
½ teaspoon dried rosemary or 1 teaspoon fresh chopped rosemary
1 bay leaf
A handful of stoned black cherries
Salt and freshly-ground black pepper to taste

Brown the chopped onion in the butter in a large frying pan, and reserve the cooked onions in the base of a casserole dish or large saucepan. Rinse the pigeons under cold water, and pat them dry with a kitchen paper towel. Cut the lemon into quarters, remove the pips and push a quarter inside each of the pigeons. Lightly brown the pigeons in butter in the frying pan and place them upright in the casserole on top of the onions. Pour the red wine into the frying pan and bring to the boil, gently rubbing the base of the pan with a wooden spoon as it boils in order to dissolve the meat and onion juices that have stuck to the base of the pan. Pour the hot wine into the casserole with the pigeons, add the bay leaf and chopped rosemary, and top up with cold water to half-cover the birds. Cover the saucepan, bring to a boil, then turn down the heat and simmer the pigeons for an hour.

After that time remove the lid and baste the birds with the remaining liquid; add the cherries and simmer for another ten minutes with the lid off. At the end of this time the sauce should have thickened and be slightly syrupy. If it is still watery, remove the pigeons and keep them warm, then turn up the heat and boil the sauce until it thickens to the consistency of gravy. Serve the pigeons with the sauce poured over, with green salad and mashed potatoes.

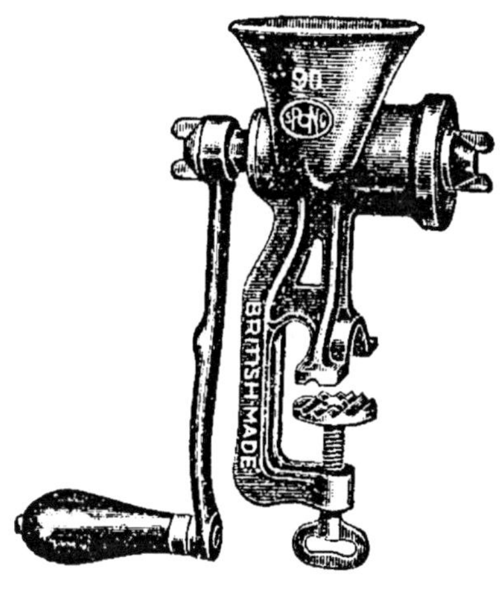

add
the final appetising touch

with Brand's A-1 Sauce
or Brand's A-1
Worcestershire Sauce
Cerebos QUALITY PRODUCTS

Guinea fowl with cream

Zimbabwe

The rich, cream sauce helps keep the guinea fowl moist. This easy recipe is based on a favourite from a small, privately-printed recipe book dating from about 1971 by Ruth Gebbie, a farmer from Marandellas, and needs simple accompaniments: mashed potatoes or crusty bread and a simple green salad.

1 large guinea fowl jointed into pieces
2 large onions
1 bay leaf
Salt and freshly-ground black pepper to taste
500ml single cream

Heat the oil in the base of a large casserole dish, and brown the onions until light golden. Add the guinea fowl and cook, turning constantly, until browned. Pour in the cream, add the bay leaf and simmer for about 45 minutes or until very tender.

Giraffe sausage

Tanzania

A favourite of Afrikaans settlers in East Africa; giraffe is tasty but tough and stringy, so making boerewors with the meat is an excellent option. I am told that this also works very well with zebra meat.

1.5kg giraffe meat
1.5kg topside of beef
600g sheep's tail fat or pork fat
2 tablespoons salt
1 teaspoon freshly-ground black pepper
1 teaspoon ground allspice
1 teaspoon fresh thyme
1 tablespoon ground coriander
50g sausage casings

Soak the sausage casings in salted water and rinse well. Afrikaans farmers used to save the intestines of goats and sheep and dry them, and then soak them when an animal was slaughtered and sausage could be made. Coarsely mince the giraffe meat and beef, and finely cut the fat into cubes the size of a peppercorn. Mix all the spices and salt together in a cup and, using a wooden spoon, fold into the meat together with the fat until well amalgamated.

Tie one end of the casing and use a piping bag to force the meat mixture inside. Traditionally, boerewors is piped in one long sausage rather than being twisted in sections like English bangers, and the mixture should be loose enough to curl the sausage around and around in a spiral. When the sausage skin is full, tie it off at the end. Leave the sausages in a refrigerator or cold larder for at least 48 hours before using, to enable the flavours to develop.

Venison casserole

Zambia

Perfect for springbok, kudu or gemsbok, or for deer venison for those who cannot get hold of southern African game.

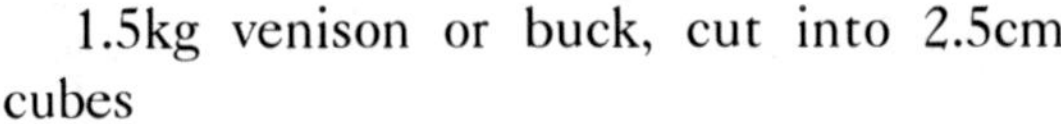

1.5kg venison or buck, cut into 2.5cm cubes
3 tablespoons plain flour
6 rashers of streaky bacon cut into pieces
2 tablespoons sunflower oil
15 shallots or pearl onions
200g mushrooms
4 carrots
4 sticks celery
2 cloves garlic
2 tablespoons chopped parsley
2 bay or myrtle leaves
½ teaspoon chopped fresh thyme
6 cloves
4 allspice
1 cinnamon stick
½ teaspoon paprika
500ml red wine
30ml port
Salt and freshly-ground black pepper to taste

If you plan to cook this in the oven, pre-heat the oven to 180°C. Chop the garlic finely and lightly fry it with the bacon, onions and mushrooms on medium heat in a little oil for about five minutes, or until the bacon is brown and beginning to crisp. Set them aside, turn the heat to full, and pour the rest of the oil into the pan to heat up. Place the flour in a large polythene bag and add a pinch of salt and a teaspoon of ground black pepper. A handful at a time, add the chunks of venison to the bag and shake them around until they are coated in flour, then take them out and set them on one side for frying. If you run out of flour, top up the bag.

Brown the meat in the frying pan, ensuring that it is cooked on all sides—you will need to do this in three or perhaps four batches—and place it in a large ovenproof casserole. Clean and chop the celery and carrots into 1cm pieces, and add them to the casserole with the herbs and spices. Pour the wine over the contents of the casserole, cover and either:

Bring to the boil on top of the stove, then turn the heat right down and gently simmer for an hour, stirring occasionally.

Or

Cook in the oven at 180°C for an hour

At the end of an hour add the port and the onion and bacon mixture. Cook it for a further 25 minutes uncovered, and at the end of that time give it a good stir and taste the sauce to establish whether you need to add more salt or pepper.

Braised neck of venison with peaches

Zimbabwe

A hearty recipe which is perfect for winter parties. The original recipe is for impala or kudu; however, it works well with farmed venison.

Most peaches in southern Africa are yellow cling peaches, known as the Kakamas peach, packed with sweet juice and bursting with flavour. Kakamas peaches descend from the trees first imported into the Cape of Good Hope by Hendrik Boom, Jan van Riebeeck's gardener, from the island of St Helena in 1654. You can of course use tinned peaches.

1 whole neck of venison, weighing about 2.5kg
4 large onions
1 tablespoon olive oil
Water or stock
4 tablespoons plain flour
6 large peaches
Salt and freshly-ground black pepper to taste
2 bay leaves
1 wine glass brandy or port (optional)

Heat the oil in a large, covered pan and brown the onions until lightly golden. Roll the venison in plain flour to which you have added half a teaspoon each of salt and black pepper, and brown the venison in the oil, turning constantly. When nicely browned, add the bay leaves and carefully pour in enough water or beef stock to come halfway up the neck; simmer for about two hours, turning the neck over occasionally.

In the meantime, pour boiling water over the peaches and leave them for one minute before peeling them—the skin should lift off easily. Cut them into slices and discard the stone. Reserve the sliced peaches, and add them to the stock 45 minutes before serving. When the venison is ready to serve, lift out the meat, strain out the peach slices with a slotted spoon, turn up the heat and leave the stock to bubble and reduce to the consistency of gravy. You can also add a wine-glass of brandy or port to the stock at this stage if you like. Carve the meat from the bone, garnish with the peach slices and serve the sauce separately. This dish is very good served with roast potatoes and a plain watercress or spinach salad.

FRESH FISH

EVERY DAY.

READY CLEANED FISH,

AT LOW PRICES,

14, DARLING STREET

(ADJOINING MASONIC HOTEL),

Large Stock of Salt Fish always on Hand.

CAPE FISH COMP.

A. W. AYLES, Manager.

Frikkadels

South Africa

There are a variety of recipes, mostly of Malay and Dutch colonial origin, and still popular in Cape Muslim culture, for frikkadels—spicy rissoles or croquettes of minced beef, mutton or fish. They are served on their own as snacks or canapés; in a curry sauce to make a substantial main dish, and are also prepared in vine leaves: a method of cooking rissoles that was popular in seventeenth-century Holland but has now largely disappeared except in South Africa. A version is also made where Savoy cabbage leaves are stuffed with spiced mincemeat, and the parcels cooked in stock (known as *oumens onder die kombers*, or 'old men under the blankets'!). This is based on Mrs E. J. Dijkman's 1890 recipe.

Fresh vine leaves
500g minced beef
½ teaspoon ground nutmeg
½ teaspoon ground cloves or allspice
1 teaspoon chopped fresh thyme leaves
1 slice fresh white bread with crusts cut off
1 beaten egg
1 tablespoon vegetable oil
1 cup water
Salt and freshly-ground black pepper to taste

Preheat your oven to 190°C. Thoroughly wash the vine leaves and pat them dry with kitchen towel. Rub the inside of each leaf with a little vegetable oil. Mix together all the other ingredients by hand, amalgamating them well into a paste. Place a lump of meat mixture the size of a walnut in the middle of each leaf and then fold up the leaf to totally enclose the meat. Place the parcels into a large, lidded casserole dish: ensure that the final fold of the leaf is on the bottom of the parcel so that the weight of the parcel keeps the leaf sealed. Pack together the parcels as closely as possible. When the dish is full, pour in a cup of cold water and cook, covered, for 50 minutes in a medium-hot oven. Mrs Dijkman recommended that, after dishing up the rissoles, one could make a rich gravy by quickly boiling up the juices in the bottom of the casserole together with a lump of butter rolled in plain flour.

PAGODA
RESTAURANT

NAIROBI'S PREMIER
CHINESE
RESTAURANT

Whether you are a connoisseur of authentic Chinese dishes, or just bent on a pleasant lunch and a leisurely, intimate dinner, the Pagoda cuisine and atmosphere will please you.

Private Dining Rooms for Special Parties

Open Monday to Saturday: 10 a.m. to 2.30 p.m.
6.30 p.m. to 11.30 p.m.
Closed Sundays

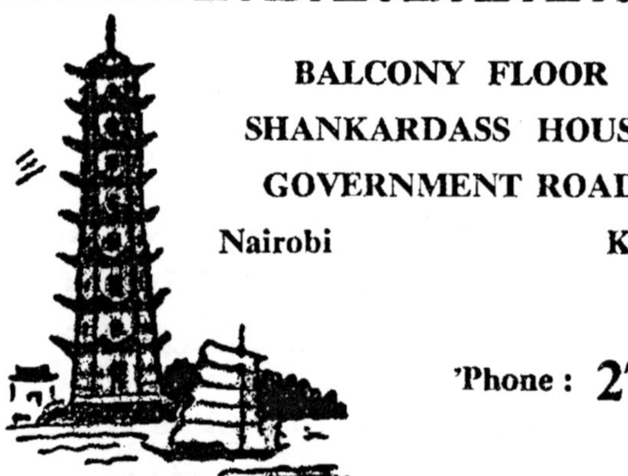

BALCONY FLOOR
SHANKARDASS HOUSE
GOVERNMENT ROAD
Nairobi KENYA

'Phone : 27036

Frikkadel curry

South Africa

A lovely, elaborate mix of flavours in this dish. You can also try it with lamb or mutton.

Frikkadels

600g minced beef
½ teaspoon ground white pepper
1 teaspoon salt
1 clove garlic, crushed
½ teaspoon ground cinnamon
½ teaspoon ground nutmeg
1 egg, beaten

Sauce

30ml sunflower oil
2 large onions, thinly sliced
1 tin chopped tomato
½ teaspoon turmeric
½ teaspoon salt
1 clove garlic, crushed
1 green chilli, halved
2 bay leaves
1 teaspoon ground cumin
1 teaspoon ground coriander seed
1 tablespoon garam masala
100ml cold water

Combine the ingredients for the frikkadels and form into walnut-sized balls. Heat the oil in a large saucepan and braise the onions until golden. Add the garlic, chilli, herbs, spices and seasoning, and cook for 30 seconds before adding the tomato and water, and cook in a covered pan for about fifteen minutes over medium heat. Gently lower in the frikkadels and cook for a further 25 minutes, adding a little more water if the sauce looks too dry.

Stewed oxtail

Zimbabwe

Deeply unfashionable, but cheap and delicious: a traditional Afrikaans dish from the district around Melsetter. The allspice and cloves are unusual additions, but are very typical of Cape cookery.

2 oxtails, cut into joints
100ml cooking oil
2 large onions, roughly chopped
6 bay leaves
4 cloves of garlic, roughly chopped
4 large carrots, peeled and cut into discs
Juice of 1 lemon
6 cloves
6 allspice
Salt and black freshly-ground black pepper to taste
Worcestershire sauce
6 waxy potatoes, peeled and halved
125ml brandy

For this dish you will need a large casserole dish or heavy saucepan. Brown the oxtail and onion quickly over high heat. Add the bay leaves, garlic, cloves, lemon juice, salt, pepper, Worcestershire sauce and carrots, and cook for a further 2 minutes before carefully adding enough water to barely cover the ingredients. Leave the pot to simmer on a very low heat for four hours, then add the potatoes and the brandy and let it simmer for a further hour, or until the potatoes are done and the meat is very tender.

Sosaties

South Africa

It wasn't until I was reading Hilda Gerber's *Traditional Cooking of the Cape Malays* that the penny finally dropped—the name comes from the same Malay root as *satay*, and sosaties in fact probably originate from Java. Sosaties are perfect for a barbeque, but can also be roasted, grilled or even pan-fried. Hilda Gerber also gives a recipe for lamb chops, left to season overnight in a sosatie marinade and then simply simmered in the marinade for 45 minutes. This recipe is traditionally made with orange or lemon leaves, but unless you are lucky enough to have a lemon or orange tree in your garden or conservatory that you don't mind denuding for the sake of this recipe, you will have to stick to lime and bay leaves from your local supermarket.

1kg leg of lamb, boned and cut into bite-size cubes
500g onions, thinly sliced into rings
125ml sunflower oil
1 packet bamboo satay skewers
20 lime leaves

Marinade

4 bay leaves
1 teaspoon chopped fresh thyme
2 cloves crushed garlic
1 teaspoon curry powder
The juice of one lemon
1 tablespoon soft brown sugar
2 tablespoons fresh or block tamarind dissolved in 4 tablespoon boiling water, or 3 tablespoons prepared tamarind paste
½ teaspoon salt
1 teaspoon freshly-ground black pepper

If using fresh tamarind, dissolve in boiling water and leave to soak for ten minutes. Strain through a sieve to remove fibre and seeds before using. Combine the marinade ingredients and meat and mix well. Leave in a refrigerator for at least 4 hours, but preferably overnight (one recipe from 1890 suggests that the meat is marinated for "nearly a week", adding that "when the weather is cool it will keep even longer"! Probably best to stick to overnight.). The following day thread the meat onto the satay skewers; alternate by folding a lime leaf and threading it onto the skewer after every two or three cubes. Reserve the remains of the marinade. Cook the sosaties—either by roasting in the oven for 25 minutes at 200°C, by shallow-frying on all sides for about 20 minutes, or by grilling under a hot grill for 14-20 minutes, turning regularly. Once cooked, braise the onions until transparent and add the remains of the marinade. Cook for five minutes, and then return the sosaties to the pan and cook for a further five minutes. Serve with rice or mashed potatoes.

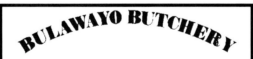

Bobotie

South Africa

Bobotie is a dish of some antiquity: it has certainly been known in the Cape since the seventeenth century, when it was made with a mixture of mutton and pork. Nowadays it is more likely to be made with beef or lamb, although pork lends the dish moistness. Early recipes incorporated ginger, marjoram and lemon rind; the invention of curry powder has simplified the recipe somewhat but the basic concept—minced, spiced meat cooked in a savoury custard—remains the same. Traditionally, bobotie incorporates dried fruit like raisins or sultanas, but the sweetness that they lend is not to everybody's taste.

Bobotie was transported by South African settlers to colonies all over Africa, and recipes for it can be found originating from Kenya, Botswana, Zimbabwe and Zambia. There is also a delicious variation that was popular among the Boer settlers who settled in the Chubut Valley in Argentina in the early twentieth century, in which the bobotie mixture is packed inside a large pumpkin, and the pumpkin baked until tender.

1 kg minced beef
1 slice of white bread, crust removed
200ml milk
2 eggs
100g butter
20ml lemon juice
1 onion, finely chopped
2 cloves crushed garlic
½ teaspoon mild curry powder
½ teaspoon ground turmeric
¼ teaspoon cumin seeds
½ teaspoon black pepper
1 teaspoon salt
1 tablespoon chopped, blanched almonds
6 fresh orange or bay leaves
50g seedless raisins (optional)

Preheat your oven to 170°C. In a shallow dish, pour 100ml of milk over the bread and leave to soak. In a frying pan melt the butter over a medium heat, and add the onion and garlic. Cook for a minute or two until the onion begins to colour, and then add the curry powder, turmeric and pepper. Cook for another minute, stirring well, and remove from the heat. Drain the milk from the bread and add the soaked bread to the mince, then add the cooked onion mixture, salt, lemon juice and almonds, and the raisins if you decide to include them. Mix the meat mixture well, kneading it with your hands to amalgamate the flavourings.

> If I am cooking South African dishes I choose pumpkin soup and bobotie—easy to make and always sure-fire winners!
>
> *Prue Leith CBE, South African-born food writer, restaurateur, and patron of the Prue Leith Chef's Academy in Centurion, Pretoria, South Africa.*

Generously grease a baking dish and scatter the cumin seeds inside. Spoon in the meat mixture, pressing it down to ensure a flat surface, and bake for 40 minutes or until it begins to colour on the top. Beat together the remaining 100ml milk and the two eggs and pour the mixture over the meat. Roll the orange or bay leaves into cylindrical 'cigars', and poke them into the mixture so that a little of the leaf roll protrudes above the surface of the egg custard, and bake the dish for another 10 minutes.

Boerewors

South Africa

Old recipes for boerewors are notable for a larger proportion of fat, and more spices, vinegar and sometimes wine are added. These adjustments without doubt improved the keeping qualities of the sausage, and often it was also either wind-dried (when it is known as *droëwors*—dry sausage) or smoked to preserve it. Traditionally, the meat was pounded or chopped instead of being minced, and the proportions and ingredients vary. Some recipes call for a 40/40/20 mixture of pork, mutton and beef, with pork fat added, and the term was also used to refer to a game sausage made with a mixture of fat and lean game: zebra and kudu, for example.

1.5kg pork
1.5kg topside of beef
600g sheep's tail fat or pork fat
2 tablespoons salt
1 teaspoon freshly-ground black pepper
1 teaspoon ground allspice
1 teaspoon fresh thyme
1 tablespoon ground coriander
1 tablespoon malt vinegar
50g sausage casings

Soak the sausage casings in salted water and rinse well. Farmers used to save the intestines of goats and sheep and dry them, and then soak them when an animal was slaughtered and sausage could be made. Coarsely mince the pork and beef, and finely cut the fat into cubes the size of a peppercorn. Early settlers used to stamp the meat in a mortar, or chop it finely on a *hackebord*—a large chopping board. Mix the thyme, spices and salt together in a cup and, using a wooden spoon, fold into the meat together with the fat until well amalgamated.

Tie one end of the casing and use a piping bag to force the meat mixture inside. Traditionally, boerewors is piped in one long sausage rather than being twisted in sections like English bangers, and the mixture should be loose enough to curl the sausage around and around in a spiral. When the sausage skin is full, tie it off at the end. Leave the sausages in a refrigerator or cold larder for at least 48 hours before using, to enable the flavours to develop. Nowadays boerewors is usually grilled or fried, but a favourite cooking method used to be to boil the sausage in hot water for 15 minutes.

Beef and lemon casserole

Botswana

Before electric refrigeration, beef was dried to make biltong, the traditional southern African beef jerky, or was eaten immediately after slaughter rather than being aged by hanging, as is common in cooler climates. Slow-cooking recipes were popular, to make the fresh, tough beef more palatable, and this recipe from Botswana is typical. There was also a belief that even slightly 'off' meat would regain its freshness, or at least lose some of its gaminess, if cooked with lemon; another settler trick was to soak the meat for a couple of hours in salt water to which a couple of handfuls of charcoal had been added. This recipe works well with a cheaper cut like topside.

1.5kg topside of beef, cut into two-inch cubes
1 large unwaxed lemon
1 large onion
200ml water
1 tablespoon of plain flour
Salt and freshly-ground black pepper to taste

Preheat your oven to 160°C. Heat a frying pan, and brown the beef on all sides in a little oil. If your pan is small, you may need to brown the beef in batches—the important thing is to have a hot pan so that the outside of the beef browns properly. Slice the onion thinly into rings, and slice the lemon into discs, removing the seeds. Layer the beef in a casserole dish, interspersing the layers with layers of mixed onion rings and lemon slices. Cover with 200ml cold water, and season with black pepper and salt. The water should just about cover the meat. Cook at 160°C for 1½ hours. After that time, mix a tablespoon of plain flour with a tablespoon of cold water, and pour the mixture into the stew, stirring gently to mix, then return the casserole to the oven for a further 15 minutes—this thickens the gravy. Serve with rice, or a green salad and French bread.

Stuffed pawpaw

Uganda

Try to get hold of a large Caribbean or African pawpaw for this dish—you will need to visit a market or fruit and vegetable shop—since supermarket pawpaws are invariably too small.

250g minced lamb or beef
1 large pawpaw
2 onions, finely chopped
1 teaspoon chopped green chilli
½ teaspoon grated nutmeg
Salt and freshly-ground black pepper to taste
Oil for frying

Pre-heat the oven to 190°C. Peel the pawpaw; cut an inch from the stalk end, and scoop out the seeds with a spoon. In a frying pan fry the onions until golden, then add the minced meat and chilli and fry until brown. Season with nutmeg, salt and pepper, and pile the meat into the pawpaw. Stand the pawpaw upright in an ovenproof bowl and bake it for 15 minutes or until tender. Serve with rice and green salad.

Denningvleis

South Africa

Dendeng is the Malay term for dried buffalo meat, and this dark, aromatic stew, with the background pungency of chilli and tamarind, remains a favourite dish among the Cape Muslim community. One of the best plates of denningvleis I have enjoyed was at the old *Kaapse Tafel* restaurant—now, sadly, closed—in central Cape Town, located just a short walk from the original Dutch East India Company's gardens on the slopes of Table Mountain.

1kg leg of lamb, boned and cubed
400g onions, sliced into rings
3 cloves garlic, crushed
1 teaspoon chopped red chillies
1 teaspoon salt
1 teaspoon crushed black peppercorns
1 teaspoon ground allspice
4 bay leaves
1 tablespoon soft brown sugar
75ml tamarind puree (either soak 2 tablespoons of solid tamarind in 75ml hot water and then sieve to a puree, or use bottled tamarind puree)
1 teaspoon malt or balsamic vinegar

Mix all the ingredients except the meat and onions, to make a marinade paste. Coat the cubes of lamb with the paste and leave to stand for a couple of hours. In a frying pan over a high heat, flash-fry the lamb pieces, browning them quickly on all sides. Put the lamb in a large saucepan, add the chopped onions and cook over a low/medium heat for about 40 minutes. Keep the saucepan covered after the first five minutes, stirring occasionally. If necessary, add enough water to keep the meat moist.

Pienang curry

South Africa

Pienang or Penang curry is another traditional Cape Muslim dish that probably originates from Java; it is almost certainly related to the Singaporean dish *pindang seruni*, a spicy lamb stew. It is an aromatic, dry curry, made with lamb and flavoured with star anise and turmeric.

500g lamb, boned and cubed
2 onions, finely chopped
200ml water
1 tablespoon oil
2 blades lemon grass

Marinade

3 cloves of garlic, crushed
½ teaspoon turmeric
3 heads of star anise
1 teaspoon medium curry powder
3 bay leaves
30ml tamarind puree or malt vinegar
30g soft brown sugar

Mix the marinade ingredients and rub thoroughly into the meat. Leave the meat to stand for at least two hours. In a large saucepan, fry the onions over medium-high heat until golden brown, then add the meat, water, and lemon grass and allow to cook at full heat for five minutes before turning the heat down. Cook the meat at a low heat for about 40 minutes until the meat is tender and most of the liquid has evaporated. This is delicious served with mashed potato and mashed butternut.

Skilpadjie

South Africa

This delicacy is also known as *skilpadjie*, or 'little tortoise'; and the appearance of the dish, with its mottled surface from the honeycombed texture of the caul fat, makes the name particularly apt. It is not dissimilar to the Italian delicacy *fegatelli*—liver in caul fat—from which the English liver meatballs known as faggots take their name. Caul fat itself is a membrane, laced with pure white fat, which encloses the internal organs of domestic animals—many traditional butchers stock it, or can at least obtain it with a couple of days' notice. Currants are a traditional addition to *skilpadjie*, but the combination of liver and dried fruit is not to everyone's taste.

Skilpadjies are rich, and benefit from simple accompaniments: try onion gravy, white rice and a fresh green salad.

4 pieces pork caul fat, approx 30cm square
100g minced beef or venison (ostrich is also very good)
50g unsmoked streaky bacon
500g ox liver
30g butter
1 small onion, finely chopped
1 clove garlic, crushed
½ teaspoon freshly-ground black pepper
½ teaspoon ground nutmeg
½ teaspoon salt
½ teaspoon chopped fresh marjoram
1 tablespoon currants (optional)

Finely chop the ox liver and streaky bacon into chunks about the size of a peppercorn, and mix them with the minced beef. Add the other ingredients, keeping the pieces of pork caul soaking in a bowl of iced water. Mix the meats well and divide into four portions. Take out the first piece of caul and dry it off with kitchen towel. Spoon the minced meat mixture into the centre of the caul, and fold over the edges to make a sealed parcel—you can secure the edges with a cocktail stick. Repeat with the remaining caul pieces until you have four parcels. These are best roasted in the oven for an hour at 180° or, even better, barbequed: they require long cooking at a comparatively low temperature, and should be tested with a skewer before serving: drive the skewer into the centre of the parcel and lay it gently against the inside of your wrist for a moment. If the tip of the skewer is hot, the *skilpadjie* is cooked through; if it is warm or cold, it needs to cook for longer.

Dutch roast beef

Zimbabwe

The first Afrikaners to settle in Zimbabwe arrived in the early 1890s on the Moodie, Martin and Edenburg Treks from South Africa. The farmers who emigrated from the Orange Free State and Natal were almost all poor: by the end of the 19th century, many Afrikaners were reduced to the status of *bywoners*, or sharecroppers, by the Roman Dutch inheritance laws which divided a man's farm between his children, so the offer of land from the British South Africa Company proved immensely attractive.

The description of this simple, spiced meat loaf as Dutch Roast Beef is a sly term used by the English-speaking settlers for what is actually a delicious recipe, not unlike bobotie, which is traditionally made with mutton.

750g minced stewing steak
1 thick slice of white bread
2 tablespoons soft butter
300ml milk
1 beaten egg
Salt and freshly-ground black pepper to taste
1 generous pinch ground allspice
½ teaspoon dried mixed chopped herbs—thyme, rosemary and sage—or 1 teaspoon fresh herbs

Pre-heat the oven to 190°C. Tear the bread into rough pieces and place in a mixing bowl. Bring the milk to the boil before pouring onto the bread, and beat well with a fork until the bread is broken up. Add the mince and seasoning, and mix well before adding the beaten egg and continuing to mix. Form the mince into an oblong shape and dot the top with butter. Roast for one hour, basting regularly. Serve with gravy, mashed potatoes and peas.

Monkey gland steaks

Zimbabwe

Meikles, in Harare, is one of the greatest hotels in Africa. It is—quite rightly—famed for the high quality of its cuisine, but Rhodesia's cultural isolation and the innate conservatism of its white population meant that even as late as the 1980s and 1990s the menu in Meikles' main restaurant was so dated that it could easily have been lifted from that of a grand London hotel of the 1960s: Avocado Ritz; Peach Melba; Beef Wellington and, of course, Monkey Gland Steaks. (A southern African favourite: during the Second World War the Criterion Hotel in central Johannesburg overcame the beef shortage by serving whale steaks with Monkey Gland sauce.)

4 fillet steaks
1 teaspoon olive oil
1 small onion, very finely chopped
1 clove garlic, very finely chopped
1 large tomato, peeled, seeded and finely chopped
1 tablespoon white wine vinegar
1 tablespoon cold water
1 teaspoon coarsely-ground black pepper
1 tablespoon sun-dried tomato paste
1 tablespoon Worcestershire sauce
1 tablespoon dark brown sugar
1 teaspoon soy sauce
1 teaspoon Tabasco sauce

Gently sauté the onions and garlic until soft and golden, then add all the other sauce ingredients and simmer briskly for 3 minutes, stirring occasionally. Reserve the sauce on a low heat, and grill the steaks; when cooked, spoon the hot sauce over them, and serve with saffron rice or a baked potato.

Mincemeat curry

South Africa

This curry is called keema curry by South Africans of Indian descent (*keema* is a Hindi word meaning minced lamb), and is sometimes served wrapped in a hot, freshly-made roti to make the takeaway known as a salomi. The tomato paste is almost as unfashionable an ingredient as the curry powder, but it is important for the richness and consistency of the dish.

500g minced mutton or beef
1 large onion, finely chopped
2 cloves of garlic, crushed or pounded to a paste
1 tablespoon of medium curry powder
1½ tablespoons of tomato paste or sun-dried tomato paste
2 whole cloves
2 cardamom pods
1 5cm length of stick cinnamon
3 tablespoons of ghee or vegetable oil
Salt and freshly-ground black pepper to taste
1 tablespoon lemon juice
2 tablespoons natural yoghurt

> "In the Indian area you could get a really hot chilli curry and rice, as opposed to the insipid Raj-English curry elsewhere in white cafes.
>
> *Sylvester Stein, former editor of* Drum *magazine, describing his childhood in 1920s Durban, South Africa* ."

Pound the dry spices in a mortar until crushed and broken. Heat the oil or ghee and fry the onion and garlic for about one minute before adding the tomato paste, spices and curry powder and cook for about five minutes, stirring constantly. Add the meat and fry for about twenty minutes or until the meat is thoroughly cooked, then add the lemon juice and yoghurt just before serving.

THE SHOPPING CENTRE

NAIROBI,

Complete House Furnishers.

DEPARTMENTS.

Haberdashery.	Hardware.
Gent's Outfitting.	China and Glassware.
Boots and Shoes.	Lampware.
Furnishing Drapery.	Electro-Plate.
Furniture.	Silverware.
Carpets and Linos.	Fancy Goods.
Toilet Requisites.	Tobacco.
Sports Goods.	Wines and Spirits.

Houses Furnished on the Hire Purchase System.

Goan pork vindalho

Tanzania

The Portuguese love pork in all its variations; pork remains a popular meat in Goa, on the Western India coast, which remained a Portuguese possession until the Indian Army reclaimed the territory in 1961. Goa is also the original home of the vindaloo, better known there as *vindalho*.

This highly-spiced pork curry recipe has an astonishing depth of flavour and is based on a recipe from a promotional leaflet produced by Goa Tourism in the early 1990s. It is typical of the Goan curries enjoyed in East Africa.

1kg lean pork, cleaned and diced into 2cm squares
10 cloves of garlic, crushed
A 2.5cm piece of ginger, peeled and chopped fine
2 red chillies, seeded and chopped
A 2.5cm piece of cinnamon stick or 1 teaspoon ground cinnamon
1 teaspoon mustard seeds
1 teaspoon cumin seeds
1 large onion, finely chopped
15 black peppercorns
6 cloves
2 tablespoons oil
2 tablespoons coconut milk (or 1 tablespoon coconut cream + 1 tablespoon warm water)
½ cup warm water
1 bay leaf
1 teaspoon malt vinegar or lemon juice
1 teaspoon brown sugar
1 teaspoon salt taste

Grind together, using a pestle and mortar or a food processor, the cloves, peppercorns, cumin, mustard seeds, cinnamon, chillies, ginger, salt and garlic. Add the sugar and vinegar or lemon juice, and rub the mixture over the pork pieces, leaving the pork in the refrigerator to stand in the marinade for 3 to 5 hours. Heat the oil in the bottom of a large saucepan, at high heat, and add the pork and whatever is left of the marinade in the bottom of the container, stirring well to brown the pork and cook the spices. After a couple of minutes' cooking, add the chopped onion and cook for a further minute, before adding the water and coconut milk (or coconut cream and water) and the bay leaf. Cover the pan and reduce the heat, and simmer the contents for 25 minutes or until tender. Serve with rice or Indian breads.

Bunny chow

South Africa

Bunny chow is a well-known Durban delicacy, and consists of a small sandwich loaf of white bread. The top of the loaf is cut off, the contents scooped out, and the loaf filled with the curry of your choice. The top of the loaf is then replaced. A half bunny is a more practical size for one person, but the challenge remains the same—to eat the curry and bread before the sauce begins to soak through the bottom of the loaf.

Smoorvleis

South Africa

'Smoorvleis' means smothered meat. This is a more elaborate version of a basic Malay mutton stew enjoyed by slaves; the addition of marsala or sherry indicates that this particular recipe was unlikely to have been served to Muslim servants.

1 kg mutton or pork, boned and cubed
2 onions, cut into thin rings
½ teaspoon salt
1 teaspoon freshly-ground black pepper
2 teaspoons soft brown sugar
1 whole red chilli
4 cloves
1 blade of mace
A piece of root ginger 2.5cm long, peeled but left whole
25g unsalted butter

Place all the ingredients in a large saucepan and leave it covered on medium-high heat. When the butter has melted and you can hear the onions beginning to sizzle, and turn down to a low heat. Leave the ingredients to cook, covered, for 1½ hours. Do not take the lid off the pan in the meantime, but shake the pan gently every few minutes to prevent the contents from burning. Five minutes before serving, remove the pan lid, add 2 tablespoons of marsala or medium sherry, and bring the contents of the pan to a boil in order to drive off the alcohol and reduce the sauce. Serve with rice or mashed potato and salad.

Durban meat curry

South Africa

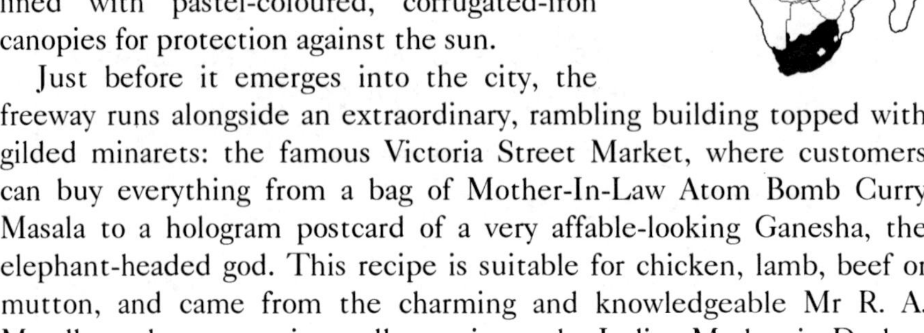

The freeway into Durban descends towards the city above a grid of broad Victorian streets, lined with pastel-coloured, corrugated-iron canopies for protection against the sun.

Just before it emerges into the city, the freeway runs alongside an extraordinary, rambling building topped with gilded minarets: the famous Victoria Street Market, where customers can buy everything from a bag of Mother-In-Law Atom Bomb Curry Masala to a hologram postcard of a very affable-looking Ganesha, the elephant-headed god. This recipe is suitable for chicken, lamb, beef or mutton, and came from the charming and knowledgeable Mr R. A. Moodley, who ran a spice stall upstairs at the Indian Market in Durban for over 30 years.

1 kg chicken, lamb, mutton or beef, cut into cubes
1 onion
2 tomatoes, skinned and chopped
2 cloves garlic, crushed into a paste
1 2.5cm length of ginger root, chopped and pounded to a paste
4 teaspoons Durban masala (you can use any medium curry powder)
1 teaspoon ground turmeric
2 teaspoons garam masala
1 stick cinnamon
6 curry leaves
2 tablespoons ghee or vegetable oil
Fresh coriander for garnish
Salt to taste

In a large pan, heat the oil or ghee and add the cinnamon stick, finely-chopped onion and curry leaves. Fry until the onion is light golden brown. Add the curry powder, turmeric, ginger, garlic and tomatoes. Cook and stir into a puree. Add the meat and salt to taste and cook on a medium heat until the meat is tender.

When the meat has cooked, add the garam masala mixture, and simmer for a further 10 minutes on a low heat. Garnish with fresh coriander leaves before serving.

Swart suur

South Africa

'Black-sour': a luxurious stew, in which ribs of lamb or mutton are braised with spices, tamarind and red wine to create a concentrated, spicy casserole.

1kg rib of lamb, cut into cubes but not boned
2 onions finely chopped
1 clove crushed garlic
½ teaspoon salt
1 teaspoon freshly-ground black pepper
2 tablespoons fresh or block tamarind dissolved in 4 tablespoon boiling water, or 3 tablespoons prepared tamarind paste
400ml red wine
1 tablespoon brandy
1 teaspoon ground nutmeg
½ teaspoon ground cloves
½ teaspoon ground allspice
1 whole chilli
2 tablespoons oil

Heat the oil in a large saucepan and, at high temperature, toss the lamb, onions and garlic until the meat begins to brown. Add the wine and the remaining ingredients, bring to the boil before turning down the temperature and simmering for one hour, stirring occasionally. Serve with almond rice or mashed potatoes and salad.

Snyboontjies (green bean) bredie

South Africa

Bredies are traditional South African stews that demonstrate a distinct Malay or Cape Muslim influence. Typically they are made with mutton or lamb and a single vegetable such as tomato or spinach—bredie is said by several historians to have been a word used by Malay slaves at the Cape to refer to spinach (the modern Bahasa Melayu word for spinach is *bayam*, but bredie is probably related to the word *berdaun*, which means 'leafy', or 'with leaves').

Even fruit is used: traditional bredies include a delicious variety cooked with quinces. During slow cooking the mutton becomes tender and its accompanying vegetables break down, so that you end up with a rich casserole and thick gravy, strongly flavoured with the vegetable pulp.

1 kg mutton or winter lamb
1 kg green beans, chopped into 5cm pieces
2 large onions, chopped
6 medium, waxy potatoes, peeled and chopped into 4cm cubes
1 teaspoon chopped thyme or marjoram
1 tablespoon chopped parsley
1 teaspoon salt
1 teaspoon freshly-ground black pepper
1 tablespoon oil for frying
220ml cold water

Fry the onions over medium heat until translucent. Add the meat and cook until the meat begins to brown (you may need to cook the meat in batches unless you have a large pan). Remove from the heat and add the salt, pepper and chopped herbs, and stir to mix. Fill a large saucepan or casserole dish with the cooked meat, potatoes and beans; first a layer of potatoes, followed by a layer of meat, followed by a layer of beans, proceeding until all the ingredients are used up, and pour the cold water over the top before covering the dish. Cook the bredie on the stove on a very low heat, simmering for 2 hours.

Cabbage bredie

South Africa

1 kg mutton or winter lamb
1 large white cabbage
2 large onions, chopped
6 medium, waxy potatoes, peeled and chopped into 4cm cubes
1 teaspoon chopped thyme or marjoram
1 teaspoon salt
1 teaspoon freshly-ground black pepper
1 tablespoon oil for frying
1 tablespoon cold water

Fry the onions over medium heat until translucent. Add the meat and cook until the meat begins to brown (you may need to cook the meat in batches unless you have a large pan). Remove from the heat and add the salt, pepper and chopped herbs, and stir to mix. Fill a large saucepan or casserole dish with the cooked meat, potatoes and cabbage; first a layer of potatoes, followed by a layer of meat, followed by a layer of cabbage, proceeding until all the ingredients are used up, and pour a tablespoon of cold water over the top before covering the dish. Cook the bredie on the stove on a very low heat, simmering for 2 hours.

Tomato bredie

South Africa

A great autumn dish, tailor-made for using up the annual, autumn glut of tomatoes.

1 kg mutton or winter lamb
1.5 kg fresh tomatoes, skinned and drained in a colander to remove the excess juice
2 large onions, chopped
6 medium, waxy potatoes, peeled and chopped into 4cm cubes
1 teaspoon chopped thyme or marjoram
1 tablespoon chopped parsley
1 bay leaf
1 teaspoon salt
1 teaspoon soft brown sugar
1 teaspoon freshly-ground black pepper
1 tablespoon oil for frying

Fry the onions over medium heat until translucent. Add the meat and cook until the meat begins to brown. Add the salt, pepper, bay leaf and chopped herbs, and stir to mix. Add the tomatoes and sugar, bring all to the boil, then turn down the heat, covering the dish, and leave to cook, simmering gently for 1½ hours. Add the potatoes and cook for a further 30 minutes before serving. The tomatoes should cook down to form a thick gravy: if the sauce becomes too dry, add a little water.

Waterblommetjie bredie

South Africa

One of the more unusual bredie ingredients is *waterblommetjie*, or *Aponogeton distachyos*, an aquatic plant found only in South Africa, whose flowers are used in *waterblommetjie* bredie, and which lend a distinctive taste—something like asparagus—and glutinous quality to the stew. Some South African food shops overseas sell All Gold tinned *waterblommetjie* flowers, and these are perfect for use in bredie. A traditional remedy for burns, scalds and grazes is to apply the juice from fresh *waterblommetjie* stems.

1 kg mutton or winter lamb
2 tins *waterblommetjie* flowers
2 large onions, chopped
6 medium, waxy potatoes, peeled and chopped into 4cm cubes
1 teaspoon chopped thyme or marjoram
1 handful sorrel leaves or 1 tablespoon lemon juice
1 teaspoon salt
1 teaspoon freshly-ground black pepper
1 tablespoon oil for frying
1 tablespoon cold water

Rinse the *waterblommetjie* flowers in cold fresh water and drain them in a colander. Fry the onions over medium heat until translucent. Add the meat and cook until the meat is just beginning to brown.

Add the salt, pepper and thyme, and stir to mix. Add the waterblommetjie flowers and a tablespoon of water, bring all to the boil, then turn down the heat, covering the dish, and leave to cook, simmering for 1 hour on the stove. At the end of that time, add the potatoes and sorrel or lemon juice and cook for a further 20 minutes before serving.

N.º 1501

Hotel Santa Cruz

Endereço Telegráfico: "SANCRUZ"
C. Postal 210 – Telef. PBX 27161
AVENIDA 24 DE JULHO N.º 1417
LOURENÇO MARQUES

EXMO. SR. (Mr.) P. Martin

MES MONTH	March 1972										
DIAS DAYS	31										
Alojamento Room	180	00									
Pensão Completa Room & Full Board											
Restaurante Restaurant											
Bar Bar											
Telefone Telephone											
Lavandaria Laundry											
Diversos Extras											
Total Diário Day's Total	180	00									
Transporte Carried											
SOMA											

OBRIGADO — Thank you
ATÉ BREVE — Please call again!

TOTAL:

ESC.	180	00
DEPÓSITO		
	180	00

REPUBLICA PORTUGUESA — DEFESA NACIONAL — 2$00 — MOÇAMBIQUE
REPUBLICA PORTUGUESA — DEFESA NACIONAL — 1$00 — MOÇAMBIQUE
0$10 MOÇAMBIQUE — DEZ CENTAVOS
0$10 MOÇAMBIQUE — DEZ CENTAVOS

Lamb xacuti

Tanzania

A favourite from the Goan community of East Africa, this has an elaborate masala of dry spices which is added to the lamb. If you can't face the measuring and grinding involved, just use a commercial garam masala and add 50g of desiccated coconut and a fresh red chilli; but it really is worth the effort of making a fresh masala. This recipe is based on an original recipe from the brilliant Indian chef P. Soundararajan, founder of the South India Culinary Association.

1 kg lamb cut into small cubes
200g chopped, peeled tomatoes
250g finely chopped onion
1 tablespoon oil or ghee
Salt to taste

Marinade:

2.5cm peeled, chopped ginger
4 cloves roughly chopped garlic
1 seeded and roughly chopped mild green chilli
½ teaspoon sea salt
Juice of 2 large lemons

Masala:

3g cardamom
3g cloves
3g cinnamon
3g aniseed
10g cumin
3g *ajwain* (nigella or black onion seed)
5g sesame seeds
1g mace or nutmeg

5g white poppy seeds
3g fenugreek seeds
2g mustard seeds
2g black peppercorns
50g desiccated coconut
1 chopped red chilli
30g coriander seeds
10g turmeric

Crush together the ginger, garlic and green chilli and grind into a paste in a food processor or pestle and mortar. If you add the sea salt at this stage you will find that both the ginger and garlic will grind down more readily. Thin with the lemon juice, and rub over the meat, leaving the meat to marinade in the paste for at least one hour.

For the masala, first measure out the spices. If you don't have the facility to measure such small weights, then you can use the rough rule of thumb that 1 teaspoon equals roughly 3g of dry spices. Place all the ingredients into your thickest-bottomed pan and heat, stirring every ten seconds, until the spices are hot and there is the faintest haze of smoke coming off. The smell will be glorious. Tip the spices into a metal or china bowl, and once fully cooled grind in a food processor into a powder. You can use a pestle and mortar, but be prepared for at least 15 minutes' hard work.

In a large, shallow, hot pan, fry the onions until opaque. Add the meat and sauté it until the lamb is beginning to brown on all sides. Add the masala and continue to cook on a high heat, turning the meat almost continuously, for a further two minutes. Add the tomatoes and turn down the heat, and simmer for about 20 minutes before serving.

Steak cooked in milk

Malawi

Because of the difficulty in a hot climate of hanging meat to mature, steak tended to be eaten immediately after slaughter and was consequently tough and flavourless. This led to a variety of colonial-era recipes in which the meat is cooked in liquid to make it tender and bring out what little flavour it has. Another solution was to wrap the leaves in pawpaw leaves for 24 hours: it was believed that the papain (a natural digestive enzyme found in pawpaw) in the leaves would tenderise the meat.

900g stewing steak
2 tablespoons plain flour
220ml milk
4 large onions
1 tablespoon butter for frying
Salt and freshly-ground black pepper to taste

Preheat your oven to 160°C. Cut the meat into 2.5cm squares and roll in flour that has been seasoned with salt and plenty of black pepper. Heat your largest frying pan and add the butter, then add the finely-chopped onions and the steak and cook until the onions are golden brown and the steak is coloured. Add the milk gradually, stirring thoroughly to absorb the flour, and you will find that it thickens to form a sauce. When all the milk has been added to the pan, transfer all of the contents into a casserole and cook in the oven for a further 1½ hours, or until the meat is tender.

NEW
The Safari Revolution
Men's Safari Suit, 3-piece, exclusively styled for Ramji's in wash and wear export selection. Only for professional men. Price $35,95
2-piece Safari Suits, long jacket, with shorts. Priced from $16,95
Plus 1 rack Safari Suits. Special Offer for size 34 and 36.
Only $9,95
About 80 Ladies' Tops reduced by 50%. Priced from $2,00
by ARCHER
The finest range of BUNNY SAFARI SUITS, exclusively styled, with Short Shorts and Saddle Stitching. Super value at $15,95
RAMJIS
Grey Street, 11th Avenue
tel. 60453
1 Rack Bunny Safari Suits.
SPECIAL OFFER at
$7,95

Lamb breyani

South Africa

Breyanis are an important feature of Cape cuisine. Closely related to the biryani or buryani from central India, they consist of spiced meat, fish or vegetables cooked and served in layers with rice.

Breyanis are great for dinner parties because, once prepared, they cook in a single pot and need no last-minute titivation. My cousin's wife, Jasmine, maintains that the secret of a breyani lies in marinating the meat beforehand, and making sure that the pot is not opened during cooking.

Marinade

A piece of ginger root 2.5cm long, peeled and finely diced
3 cloves garlic, crushed
1 teaspoon salt
3 sticks cinnamon or cassia
5 crushed cardamom pods
2 green chillis, seeded and chopped
1 teaspoon ground turmeric
3 tablespoons garam masala
5 cloves
5 whole allspice
A couple of strands of saffron
1 tomato, peeled and chopped
300ml plain yoghurt

1 kg cubed lamb or mutton (winter lamb)
130g cooked or tinned brown lentils
6 potatoes, peeled and cut into 2.5cm cubes
500ml cold water
500g basmati rice
3 tablespoons sunflower oil
300ml hot water

50g butter or ghee

Beat together the ginger, salt and garlic with a pestle and mortar. Combine with the rest of the marinade ingredients and add to the meat, turning and mixing thoroughly in order to cover all the lamb. Leave to marinade in the refrigerator for at least 3 hours or overnight.

Place the rice in a sieve and rinse it until the water runs clear. Heat 50ml of oil in a deep frying pan over high heat and add the rice. Stir well to coat the rice with hot oil, and then add 500ml cold, salted water. Bring to the boil and boil for 5 minutes. Remove from the stove, drain and leave to cool.

Heat the remaining oil in a pan and fry the potatoes until browned. Remove them with a slotted spoon and set them aside to cool. Add the onions to the remaining oil and fry them until golden brown. Remove about a quarter of the onions with a slotted spoon and set them aside. To the remaining onions, add the meat and marinade and cook for about 25 minutes on medium-low heat, stirring occasionally.

Now it is time to build up the layers of the breyani, ready for cooking. In a large saucepan, cover the base of the saucepan with a single layer of cooked potatoes. On top of the potatoes sprinkle half the reserved rice, and sprinkle that with ½ teaspoon salt. Next pour in the meat and sauce, and arrange the pieces of meat over the rice so that it is evenly spaced in a single layer. Sprinkle the lentils over the meat, and then cover the meat with the remaining rice and salt. Dot the top with specks of butter or ghee, and spread the reserved onions over all before sprinkling the hot water over the top. Close the saucepan, making sure that it is sealed tightly—I use a sheet of aluminium foil, shiny side down, laid over the top of the saucepan, then the lid on top of it, and then crimp the edges of the foil down over the sides of the saucepan for a close seal.

Cook the saucepan on high heat for five minutes, then turn down the heat to its lowest setting and simmer it for 45 minutes, without opening the lid.

Stewed trotters

Kenya

A favourite of the East African Afrikaans community, this version is based on a recipe given in the classic South African cookery book *Cape Cookery* by C. Louis Leipoldt.

Six pigs or sheep's feet, cleaned, scraped and washed
3 large onions, thinly sliced
A blade of mace or ½ teaspoon of ground nutmeg
A sprig of fresh rosemary
Salt and freshly-ground black pepper to taste
3 tablespoons red wine
The yolks of two eggs
Juice of a large lemon
A generous handful of fresh white breadcrumbs

Cut the feet in pieces and boil them in salt water until the flesh floats off the bone—this will take about two hours. Strain the liquid and remove the flesh, and place in a casserole dish with the rest of the ingredients. Bring the contents to the boil before reducing the heat and gently simmering for 30 minutes, stirring occasionally. At the end of that time add the breadcrumbs, stir well to amalgamate the mixture, and leave to stand for three or four minutes. Beat together the egg yolks and lemon juice and stir vigorously into the stew, and serve with mashed potatoes or butternut.

Pork stew with cockles

Angola

Another traditional recipe that uses the superb shellfish of the Atlantic and Indian Ocean, combined with the favourite Portuguese meat—pork. In Cape Town I was told that many South Africans and Mozambicans of Madeiran descent use limpets in the stew instead of cockles or clams.

800g loin of pork, boned and cut into 2cm cubes
35 cockles, shelled, rinsed and left to soak
3 onions, finely chopped
1 tablespoon olive oil
2 cloves garlic, finely chopped
200ml dry white wine
150g peeled, chopped tomatoes
A handful of chopped coriander
1 bay leaf
Salt and freshly-ground black pepper to taste

In a heavy-bottomed, deep pan or casserole, heat the oil until just smoking, and add the pork, onions and garlic. Cook for about ten minutes until the meat is brown on all sides, and add the bay leaf, tomatoes and white wine. Turn down the heat and leave to simmer for 1½ hours, adding liquid if the stew seems to be getting too dry. After 1½ hours drain the cockles and add them to the stew, along with the coriander, and simmer for a further ten minutes before serving.

The Perfect Stove.

We believe the NEW PERFECTION OIL STOVE is the best all-round oil cooking stove that has ever appeared, from the standpoint of efficiency, simplicity, and durability. It is as near perfection as human skill and modern machinery can make it.

With these stoves there is no time lost in lighting, good working flame is obtained as soon as the stove is lighted, and after use it may be instantly extinguished, thereby saving fuel.

If you turn it too high or too low it goes out. Can be lighted and extinguished immediately. There's no waiting for the flame to burn up on this New Stove.

Housewives should note that the tops of these New Stoves have been extended six inches over the reservoir, giving 84 square inches more top service. Yet the Stove takes up no more room.

WICKS LAST SIX MONTHS with ordinary care. No trouble in rewicking. Wicks are supplied complete with carrier. You simply lift the old wick and carrier out and drop in the new wick and carrier.

Model No. 2
49s 6d

Write for descriptive Booklet which gives full particulars.

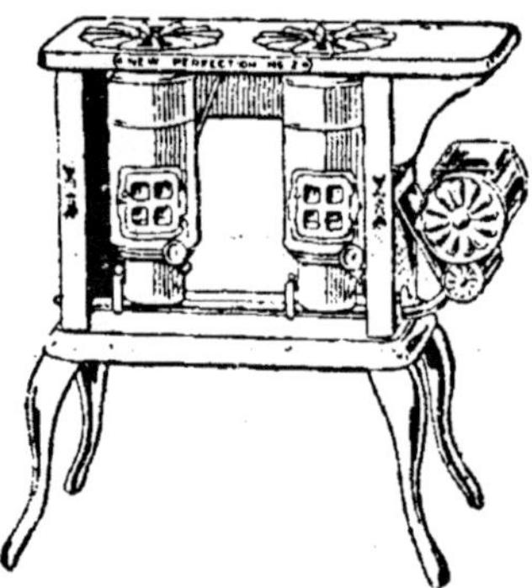

Why not do ALL your Shopping by Post with

Stuttaford's

STUTTAFORD & CO., LTD. (INCORP. IN C.C.)

JOHANNESBURG.

A selection of salads, sauces and other accompaniments.

Potato salad

South Africa

South African potato salad is very different from the mean, pallid version, made with undercooked potatoes and vinegary salad cream, which you are often served in Britain.

1 kg baby new potatoes
6 spring onions
A handful of chives
A large handful of parsley
8 anchovies
1 tablespoon of capers
2 hard-boiled eggs
1½ tablespoons of good-quality mayonnaise
Salt and freshly-ground black pepper to taste

Boil the new potatoes in salted water. When done, drain into a colander and leave to dry. In the meantime, coarsely chop the spring onions, herbs, anchovies, capers and eggs. When the potatoes are cool halve them, pile them into a bowl and grind plenty of black pepper over them, then add the mayonnaise and turn the potatoes to cover them evenly. Add the chopped flavourings and continue to turn the potatoes to mix the ingredients without breaking the potatoes.

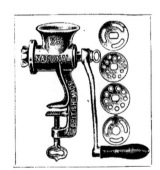

Red cabbage with bacon

Zimbabwe

Perfect as a side dish with game, pork or goose, and excellent as a salad served with cold meat. The vinegar helps to reduce the smell from the cabbage while it cooks, but the younger and smaller the cabbages you choose, the less they will smell. This used to be one of my family's favourite accompaniments with any sort of buck venison.

900g fresh red cabbage
2 large green cooking apples
1 large onion
150g streaky bacon
2 tablespoons white wine or cider vinegar
1 tablespoon brown sugar
10 juniper berries
5 cloves
1 bay leaf
Salt and freshly-ground black pepper to taste

Remove the outer leaves from the red cabbage and quarter it. Cut out the tough core in each quarter, then halve each quarter and slice thinly across the layers, before rinsing the sliced cabbage thoroughly to remove any traces of soil. Dice the onion. Peel and core the cooking apples, and chop roughly. Put all ingredients except the bacon, salt and pepper into a saucepan and add cold water so that they are just covered. Bring to the boil, then turn down the heat and leave the pan to simmer for an hour, stirring occasionally.

In the meantime cut the bacon into bite-sized pieces and fry it until crisp. After an hour the liquid should have almost evaporated. At this stage you can either let the cabbage cool and serve it as a cold side dish or salad, adding the seasoning and bacon just before serving; or you can season it with the salt and pepper, add the bacon pieces and serve the cabbage hot.

Mielie fritters

Zimbabwe

These fritters are brilliant with gammon or sausages.

2 boiled mielie cobs or corncobs
75g plain flour
1 egg
Salt and freshly-ground black pepper to taste

Mix together the flour, egg and season with salt and pepper. Cut the cooked kernels from the mielie cobs with a sharp knife, and stir into the batter mix. Drop spoonfuls of the mixture into a pan of very hot fat, fry on both sides until golden brown and then drain on kitchen paper.

Victoria Falls bacon and mielie fritters

Zimbabwe

These fritters were a favourite hot dish served at breakfast at the Victoria Falls Hotel in the 1950s. They are identical to the previous recipe, but with a couple of rashers of smoked bacon grilled, cut into dice and added to the batter mix.

SUPER BRAAI

THIS SUNDAY and TUESDAY, Sep. 12th.

SUPER MEATS . . .
FINE ENTERTAINMENT,
SUPER FUN FOR THE WHOLE FAMILY!

PLUS —

KENNY OLIVER
INTERNATIONAL ENTERTAINER
Versatile Singer/Guitarist
— from 12.30 - 2.00 p.m.

Holiday Inn®

THE HOSTS WITH THE MOST

e e77977/FZ

Lentil cakes

Nigeria

These little fritters are comparatively quick to make and are particularly good as a side dish for stews or casseroles. They also keep well in the fridge and are tasty cold. If you are planning to eat them cold, put in slightly more seasoning—a little chopped chilli or curry paste is a pleasant addition. This recipe is based on one in Muriel Tew's 1920 guide for colonial cooks in West Africa, and is clearly related to both the Ghanaian fritters known as *akara* and the Jamaican fritters called akras.

125g red lentils
1 onion
½ teaspoon finely-chopped garlic
5 tablespoons fresh breadcrumbs
2 eggs
Salt and freshly-ground black pepper to taste
Oil for frying

Drain the lentils and rinse them under fresh water. Place in a saucepan and add 600ml of water. Bring to the boil, then turn down the heat and simmer for 40 minutes, by which time the lentils will be soft and will have absorbed all the water. Place in a large mixing bowl. Chop the onion very finely and fry with the garlic until the onion becomes translucent—just a couple of minutes should do the trick. Add the onion to the lentils and stir in half of the fresh breadcrumbs. Break both eggs into a jug and lightly whisk with a fork, and then stir half of the beaten egg into the lentil mixture and season with salt and pepper. Form the paste into small cakes about the size of fishcakes. Pour the remaining beaten egg into a shallow dish and scatter the remaining breadcrumbs on a dinner plate. Dip each cake into the beaten egg and then into the breadcrumbs, and shallow fry in the hot oil until golden brown.

Steamed mielie bread

Zimbabwe

A very traditional recipe, particularly popular among the Afrikaans-speaking Rhodesian community, and often served as a side dish with rich meat dishes like ox-tail. This bread is particularly good when made with fresh maize—buy two corn cobs and strip the soft, sweet kernels off the cobs with a sharp knife before mincing them or putting them through a food processor using a coarse blade. If you cannot find fresh, white maize or corn-on-the-cob, a tin each of creamed sweetcorn and non-creamed sweetcorn, mixed, gives more or less the right texture. This recipe is closely related to a traditional Zulu savoury recipe made without the addition of sugar and eggs.

400g fresh maize, cut straight off the cob and minced in a food processor (or a tin each of creamed sweetcorn and non-creamed sweetcorn)
1 teaspoon salt
1 tablespoon melted butter
1 tablespoon light brown sugar
1 medium egg, beaten
2 teaspoons baking powder

Favourite food from childhood? Maltabela porridge and mielie bread, eaten on freezing mornings on a holiday riding farm in what was the Northern Transvaal.

Prue Leith CBE, South African-born food writer, restaurateur, and patron of the Prue Leith Chef's Academy in Centurion, Pretoria, South Africa

Thoroughly mix all the ingredients in a bowl and pour into a greased pudding basin. Cover the basin with a disc of greaseproof paper, and wrap aluminium foil around it, then place in a saucepan and fill the saucepan with boiling water to come two-thirds of the way up the side of the basin. Steam the bread for about 2 hours, making sure that the water in the saucepan is topped up regularly as it boils away. Like polenta, anything left over is good sliced into one-inch thick slices and fried in bacon fat—try it with bacon and eggs.

In my great-grandmother's handwritten recipe book I see there is also a recipe for mielie bread made with stiff maize porridge to which is added a yeast 'sponge' and enough additional wholemeal flour to make a dough which is baked like normal wheat bread.

The Masonic Hotel,

CAPE TOWN,

ESTABLISHED 1859.

THIS First-class Family and Commercial Hotel is situateed in a central position facing the Parade and close to the Railway Station, with Tramway Cars passing from the Docks.

Private Sitting Rooms and Dinners; Wines of the choicest quality; Table d'Hote; Luncheons à la Carte; Billiards

TERMS MODERATE.

F. W. PRATT, Manager.

Pineapple-glazed duck or chicken stuffing

Zimbabwe

This is especially good with duck, and is delicious when made with the little, intensely-flavoured Queen pineapples—the acidity of the pineapple cuts some of the fattiness of the duck, and the papain enzyme found in pineapple helps to tenderise any tough fowl.

2 cups (about 100g) fresh white breadcrumbs
1 tablespoon chopped chives
1 small pineapple, finely chopped
500ml water
100g Demerara sugar
1 tablespoon olive oil
1 egg
Salt and freshly-ground black pepper to taste

Prepare the duck or chicken for roasting as usual, ensuring that you cook it in a deep roasting pan. Mix together the breadcrumbs, chives, olive oil, salt and pepper and half of the chopped pineapple, and use this mixture to stuff the bird for roasting.

While the bird is cooking, simmer the remaining pineapple with the Demerara sugar and water in an open pan for 20 minutes. Half an hour before the bird is ready, pour the stewed pineapple and juices over the bird, and baste it well. Use the remaining juices in the roasting pan for gravy.

Peanut stuffing

Malawi

Many poultry stuffings include nuts, and this simple version is a favourite of mine.

175g roasted peanuts
30g fresh breadcrumbs
100g melted butter
1 onion
1 egg
Salt and freshly-ground black pepper to taste

Chop the peanuts roughly and the onion finely, and mix all of the ingredients together. Use this mixture to stuff the bird before roasting.

Glazed sweet potatoes

Kenya

An excellent recipe adapted from one in the venerable *Kenya Cookery Book and Household Guide.*

1 kg sweet potatoes
½ cup unsalted butter
2 tablespoons brown sugar
Salt and freshly-ground black pepper to taste
Ground nutmeg

Peel the sweet potatoes and boil in salted water until soft, exactly as for ordinary potatoes. Leave to cool. Once cold, pre-heat the oven to 220°C. Gently melt the butter in a pan and dissolve the sugar in the butter. Cut the potatoes into slices about 2.5cm thick and dip in the butter mixture. Lay the dipped slices in a baking pan and bake for about 20 minutes, by which time the potatoes should be a glossy, golden colour. Sprinkle with ground nutmeg before serving.

Irio

Kenya

Another example of an indigenous, East African food widely adopted by white Kenyan settlers—usually as a side vegetable on a European-style, 'meat and two veg.' menu.

Irio is a staple starch dish, probably originally made with millet, beans and a green-leaf relish like the southern African *moroko*, and later with maize and potatoes, mixed with spinach or pumpkin-leaf: in this basic form, similar dishes are found across central and southern Africa. Its appeal to white settlers is probably not unconnected with the fact that it is rather similar to the English dish bubble-and-squeak.

This recipe uses maize and green peas, which combine to give a sweet flavour and striking appearance to the *irio*.

2kg floury potatoes—King Edward for preference
300g fresh or frozen green peas
3 fresh corncobs (if unavailable, you could use a tin of creamed corn, but it really is much nicer made with fresh maize)
50g butter
A handful of fresh spinach leaves
Salt and freshly-ground black pepper to taste

Wash and peel the potatoes and cut into chunks. Arrange them at the bottom of a large saucepan. With a sharp knife, cut the sweet kernels off the corncobs, making sure not to cut too deep into the inedible and fibrous core, and add to the potatoes. Fill the pan to cover the vegetables, and add a pinch of salt, before bringing to the boil. Turn the heat down slightly and boil for twelve minutes, or until the potatoes are just cooked through. Add the peas and cook for a further two minutes, then drain and switch off the heat. While the vegetables are draining, place the butter and spinach in the bottom of the pan and allow the residual heat to begin melting the butter. Add the cooked vegetables, and thoroughly mash all together with a potato masher. Add salt and black pepper to taste. Kenyans swear by Mchuzi seasoning, made by

Royco, which gives a particularly spicy and tasty finish to *irio*—you may find Mchuzi in African or Caribbean grocery stores.

THE CLACHAN.

The Cantiest Wee Howff in Beira for the best brands o'

BARLEY BREE, YILL, WINES, BRANDIES.

Reading Room wi' latest Papers and Periodicals.

"Inspiring, bold John Barleycorn!
What dangers thou can'st mak' us scorn!
Wi' tippeny we fear nae evil,
Wi' usqueba we'll face the devil!"

"Freedom and whusky gang thegither." "Tak' aff your dram."

CARMICHAEL & CO., Proprietors, Rua Cons. Ennes.

Coriander and mint chutney

Kenya

A cool and refreshing chutney which is perfect with any curry.

1 large bunch of chopped coriander, with roots and stems
1 handful chopped mint leaves
2 green peppers, seeded and chopped
1 clove garlic
1 chopped tomato
1 sweet green apple, peeled and cored
½ teaspoon salt
½ teaspoon cumin seeds
½ teaspoon coriander seeds
Juice of a large lemon

Combine all of the ingredients in a blender or food processor and puree them until fairly smooth.

Leipoldt's curry paste

South Africa

Probably the most creative and exciting cookery writer in southern Africa was the Afrikaans poet, surgeon and writer C. Louis Leipoldt. His best-known cooking work was the book *Kos vir die Kenner*—'Food for the Connoisseur'—published in 1933, and it is pleasing to see that his wartime cookery columns from the Afrikaans magazine *Huisgenoot* have now been published as a book.

Part of the joy of reading Leipoldt's work comes from the evident pleasure he took in cooking, and this is always enhanced by the depth and breadth of his scholarship. I came across his recipe for curry paste in the book *Cape Cookery*, first published 30 years after his death, and, with some adaptations, have used it ever since. It takes perhaps fifteen or twenty minutes to put together, but will happily keep in the fridge for a week—or longer, if you pour an inch of olive oil over the top of the paste. Use this paste to make curries, or smear it over fish or meat before grilling, frying or braai-ing.

Fresh ingredients

60g ginger root, peeled and finely sliced
2 red chillies, seeded and finely chopped
4 cloves garlic, finely chopped
2 tablespoons tamarind paste
1 handful coriander leaves and stalks, finely chopped
1 teaspoon sea salt

Dry ingredients

The seeds from 8 cardamom pods (discard the greenish, outer husk)
1 teaspoon black peppercorns
6 cloves
1 small blade mace
2 teaspoons fennel seeds

3 teaspoons cumin seeds
3 teaspoons coriander seeds
1 teaspoon ground turmeric

Place the dry ingredients into your thickest-bottomed pan and heat, stirring every ten seconds, until the spices are hot and there is the faintest haze of smoke coming off. Tip the spices into a metal or china bowl, and once fully cooled grind in a food processor into a powder . You can use a pestle and mortar, but be prepared for at least 15 minutes' hard work.

In a pestle and mortar grind together the ginger, chillies, chopped coriander, garlic and sea salt. When they are reduced to a paste, add the tamarind paste and the powdered spices, and mix thoroughly. Store surplus paste in a jar with an inch of olive oil poured in above the level of the paste.

Peri-peri sauce

Mozambique

Capsicum, or chilli peppers, are native to South America, and were first brought to Europe by the Spanish and Portuguese in the early fifteenth century. From there, plants were quickly exported to Portuguese possessions across the Indies, India and Africa (it is interesting to reflect that curries have had their characteristic fire provided by capsicum peppers for only about 500 years; before then, the heat in Indian food came from ginger and black peppercorns).

This sauce, known as *Molho de Piri-Piri*, is one of the universal sauces of African settler cooking: variations are found from Kenya down to the Cape and up again in Guinea and Cape Verde. The name, too, is rendered variously as peri-peri, piri-piri and pili-pili, with the tiny, scarlet peppers being known as *pilipili manga* or *pilipili hoho* in Swahili.

You can use this sauce as a marinade, or offer it at the table as a side or dipping sauce. There are a number of good commercial versions available on the market, and the South African restaurant chains Nando's and Steers both have bottled versions for sale. The finest commercially-made sauce is probably Nali Sauce from Malawi, which comes complete with a warning in English and Nyanja on the bottle, '*Abale samalani* – Friends take care'. It is not easy to find, but some shops in Europe and the USA offer it by mail order.

100ml (slightly less than half a cup) light olive oil

6 tablespoons finely minced peri-peri chilli pepper, fresh or dried. If you can't find peri-peri chilli pepper you can try the little, Thai, red birds-eye peppers

½ tablespoon ground paprika

1 clove garlic, crushed to a paste

1 teaspoon salt

½ teaspoon chopped oregano or thyme

The juice of a large lemon

This sauce is best made in an electric blender or food processor; if making it by hand, make sure you chop the chilli as finely as possible.

Blend together the chilli, garlic, paprika, salt, thyme and lemon juice into a coarse paste. Leave the blender going, and gradually add enough olive oil to give the sauce the consistency of thick pouring custard. You can keep this sauce in a jar in the fridge: it will improve with age and can happily be used up to about a month old—after that the oils in the garlic tend to get a slightly rancid note. In addition, because the 'hot' component of chilli pepper dissolves and is more easily transmitted in oil, the sauce will taste more fiery after it has stood for a while.

As always when using chilli, don't rub your eyes while chopping, and if you have sensitive skin make sure you wear disposable gloves or protect your hand with a polythene sandwich bag. And, as any chef will tell you, if you have been handling or chopping chilli make sure you wash your hands thoroughly before using the lavatory.

Fried pawpaw

Malawi

This makes a very unusual vegetable to accompany roast meat and is particularly good with chicken or guinea fowl.

One pawpaw, not too ripe
2 tablespoons fresh breadcrumbs
1 tablespoon flour
1 egg, beaten
Oil for deep-frying

Peel and halve the pawpaw, removing the seeds and cutting the fruit into slices about 2.5cm thick. Toss the slices in flour before dipping them in beaten egg and then coating them in breadcrumbs.

Deep fry in hot oil until golden, and drain on kitchen paper.

Yellow rice I

South Africa

A tasty and attractive accompaniment to all manner of curries, bredies and casseroles.

200g white long-grain or Basmati rice
65g seedless raisins
4 cloves
1 tablespoon brown sugar
1 stick cinnamon
1 teaspoon salt
1 tablespoon ground turmeric
1 piece star anise
1 tablespoon split, blanched almonds
1 tablespoon ghee or vegetable oil
1 bay leaf
Boiling water

Boil a kettle so that you have hot water to hand. Heat the ghee or oil in a heavy-bottomed pan, then carefully add the cinnamon, star anise and cloves and fry for one minute. Add the dry rice and fry, stirring constantly, for another minute or until the rice appears glossy and opaque. Add boiling water from the kettle, pouring in carefully as the oil will hiss and spit, and two-thirds fill the pan; add the salt and turmeric, and leave to boil. After ten minutes add the raisins, sugar and bay leaf, and boil for a further three minutes before sieving. Fluff the grains with a fork and sprinkle with almonds.

Yellow rice II

Malawi

This recipe for yellow rice is not quite as rich or elaborate as the preceding Cape recipe.

200g white long-grain or Basmati rice
100g seedless raisins
1 tablespoon brown sugar
1 stick cinnamon
1 teaspoon salt
1 tablespoon ground turmeric

Rinse the rice and put it into a pan with the other ingredients. Add 800ml cold water, bring to the boil and cook until the rice is soft. This will take about 20 minutes. Drain off any remaining water, and fluff the grains with a fork before serving.

Coconut rice

Tanzania

A traditional accompaniment to East African curries. Use tinned coconut milk for this recipe, or use tinned coconut cream and dilute with water according to the instructions on the tin.

200g white long-grain or basmati rice
900ml coconut milk
A generous pinch of salt
1 tablespoon chopped coriander leaves

Rinse the rice and put it into a pan with the coconut milk and salt. Bring to the boil, stirring constantly. After boiling, turn the heat right down, and leave the rice to simmer for 20-25 minutes, stirring occasionally, or until the rice is soft and tender and most of the liquid has been absorbed. Garnish with coriander before serving.

Sweet potato fritters

South Africa

Jan van Riebeeck brought sweet potatoes from Java, and ordered them to be planted on Robben Island as early as 1655. These fritters are a great accompaniment to strong-flavoured or spiced stews, which can be left to stand while you make the fritters at the last minute.

500g sweet potatoes, peeled and grated
150g plain flour
1 egg, beaten
50g melted butter
½ teaspoon grated nutmeg
½ teaspoon freshly-ground black pepper
1 tablespoon chopped parsley
Pinch of salt

After grating the potatoes, place them in a bowl and pour boiling water over them to cover. Leave to stand for ten minutes. Drain the potatoes in a colander and add the rest of the ingredients, stirring well to mix. The mixture should form a stiff, semi-liquid batter: if it is too wet, add a little more flour; if too dry, add a little warm water.

Shallow-fry in hot oil and drain on kitchen paper before serving.

Sorrel and spinach salad

South Africa

Sorrel is one of the few salad greens that grows wild in southern Africa. Cape Sorrel was used by early Dutch settlers, and is still popular as a salad herb. This is one of my grandmother's recipes.

Two handfuls baby spinach leaves, washed and dried
One handful sorrel leaves, washed and dried
A tablespoonful of chopped mint leaves

Mix together and dress as usual

Cucumber salad

South Africa

2 cucumbers
1 teaspoon salt

Take two cucumbers and peel them. Slice them thinly into rounds (use a mandoline to make this job simple) and place the sliced cucumber in a colander. Sprinkle with a little salt and stir well before leaving the colander to stand in a deep dish in the fridge for an hour or two. The salt draws out the slightly bitter juice that cucumbers sometimes have, and this will drip down and collect in the dish. Just before serving, stir again and put into a serving dish.

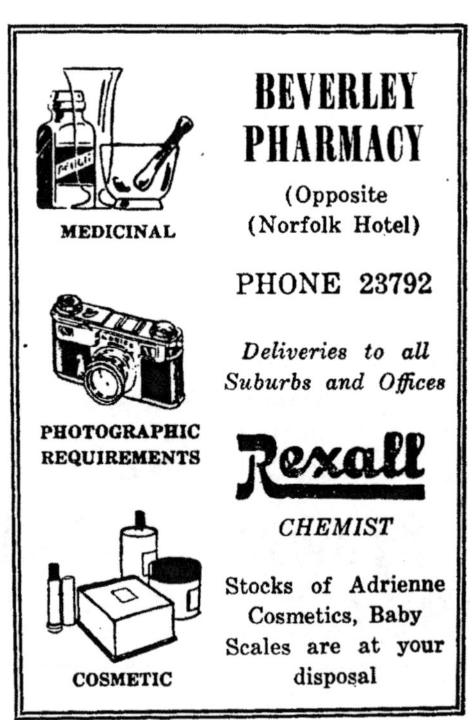

Quince sambal

South Africa

Sambals are the fresh fruit or vegetable relishes or chutneys that traditionally accompany curries. In Africa these dishes are almost as important as the curries themselves, with a dozen or more offered in some Indian restaurants in Durban or Mombasa. In private homes the variety is likely to be slightly narrower, but one is far more likely to find interesting sambals such as quince, which is also very popular in the Cape.

2 ripe quinces
1 spring onion, finely chopped
½ teaspoon of seeded, chopped green chilli
Freshly-ground black pepper and salt to taste

Peel, quarter and seed the quinces and grate them coarsely. Mix them with the remaining ingredients.

Apple sambal

South Africa

Apple sambal is another traditional Cape sambal served to accompany curries or spicy stews.

3 sweet green apples
1 teaspoon salt
1 teaspoon lemon juice
Freshly-ground black pepper to taste
½ teaspoon finely-chopped, seeded green chilli

Grate the apples coarsely and sprinkle with salt and lemon juice. Leave to stand for 30 minutes before squeezing out the excess liquid. Combine with the remaining ingredients and mix thoroughly.

Cucumber sambal

South Africa

2 sweet salad cucumbers
1 tablespoon salt
½ teaspoon finely-chopped, seeded green chilli
½ teaspoon crushed garlic
1 teaspoon balsamic vinegar

Peel and grate the cucumbers, and sprinkle with salt. Leave to stand for 30 minutes before rinsing in a colander. Squeeze out the excess water with your hands until the cucumbers are almost dry. Add the remaining ingredients and mix thoroughly.

Traditional blatjang

South Africa

In English, the name chutney is given to the sweet, fruit preserve served as an accompaniment with everything from curry to cheese sandwiches. (In India, a chutney (or *chatni*) is what southern Africans call a sambal—a relish made from fresh fruit, herbs or vegetables.) A sweet, hot sauce is known as a *blatjang* in Indonesia, and the word has been adopted by both Dutch and Afrikaans to signify a sweet pickle.

The best-known commercial blatjang from Africa is probably Mrs Ball's Chutney, originally made to the recipe of Mrs H. S. Ball (born Amelia Adkins in Fort Jackson in the Eastern Cape in 1865), who died in 1962 at the age of 97; it is now made by Unilever. However, Cape Muslim households traditionally made their own blatjang from apricot jam and chillies.

5 tablespoons apricot jam
100ml malt vinegar
100ml balsamic vinegar
70g crushed, dried red chillis
1 clove garlic, crushed to a paste
½ teaspoon salt

Mix together all the ingredients thoroughly. This blatjang keeps well in the fridge for up to three months.

Puddings

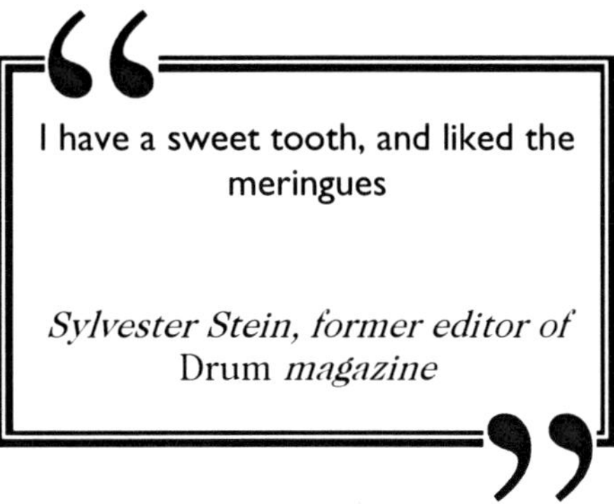
I have a sweet tooth, and liked the meringues
Sylvester Stein, former editor of Drum *magazine*

'Miss Tilsley'

Zimbabwe

The source of the name of this dish is a mystery: it is a Rhodesian version of tiramisú: made with butter instead of mascarpone, so firmer and richer than the Italian original, and containing nuts and biscuit crumbs. This recipe is adapted from one submitted to Rhodesian Woman and Home in the late 1960s.

½ packet (250g) of boudoir biscuits
110g caster sugar (the golden variety makes a pleasant change)
110g unsalted butter
2 medium eggs
25ml espresso or very strong black coffee—I use the best-quality instant coffee I can find and make it with 25ml boiling water to 1½ teaspoons of coffee granules.
50g chopped walnuts
20g cocoa powder or finely grated dark chocolate

Separate the eggs and beat the whites for 30 seconds with a fork before pouring into a shallow dish. Line the sides and base of a small soufflé dish with boudoir biscuits, dipping the edges of the biscuits into the egg white to help them stick to one another. Crush the rest of the biscuits into crumbs, either with a rolling-pin or in a food processor. Lightly beat the egg yolks and stir in the coffee. Cream the butter and sugar together in a mixing bowl, and gradually add the egg yolks and coffee, beating until the mixture is smooth and creamy. Add the nuts and stir to mix.

Pour a layer of the coffee mixture into the lined dish and then top with a layer of crushed biscuits. Pour in another layer of coffee mixture, followed by biscuits, and repeat, finishing up with a layer of biscuit crumbs on the top, which should be roughly level with the top edge of the dish. Put a sheet of greaseproof paper on top of the biscuits, then carefully put a plate on top of the paper, and place a weight on top of the plate to press down the pudding: a tin of baked beans works quite well if you don't have anything else. Refrigerate for at least 8 hours; when you are ready to serve, turn out the pudding onto a plate and either scatter grated dark chocolate over the top, or sieve cocoa powder over the top.

Chocolate Sunday pudding

Zimbabwe

A favourite southern African pudding for a winter Sunday lunch, this dish takes about fifteen minutes to put together and 45 minutes to cook. In one Zimbabwean farming family of my acquaintance, the maid would mix the pudding as Sunday's roast lunch reached the end of its cooking time, and the pudding would go into the oven while the mother of the family finished boiling the vegetables on top of the stove and began to dish up. By the time the family had finished their main course the pudding was ready.

Sponge:

1 cup plain flour
2 tablespoons cocoa
½ cup chopped walnuts or pecans
2 teaspoons baking powder
A pinch of salt
½ cup sugar
½ cup milk
2 teaspoons vanilla essence
2 tablespoons melted butter

Topping:

¼ cup white sugar
¼ cup dark brown sugar
3 tablespoons cocoa powder
A pinch of salt
1 teaspoon vanilla essence
1 cup boiling water

Preheat your oven to 190°C. For the sponge mixture, sift together the flour, baking powder, salt, cocoa and sugar. Add the milk, nuts, butter and vanilla essence and mix well. If using a food processor, add the nuts right at the end and mix them in by hand. Pour this sponge mixture into a greased baking dish or casserole. Mix together the dry topping ingredients in a cup, and gently sprinkle the mix evenly over the surface of the sponge mixture. Very gently pour or spoon the boiling water over the surface of the sponge mixture, and quickly place the casserole in the oven. Do not stir the mixture after pouring the water over it. Bake for 45 minutes at 190°C. As the sponge cooks, the topping mixture sinks down, through the sponge, and you end up with a light chocolate sponge with a rich, chocolate sauce underneath it.

Orange and lemon trifle

Zimbabwe

Having read many references to trifle in the works of the Rhodesian author Sheila Macdonald, it was pleasing to come across an Edwardian recipe for a trifle in the *Bulawayo Cookery Book and Household Guide*, submitted by Mrs Puzey—whose family for many years owned one of the country's largest motor dealers. For anyone who does not like sherry trifle this citrus fruit version provides a delightful substitute: light and creamy, with enough acidity to counter the sweet custard. Because of the difficulty in obtaining fresh dairy products in early 20th-century Zimbabwe, the original recipe did not include cream.

2 oranges
2 lemons
100ml hot water
70g sugar
5 trifle sponges, cut into quarters
475ml thick custard, made with custard-powder, cooked and allowed to cool
240ml whipping cream
Flaked, blanched almonds to decorate

In a jug, dissolve the sugar in the water and leave to cool. Squeeze the juice of the oranges and lemons and add to the sugar-water. Place the sponge pieces at the bottom of a serving dish and pour the mixture over them, then leave to soak for 20 minutes. Whisk the custard for one minute, pour the custard over the sponge and refrigerate so that the custard sets slightly. Just before serving lightly whip the cream, spread it over the top of the custard and garnish with flaked almonds.

Watermelon and lime sherbet

Mozambique

Supermarket watermelons are often under-ripe and tasteless; some of the sweetest that I have bought have come from local Turkish grocers in Hackney and Leyton, who display piles of watermelons heaped carelessly on the pavement outside their shops. Choose a dark green melon which makes a faintly musical thud when you thump it with the heel of your hand: in the Cape, the test for a ripe melon used to be to balance a straw on it—if the straw swung round slowly, the melon was ripe.

Half a small watermelon
30g caster sugar
Juice of one lime
Rosewater or orange-flower water (optional)

Cut the melon into two quarters and remove the pink flesh, cutting it into chunks. Crush the pulp roughly with a fork and remove the seeds. Stir the sugar into the lime juice to partially dissolve the sugar, and then add to the melon pulp and mix thoroughly. Freeze in a stainless metal container (not aluminium—the acid in the lime juice will dissolve it); after two hours take out the mixture and stir it with a fork to help break up the ice crystals, then replace it in the freezer. Serve this to be eaten from glasses like a sorbet; a couple of drops of rosewater or orange-flower water added to the sherbet will perfume it beautifully.

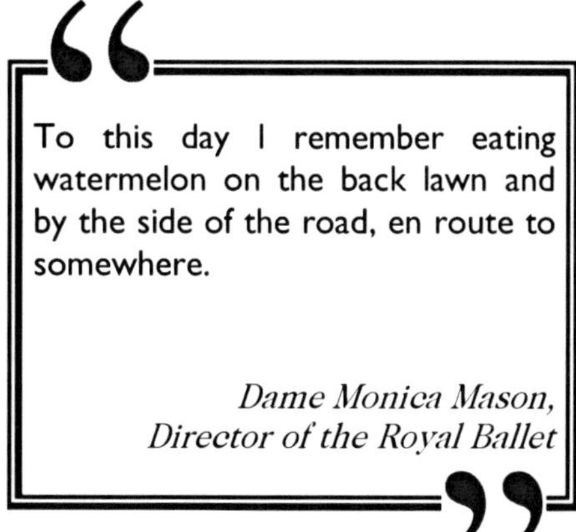

> To this day I remember eating watermelon on the back lawn and by the side of the road, en route to somewhere.
>
> *Dame Monica Mason, Director of the Royal Ballet*

Baked pineapple pudding

Zimbabwe

One of my great-aunt Iris's recipes from the Globe and Phoenix Mine in Que Que.

100g plain flour
½ teaspoon baking powder
75g unsalted butter
75g light brown sugar
2 medium eggs
One small, sweet pineapple
Pinch of salt

Preheat your oven to 190°C. Separate the eggs and lightly whisk the yolks with a fork for 20 seconds. Peel the pineapple and chop it lengthways into quarters. Discard the fibrous core, and chop the remaining flesh very finely with a knife or food processor: you should end up with about two cups full of chopped pineapple flesh. Simmer the pineapple in its own juice for five minutes in a small saucepan—this is to destroy an enzyme in pineapple which will otherwise prevent the custard from setting properly—and drain the pineapple flesh.

In a large basin, cream together the butter and sugar until smooth. Add a teaspoonful of flour to the butter/sugar mix and gradually beat in the egg yolks until creamy. Sieve the remaining flour and baking powder and gradually add it, a spoon at a time, to the batter mixture, alternating with a spoonful of the chopped pineapple and stirring constantly. Whisk the egg whites with a pinch of salt until stiff, and fold them into the mixture using a metal spoon. Pour into a buttered baking dish and cook for 30 minutes.

Mock apple pie

Nigeria

Apples simply do not grow in tropical climates, so homesick Europeans were forced to look elsewhere for substitutes. This Edwardian recipe from Muriel Tew uses under-ripe pawpaw, masquerading as cooking apples. Green mangoes were also used by many cooks.

1 medium-sized, unripe pawpaw (if you are buying pawpaws from the supermarket you will probably need two)
6 cloves
The juice of 2 limes
1 teaspoon powdered cinnamon
2 tablespoons sugar or to taste
275g sweet shortcrust pastry

Preheat your oven to 200°C. Peel and halve the pawpaw and remove the seeds. Cut the flesh into bite-size chunks. Place the flesh into a saucepan with the lime juice, cloves, sugar and cinnamon and about a tablespoon of water—just enough to prevent the flesh from catching on the base of the saucepan—and cook for five to ten minutes until the pawpaw is as soft as cooked apple. Turn the mixture out into a deep pie dish and cover with the pastry, making a couple of small holes in the pastry with a knife. Bake for about 25 minutes or until the pastry is golden brown; dredge with caster sugar while still hot.

Sutlach

Zimbabwe

The Greek island of Rhodes and the colony of Rhodesia have a curious connection that covers more than their homographic similarity.

From 1931, when the Italian Fascist governor of Rhodes introduced anti-Semitic laws to the island, many members of the 40,000-strong Sephardic Jewish community of Rhodes emigrated to Rhodesia. In 1943 the Germans occupied Rhodes, and almost the entire Jewish population of the island was deported; fewer than 200 survived. Only about 40 Jews live on Rhodes today, but Rhodian Sephardic culture still endures in its communities overseas, spread as far away as Argentina and Zimbabwe.

Sutlach is a traditional Rhodian Sephardic pudding, and a very common pudding from Sephardic households in Zambia and Zimbabwe in the 1950s. It differs from the normal Turkish version in that it does not include whole rice grains, but is more often made with rice flour.

125g rice flour
1.75 litres full-cream milk
200g sugar
1 tablespoon ground cinnamon
1 tablespoon rosewater

Put the rice flour in the bottom of a thick-bottomed pan and mix with a little of the milk to form a smooth paste. Place over low heat, add the rest of the milk and bring to a gentle simmer, stirring continuously. When the mixture thickens, add the sugar, and continue to simmer at the lowest possible heat for 15 minutes, stirring all the time. Add the rosewater just before serving, and sprinkle each portion generously with ground cinnamon.

Mango and granadilla Charlotte

Zambia

Mangoes have been grown in southern Africa since the 1870s, when they were brought from Mauritius to Natal. Early settlers in West and Central Africa used them as a substitute for apples in pies and apple puddings such as this delightful charlotte. With the availability of mangoes in British supermarkets all year round, there is no excuse for not trying this glorious pudding, with its intense, tropical fruit aromas. Use firm, green-skinned mangoes, and select heavy passion fruit with slightly wrinkled skins. If you dislike passion fruit seeds, work the pulp with a wooden spoon through a sieve beforehand to strain out the seeds.

Two large green mangoes
2 cups fresh breadcrumbs
¾ cup soft brown sugar
2 tablespoons butter
Grated zest and juice of one lemon
Juice and pulp of two passion fruit (granadillas)
½ teaspoon mixed spice

Preheat your oven to 170°C. Peel the mangoes and cut the flesh away from the stone; chop the flesh into chunks roughly half an inch cubed. Melt the butter in a small pan, and stir in the breadcrumbs. (These must be proper breadcrumbs made from fresh or stale bread—not the fluorescent orange breadcrumbs that come out of a packet.) Mix together the lemon zest, sugar and spice in a bowl. Butter a baking or soufflé dish and sprinkle one-quarter of the breadcrumb mix over the bottom of the dish. Add half of the cubed mangoes, and sprinkle with half of the dry sugar mixture, then sprinkle another quarter of the breadcrumb mix over the mangoes. Arrange the remaining mangoes over the breadcrumbs and sprinkle with the remaining dry sugar mixture. Mix together the passion fruit juice and pulp with the lemon juice, and gently pour over the mangoes in the dish. Spread the remaining breadcrumbs evenly over the top of the mangoes. Cover with aluminium foil and bake at 170°C for 50 minutes. After 50 minutes, remove the foil and leave the Charlotte for a further ten minutes or until golden brown on top. Serve hot, with cream.

Granadilla Pavlova

Zambia

Pavlova is claimed as an Antipodean dessert, but it has been part of British colonial cuisine for the last hundred years and in that time has become a favourite southern African dish. I have decided, admittedly capriciously, to classify it as Zambian—simply because my local supermarket's supply of passion fruit (which in southern Africa we call granadilla—"little grenade" in Spanish) seems always to come from Zambia.

When asked to bring a pudding to family parties, my usual trick is to make something yolk-heavy like a lemon tart or Key lime pie, and then to make a Pavlova with the spare egg whites. Pavlova is brilliant with different fruits: raspberry and pineapple are particularly good. For a lighter texture, use whipping cream on top of the meringue, but be sure not to spread the cream over the meringue until just before serving, or the meringue will lose its crispness.

4 egg whites
200g caster sugar
Pinch of salt
500ml double cream
6 passion fruit (granadillas)

Preheat your oven to 150°C. First of all thoroughly wash your whisk (hand, rotary, or electric) and mixing bowl with hot water and lots of washing-up liquid to get rid of any traces of grease, and wipe dry with a clean paper towel. It goes without saying that you must ensure that there are no traces of yolk in the egg whites: if the egg whites become contaminated by yolk or grease they simply will not whisk properly.

Mark with light pencil or with a pin a 25cm diameter circle on a piece of non-stick baking parchment, and place it flat on a baking tray. Whisk the egg whites with the salt until they stand in stiff peaks. Gradually add the sugar, whisking all the time, until the mixture is stiff, glossy, white and opaque, and the sugar has entirely dissolved. Spoon or pipe the meringue within the marked circle so that you have a circular, roughly flat 'plate' of meringue a little under 25cm in diameter, and about 1.5cm high. Bake in the middle of a cool oven (150°C) for 1 hour, then turn down the oven to its lowest possible temperature and cook for a further hour, and then switch off the oven and leave the meringue in the oven until totally cold.

Remove the paper and place the meringue disc on a plate. Just before serving, whip the chilled double cream until fairly stiff, and spoon or pipe over the Pavlova. The edges of the pile of cream should be slightly higher than the centre, so that the granadilla stays on top of the cream until the Pavlova is cut. Slice the granadillas in half and scoop the juice, flesh and seeds into a bowl; mix lightly with a fork and spoon the granadilla onto the top of the Pavlova.

Baked lemon pudding

Zimbabwe

This Edwardian recipe originates from Mrs Sly, who was the wife of Mr Sly of Haddon and Sly—Bulawayo's foremost department store. It makes a simple and very tasty hot winter pudding.

Grated zest and juice of 2 lemons
75g cake crumbs (trifle sponges, grated, or whizzed in a food processor, are ideal)
100g caster or vanilla sugar
3 eggs
100ml milk
Pinch of salt
A 23cm shortcrust pastry case, baked blind and left to cool

Pre-heat the oven to 180°C. Separate the eggs and whisk together the sugar and egg yolks until pale. Add the lemon juice and zest, milk and cake crumbs. Whisk the egg whites with a pinch of salt until stiff, then fold into the lemon mixture. Pour into the pastry case and bake for 25-30 minutes or until golden.

How perfect is
"Bear Brand" Milk!
Capable of being easily transported and stored for a long time in any climate without possibility of deterioration, this genuine mountain milk is always ready for immediate use, a never ceasing source of delightful refreshment. The last drop is as delicious as the first, containing as it does the wonderful aroma of pure Swiss Mountain Milk. Look for the BEAR BRAND trade-mark on the tin, there is no better milk in the tropics.
ALTHAUS
BEAR BRAND
Natural Swiss Milk

Banana and wineberry fool

Kenya

Wineberries look and taste very similar to raspberries, and grow on very long, bristly canes that look like bramble stems covered in red fur. This recipe can be made very successfully with fresh or frozen raspberries.

250g fresh or frozen wineberries or raspberries
2 ripe bananas
75g caster sugar
450ml whipping cream

Mash the berries roughly with the sugar and stir with a wooden spoon to dissolve the sugar. Mash the bananas roughly with a fork and combine with the berries. Whip the cream until it forms soft peaks that hold their shape, and stir in the fruit mixture. Place in a large bowl or into small serving bowls and chill before serving.

For an even more decadent pudding rather like the original Eton Mess, use less sugar and gently fold in two or three large meringue nests broken into pieces about the size of a walnut.

As a child a special treat was banana and wineberry fool. The remark of one of my childhood friends when he was asked if he would like some more became a family saying. He said, "Oh, I'm full... but maybe I could if I stood up!"

Dr Roger Leakey, Kenyan-born expert in terrestrial ecology and tropical agroforestry

Dop flame pudding

Zimbabwe

From the *Bulawayo Cookery Book and Household Guide*, unattributed, but almost certainly contributed by Major Robert Gordon, a Bulawayo resident who won his D.S.O. during the Anglo-Boer War and later went on to command the Northern Rhodesia Regiment at the start of the First World War. 'Dop' is Cape brandy.

'Cut up a tinned sponge cake in neat pieces and arrange on a tin dish, saturate with good Cape Dop just before serving, pour some round and set alight. Serve while blazing.'

Torta de laranja (orange torte)

Mozambique

When the scientist J. Stark Brown visited Africa in 1905 with the British Association for the Advancement of Science, his disappointment with the generally dire standard of British colonial cookery was underlined by a meal he and his party enjoyed across the border, as guests of the Portuguese administration in Beira in Portuguese East Africa:

> 'The lunch itself was good and quite different in style from those we had lately eaten, for the cooking was foreign and many of the dishes unknown to us. One of the sweets I marvelled at; it was something between a plum-pudding and a baked jam-pudding, garnished with stewed peaches and apricots, and covered with syrup; a rich fare, but really very nice.'

The pudding must have been a something like that Portuguese favourite, *Torta de Laranja*: a grand version of jam roly-poly in which an eggy sponge is rolled up with sugar, the sugar forming an orange filling as the sponge cools. The cook may have added the peaches and apricots to the sugar when the torte was rolled up, in which case the filling would have been studded with pieces of sticky fruit, revealed only when the torte was cut and served. I have tried serving *Torta de Laranja* with an ice-cold orange syrup, but that really does make a rich and over-sweet pudding; my preference is for single cream, or nothing at all.

350g caster Sugar
4 eggs
Juice and zest of one large orange
1 teaspoon orange-flower water (optional)
1 teaspoon ground cinnamon
1 tablespoon flour

Preheat the oven to 220°C. Butter a large Swiss roll tin, and cut out a rectangle of baking parchment to cover the bottom of the tin exactly.

Butter and flour the baking parchment and lay it in the base of the tin. Beat the eggs lightly with a fork, then add 175g of the caster sugar and whisk vigorously with a hand or electric beater for at least five minutes, until the mixture is pale and creamy and the sugar is fully dissolved. Add the flour, orange juice and zest, and cinnamon (and orange-flower water if you choose to use it), and whisk for another two minutes. Pour the batter into the tin and bake for 12-15 minutes, or until risen and lightly golden.

Lay out a clean dishcloth on the kitchen counter-top. (Make sure that it is absolutely clean and fresh and does not smell of washing powder or fabric conditioner!). When the torte is cooked, quickly run a knife around the edge of the Swiss roll tin and turn the torte out onto the cloth. Dredge the remaining 175g caster sugar over the surface of the torte. Raise the edge of the dishcloth nearest to you, and roll the torte over on itself inside the dishcloth like a Swiss roll or jam roly-poly, with the sugar inside the torte. Once rolled, fold the ends of the cloth and leave the torte to cool, during which time the sugar will partially melt and form an orangey filling. To serve, cut into slices at a slight angle, and serve with cream.

Bread pudding

Angola

A delightful recipe; this rich but not over-sweet chocolate pudding originates from the settlers who emigrated from rural Portugal to make their homes in Angola. The port is important not only to add an extra depth of flavour, but also because its acidity reacts with the baking powder and helps the pudding to rise.

375g day-old white bread
350ml milk
2 beaten eggs
150g sugar
4 tablespoons of ruby port (sweet sherry or Madeira can be substituted)
120g unsalted butter
3 teaspoons baking powder
70g cocoa powder

Preheat your oven to 190°C and grease a deep cake tin or large baking dish—a soufflé dish is perfect. Grate the bread into breadcrumbs using a food processor or coarse grater, and place in a large mixing bowl. Warm the milk until hot but not boiling, dissolve the sugar and butter in the hot milk and pour the milk over the breadcrumbs. Leave to stand for 30 minutes. Add the remaining ingredients and mix well before turning into the greased dish. Stand in a baking tray filled with water and bake for 50 minutes to an hour, or until risen and springy to the touch. Remove from the oven and leave to cool slightly before serving warm, with cream.

Melktert

South Africa

The best melkterts I have tasted are those made by my aunt Virginia, and after that probably the one served at the wonderful café at Kirstenbosch Botanical Gardens on the slopes of Table Mountain in Cape Town. In a good melktert, the butter pastry shell holds a custard filling that is unctuous and creamy, with a spicy hint of nutmeg and cinnamon. Delicious.

A 26cm blind-baked shortcrust pastry case
500ml milk
2 tablespoons sugar
1 tablespoon unsalted butter
1 tablespoon cornflour
2 beaten eggs
A stick of cinnamon
1 teaspoon ground nutmeg

Preheat your oven to 180°C. Measure 500ml milk and then take a couple of tablespoonsful and put them on one side. Heat the remaining milk, butter and cinnamon stick in a thick-bottomed pan until it almost boils. In a bowl, mix the sugar, cornflour and the reserved cold milk into a paste; pour on the hot milk and whisk all together before returning the mixture to the pan and bringing back to the boil. Simmer very gently for five minutes, stirring all the time, then remove from the heat and leave to cool, stirring every couple of minutes to prevent a skin being formed. Once cool, whisk in the beaten eggs, pour into the pastry case and bake for 20 minutes. Sprinkle nutmeg over the top and serve cold.

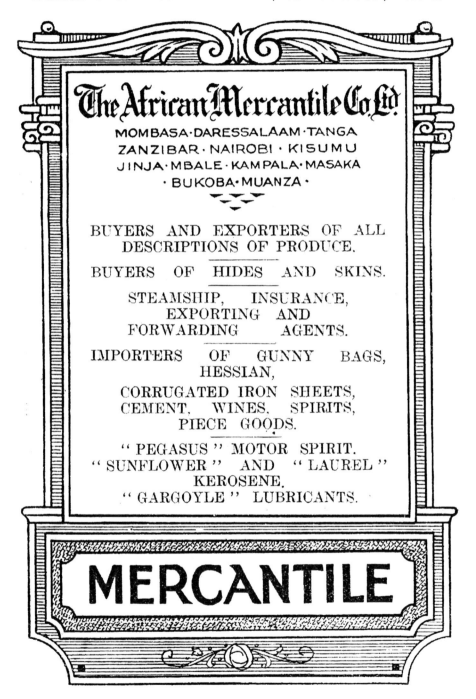

Baked plum-duff

Nigeria

A satisfying West African pudding from the British community in Nigeria; steamed plum-duff was also popular, made from the same basic cake mixture but steamed for 1½ hours.

150g plain flour
20g currants
40g sugar
20g mixed peel
1 teaspoon baking powder
½ teaspoon grated nutmeg
40g butter or margarine
2 eggs
2 tablespoons milk
A pinch of salt

Preheat your oven to 180°C and butter a shallow pie or baking dish. Sift the flour into a basin with the baking powder, salt and nutmeg. Rub in the butter or margarine with the tips of the fingers until the mixture looks like breadcrumbs. Stir in the sugar, candied peel and currants. Break the eggs into a bowl and add half the milk, whisk lightly for 30 seconds. Stir the egg mixture into the dry mix until you have a stiff batter that will stand in peaks. If too dry, add some more milk. Spoon the batter into the greased dish and smooth the top with a spoon dipped in cold water. Bake for about 20-25 minutes or until golden brown (a skewer poked into the pudding should come out clean) and serve with custard.

Baked lemon pudding

South Africa

A favourite South African pudding: I remember my aunt making this years ago in the big, white Corning-ware casserole dish, decorated with a couple of little blue daisies, that seems to have been a fixture in every white South African kitchen. This recipe makes a golden, crusty sponge with a creamy lemon custard sauce concealed underneath.

100g salted butter
100g caster sugar
2 large eggs, separated
150g self-raising flour
The grated rind and juice of a lemon
500ml milk
A pinch of salt

Preheat your oven to 180°C and grease a deep, ovenproof dish. Beat together the butter and sugar until creamy, then add the egg yolks, adding a teaspoon of flour if they look like curdling. Beat the egg whites with a pinch of salt until they form stiff peaks. Sift the flour into the butter and sugar mixture, and then add the lemon rind and juice; stir well and add half of the milk. Fold in the egg whites, and then add the remaining 250ml milk. Pour into the dish and bake for 35 minutes, or until well-risen and lightly coloured on top.

Depression pudding

South Africa

During the Great Depression, the family lived in a tin-roofed miner's cottage in Janie Street in a working-class suburb of Johannesburg. My great-grandfather bought a chest of tea, and his wife and my grandmother and great-aunt spent days in the tiny house, weighing out the tea into one-pound portions and wrapping them in blue paper. After the girls came home from school my great-grandmother would take the family by tram to the suburbs on the other side of town, where they were unlikely to see anyone they knew, where they walked up and down the streets selling tea door-to-door.

Johannesburg has cold, dry winters, and this recipe makes a wonderful, comforting pudding with a sticky, spicy sauce.

Syrup

1.25 litre cold water
300g brown sugar
1 teaspoon ground cinnamon
1 teaspoon ground allspice

Heat all ingredients together over low heat till sugar is dissolved. Boil for 5 minutes and leave to cool.

Pudding mixture

25g butter, melted
25g apricot jam
60g sugar
2 teaspoons bicarbonate of soda
25ml malt vinegar
300g plain flour
A pinch of salt
375ml milk

Preheat the oven to 180°C and butter a large baking dish. Prepare the syrup by boiling the ingredients together until the sugar is completely dissolved, and leave on one side to cool. In the meantime, in a large mixing bowl, cream together the melted butter, jam and sugar. Add the bicarbonate of soda and mix well, then add the vinegar. Quickly mix in the flour and salt and pour in the milk, mixing thoroughly. Pour the syrup into the bottom of the prepared baking dish and then pour in the pudding mixture. Bake for about 40 minutes or until golden brown.

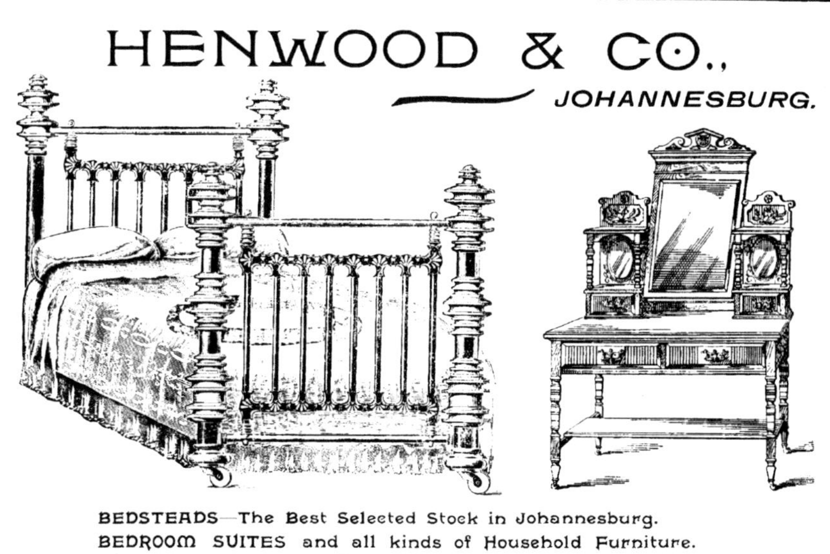

Baked tropical fruit pudding

Malawi

This simple recipe is very adaptable; the pudding can be served hot or cold, and the recipe may be used successfully with mango, banana, peach or a mix of fruits. It can also be made with pawpaw, but the chunks of pawpaw need to be cooked for five minutes before use to destroy the papain enzyme; otherwise the custard will not set.

1 mango or 2 bananas or 2 peaches
2 tablespoons of any sort of jam
1 beaten egg
120ml milk
1 teaspoon cinnamon
1 tablespoon sugar or to taste
A 23cm shortcrust pastry case, baked blind and left to cool

Preheat your oven to 160°C. Peel and stone the fruit as necessary, and cut the flesh into small chunks. Cover the base of the pastry case with jam, and scatter the fruit over it. Whisk together the milk and egg with the sugar and cinnamon until the sugar is dissolved, then pour over the fruit and bake for about 30 minutes or until the custard has set.

Rice pudding

South Africa

South African rice pudding recipes range from grand affairs studded with fruit and cooked until so stiff that they can be turned out onto a dish, to simple, domestic affairs. They are often served with preserved or crystallised fruit. This is based on one of Hilda Duckitt's 19th century recipes.

700ml milk
60g pudding rice
2 eggs
1 tablespoon butter
1 teaspoon lemon zest or powdered naartjie peel
2 tablespoons sugar

Simmer the rice in the milk until soft, then stir in the butter, sugar and lemon or naartjie peel and leave to cool. When cold, preheat the oven to 180°C and butter a baking dish. Whisk up the eggs and mix thoroughly with the cooked rice, then pour into the dish and bake for 25 minutes or until golden on top. Serve hot, garnished with a little crystallised melon or other fruit.

Christmas pudding ice cream

South Africa

There are very few parts of former British Africa where Christmas is celebrated in cold weather—the top of the Mountains of the Moon in Uganda springs to mind, perhaps?—but otherwise an African Christmas tends to be on the sultry side. Despite this, many Africans of British descent still cook a full Christmas dinner: a roast, Christmas pudding and mince pies, and in the early colonial period whole communities came together to celebrate and feast.

In 1895 in Mangwe, near Bulawayo, Mrs Prescott, a pioneer of eccentric character who farmed about twelve miles from Mangwe, invited the entire settler community back to her farm for Christmas breakfast. Her daughter remembered the menu as, 'roast and boiled meat, fowls, potatoes, cabbage, pumpkin, plum pudding, tea and coffee'. Twenty-five years later, a menu for the 1920 Christmas dinner served at the Market Grill in Bulawayo indicates a more elaborate event: eight courses begin with consommé, followed by sole or salmon, York ham, and a choice of six roasts: turkey, duckling, chicken, lamb, beef or sucking pig.

Mrs Hardman, who ran the Market Grill, then offered her customers Christmas pudding, red-currant jelly, mince pies and Christmas cake; two choices of salad (cucumber, or *à la* Duchess of Fife) and dessert: bon-bons, nuts, fruit and muscatel, which were probably fat, fragrant muscatel raisins made from hanepoot grapes from the Cape.

Jeannie M. Boggie, in her book *First Steps in Civilising Rhodesia*, tells the story of the Christmas pudding which another early Rhodesian colonist, Annie Cockin, cooked on her way to Hope Fountain mission in Matabeleland in 1877. Mrs Cockin was taken ill en route, so she and her husband stayed at Shoshong (in Botswana) with the Reverend and Mrs Hepburn, who ran the mission station there. It transpired that Mr and Mrs Hepburn had never had a plum pudding during the period that they had lived at Shoshong, so Mrs Cockin begged lemon, currants, raisins, eggs and milk from local traders, and made a Christmas pudding for the missionaries (when asked if he would have a second helping, Mr

Hepburn, with a distinct lack of grace, heaved a sigh and replied, 'It is substantial, but I will have some more.)

An anonymous writer in the *Journal of the Royal African Society* of 1903 was an official of the British South Africa Company based at Mpika in Northern Rhodesia. He described travelling five days to enjoy Christmas dinner—in full evening dress—with nine other Europeans ("(3 French, 1 Dutchman, 1 Swede, 2 Scotsmen, 1 Welshman, and 2 Englishmen) with 13 dogs and 5 cameras").

This ice cream provides an unexpected alternative to the traditional steamed Christmas pudding, which many people dislike in any case, and is perfect for a light Christmas dessert.

25g raisins
25g currants
25g sultanas
25g chopped, mixed peel
25g glacé cherries
60ml dark rum
30ml ruby port
The zest and juice of 1 orange
450ml single cream
150ml whipping cream
3 egg yolks
90g caster sugar
25g soft brown sugar
1 teaspoon ground mixed spice
1 teaspoon ground cinnamon

Mix together the dried fruit, rum, port, orange juice and zest, spice and cinnamon and leave to stand overnight in the refrigerator. The following day, whisk together the egg yolks and sugar in a mixing bowl until the mixture is creamy and the sugar is dissolved. Bring the single cream to a gentle simmer over a low heat, and slowly pour the hot cream in a single stream into the egg yolk mixture, whisking continuously. You may find it easier if you decant the hot cream into a jug beforehand. Strain this custard mixture through a sieve into a saucepan or, even better, into a bain-marie (in other words, a double-boiler or even a bowl suspended in a saucepan of warm water), and return to the lowest possible heat. Gently warm the mixture, stirring constantly, until after about 10 or 15 minutes it forms into a proper custard thick enough to coat the back of a spoon. Immediately remove from the heat and stand the pan to cool in a couple of inches of cold water—this will prevent it from cooking any more.

Whip the whipping cream until stiff, and fold into the cold custard. Fold in the fruit and spice mixture, with any remaining liquid, and mix thoroughly. Pour into a metal container and freeze for about 3 hours, then turn out into a cold bowl and beat with a wooden spoon to break up the ice crystals. Freeze for another 3 hours, then turn out again and beat with a wooden spoon once more. Return the ice cream to the freezer and leave to freeze overnight in a chilled pudding basin or bombe mould. Remove from the freezer 20 minutes before serving, turn out and garnish with holly.

Malva pudding

South Africa

Malva is probably one of the best and simplest baked puddings in the world, and unmistakeably South African. Use a good apricot jam like 'Bonne Maman' or the South African brand 'All Gold'.

2 tablespoons butter
1 tablespoon apricot jam
50g soft brown sugar
50g caster sugar
1 egg, beaten
150g plain flour
220ml milk
1 teaspoon bicarbonate of soda
1 tablespoon white wine or cider vinegar
A pinch of salt

Sauce

100g soft brown sugar
100ml warm water
250ml double cream
1 teaspoon vanilla essence
100g unsalted butter

Preheat your oven to 180°C. Cream together the butter, jam and sugar. Sift the flour with the bicarbonate of soda and salt. Whisk together the egg and vinegar, and pour into to the butter mixture, and then add the flour and milk alternately, spoon by spoon, whisking after each addition. Pour into a buttered baking dish with reasonably high sides and bake at 180°C for 30 minutes or until firm to the touch and cooked through.

While the pudding is baking, make the sauce by mixing together in a pan the sugar, water and butter and bringing the mixture to the boil. Boil until the sugar is dissolved, and then remove from the heat and add the cream and vanilla essence. Stir and leave to cool.

When the sponge is cooked, remove from the oven. Pour the sauce over the sponge and leave for ten minutes to soak, before serving warm with cream or ice cream.

Cape bread and butter pudding

South Africa

In this old Cape recipe the rosewater and citron preserve or peel add an unexpected depth of flavour to a favourite pudding.

8 slices of white bread
150g soft butter
1 tablespoon blanched, sliced almonds
100g citron preserve or mixed peel
100g currants
150g caster sugar
1 tablespoon rosewater
2 eggs
500ml milk

Preheat your oven to 180°C. Lightly butter a pudding dish. Butter each slice of bread and soak it in milk, then lay it in layers in the base of the dish, sprinkling over the almonds, sugar, currants and mixed peel between each layer. Whisk together the remaining milk with the eggs and rosewater, pour over the bread, and bake for about 25 minutes or until golden.

Lemon meringue pie

South Africa

This is a family recipe from my great-grandmother. She was a tough old woman, brought up in Natal, who remembered hearing, as a child, the sound of the guns at the siege of Ladysmith during the Anglo-Boer War.

200g digestive biscuits
75g unsalted butter
450g tin sweetened, condensed milk
The juice of 2 lemons
The zest of 4 lemons
Two eggs, separated
100g caster sugar

Pre-heat the oven to 140°C and grease a deep, 20cm baking tin. Crush the digestive biscuits in a food processor or with a rolling pin and mix with the melted butter, and use to line the base and sides of the baking tin. Beat the egg yolks until pale, and add the condensed milk, lemon juice and lemon zest, mixing until creamy. Pour the mixture into the baking tin. Whisk together the egg whites with the caster sugar until the mixture forms semi-stiff peaks. Carefully spread the egg whites over the top of the filling, and bake for about 1¼ hour or until the egg whites begin to colour slightly. Leave to cool thoroughly before serving.

My mother's cooking brought mixed results, but her pastry was always fantastic and the point is she used real lemons. You must use real lemons for Lemon Meringue Pie.

Matthew Parris, former Member of Parliament and political columnist of the Times

Butterscotch pears

Kenya

4 pears (Conference are the best variety for cooking)
Vanilla ice cream

Syrup

200g sugar
400ml cold water
A cinnamon stick

Sauce

250g unsalted butter
200g soft brown sugar
500ml double cream

Boil together the sugar and water and cinnamon stick to form a syrup, and add the peeled, cored pear halves. Cook for about ten minutes, or until the pears are soft but still hold their shape, and allow them to cool in the syrup before removing them. In a thick-bottomed pan heat the butter, cream and sugar, stirring regularly to dissolve the sugar. Allow the mixture to simmer very gently for about seven or eight minutes, stirring every couple of moments, and then leave to cool. The sauce will thicken as it cools: if it becomes too thick, add a little more cream to thin it down. Serve the pears drizzled with the butterscotch sauce, with some ice cream on the side. The sauce keeps well for up to a week in the fridge.

Baked custard pudding

South Africa

The Dutch influence shows in the flavouring of this simple custard pudding, which is great served cold with hot fruit compôte. The bay leaves perfume the custard beautifully.

900ml milk
2 tablespoons caster sugar
4 eggs
2 bay leaves
1 teaspoon ground nutmeg

Place the milk in a small pan with the bay leaves, heat until almost boiling, then remove from the heat and leave to cool thoroughly; remove the bay leaves when cold. Preheat the oven to 160°C. Whisk the eggs with the sugar, then gradually whisk in the milk. Pour into a baking dish, sprinkle with nutmeg, and stand the dish in a tray of water while baking. Bake for around 35 minutes or until golden on top and firm to the touch.

Cape brandy pudding

South Africa

A favourite Cape recipe, to be served with whipped cream or ice cream. I first tasted this pudding when my aunt cooked it at a family dinner in Johannesburg; since then I have found dozens of recipes for it.

200g stoned dates
50g raisins
1 teaspoon bicarbonate of soda
250ml boiling water
120g butter
2 beaten eggs
250g plain flour
1 teaspoon baking powder
Pinch of salt
50g chopped walnuts
50g chopped, blanched almonds

Sauce

250g soft brown sugar
15g butter
150ml water
1 teaspoon vanilla essence
175ml brandy

Preheat your oven to 180°C. Cut up the dates and place in a bowl. Sprinkle them with the bicarbonate of soda, and pour over the boiling water. Stir and leave to soak. Cream together the butter and sugar and slowly add the eggs, whisking all the time (you may find it helpful to add a spoon of flour to prevent the mixture from curdling). Sift together the flour, salt and baking powder, and add to the egg mixture. Fold in the nuts, raisins and dates, and mix thoroughly to form a batter. Bake in a greased, high-sided pan for 45 minutes or until the pudding is firm to the touch and well risen.

While the sponge is baking, mix the sauce by boiling together the sugar, butter and water in a saucepan over a medium heat. When the sugar is fully dissolved, remove the liquid from the heat and add the brandy and vanilla essence.

When the sponge is cooked, remove from the oven. Pour the sauce over the sponge and leave for ten minutes to soak, before serving warm.

Banana tart

Uganda

Some shops now stock the soft, dried Ugandan bananas imported by a fair trade company. These can be soaked in warm water and used in this recipe for a genuine East African flavour.

A 23cm shortcrust pastry case, baked blind and left to cool
6 ripe bananas
1 teaspoon lime juice
6 tablespoons caster sugar
2 eggs, separated
A small pinch of salt

Pre-heat your oven to 160°C. Mash the bananas and whisk them with the lime juice and one-third of the sugar (i.e. 2 tablespoons) until they appear smooth and frothy. Beat the egg yolks until pale and mix them into the banana mixture. Beat the whites with a pinch of salt until they form soft peaks; add the remaining sugar and continue to beat until the sugar is dissolved. Pour the banana mixture into the pastry case and top it with the egg white meringue. Spread the meringue over the banana filling, place the tart into the hot oven, and immediately switch off the oven. Leave the tart for 30 minutes before removing it and leaving it to cool.

Apricot and vanilla soufflé

Kenya

The *Kenya Cookery Book and Household Guide* contains an interesting recipe for Apricot Delight. Made with tinned apricots, it makes delightfully light, little, steamed, apricot puddings. I love anything with apricots, but I'm not keen on tins. After some time spent playing around with the recipe this is what emerged.

12 fresh apricots
1 tablespoon icing sugar
1 vanilla pod
3 eggs
200g vanilla sugar
300ml milk

Pre-heat your oven to 190°C. Butter a soufflé dish or deep, ovenproof china bowl, and dredge the inside with icing sugar; set the dish aside in a cool place. Cook the apricots, uncovered, over a medium heat. Once they begin to exude juice, break them up a little with a wooden spoon and add the whole, unbroken vanilla pod. Cook for about 20 minutes, stirring occasionally, until the apricots are reduced to a puree. Remove the vanilla pod, rinse it and set it aside, then push the apricots through a wire sieve with a wooden spoon—you should have somewhere between 250ml and 300ml of puree.

While the puree is still hot, add 125g of the sugar and stir thoroughly until dissolved. Separate the eggs and whip the whites until stiff. Fold the whites into the warm apricot puree, and heap the mixture into the buttered soufflé dish. Place the dish in a deep baking tin, and pour a little cold water into the bottom of the tin to come about a quarter of the way up the sides of the dish. Bake for 30 minutes.

In the meantime, whisk together in a bowl the egg yolks and the remaining sugar until the mixture becomes light in colour. Add 200ml of the milk, whisking continuously. Put the remaining 100ml milk to heat gently in a saucepan with the vanilla pod that you used for the apricots, and pour in the egg mixture, stirring continuously. Allow the custard to warm gradually until it begins to thicken, then remove from the heat and continue to stir it until it cools slightly and the danger of it curdling is past. Serve the custard with the apricot soufflé.

Baked banana pudding

Uganda

A wonderful winter pudding, somewhere between a bread-and-butter pudding and a hot banana trifle.

6 large, ripe bananas
3 eggs
1 tablespoon vanilla sugar
550ml milk
Apricot jam
Four or five thin slices of white bread and butter

Generously butter a pie dish or soufflé dish, and cover the bottom with thick slices of banana. Spread some thin slices of white bread and butter with a generous layer of apricot jam, and place them in a single layer—buttered side down—on top of the banana. Repeat these layers of banana and bread until the dish is three-quarters full, ending with a layer of bread. Pre-heat the oven to 180°C.

Whisk the milk with the vanilla sugar and eggs until thoroughly blended and the sugar is dissolved. Pour this very slowly over the top of the dish, making sure to cover all of the bread, and leave for 25 minutes to soak into all the layers. Place the dish in a deep baking tin, and pour a cold water into the bottom of the tin to come about a quarter of the way up the sides of the dish. Bake for 30 minutes, until the top is golden brown.

Granadilla (passion fruit)ice cream

Kenya

The writer Robin Howe once suggested that if Kenya had a national dish, it was ice cream! Colonial-era Kenya had a highly developed dairy industry, and urban centres enjoyed daily deliveries of fresh milk and cream. This is a typical recipe.

250ml single cream
150ml whipping cream
2 eggs, separated
100g caster sugar
The pulp of 10 granadillas
½ teaspoon vanilla essence
A pinch of salt

Whisk together the egg yolks, vanilla essence and sugar in a mixing bowl until the mixture is creamy and the sugar is dissolved. Bring the single cream to a gentle simmer over a low heat, and slowly pour the hot cream in a single stream into the egg yolk mixture, whisking continuously. You may find it easier if you decant the hot cream into a jug beforehand. Strain this custard mixture through a sieve into a saucepan or, even better, into a bain-marie (in other words, a double-boiler or even a bowl suspended in a saucepan of warm water), and return to the lowest possible heat. Gently warm the mixture, stirring constantly, until after about 10 or 15 minutes it forms into a proper custard thick enough to coat the back of a spoon. Immediately remove from the heat and stand the pan to cool in a couple of inches of cold water—this will prevent it from cooking any more.

Beat the egg whites with a pinch of salt until stiff, and fold into the cold custard mixture, and then fold in the granadilla pulp. Whip the whipping cream until stiff, and fold into the mixture. Pour into a metal container and freeze for about 3 hours, then turn out into a chilled bowl and beat with a whisk to break up the ice crystals. Freeze for another 3 hours, then turn out again and beat with a whisk once more. Return the ice cream to the freezer and leave to freeze overnight in a chilled pudding basin or bombe mould. Remove from the freezer 20 minutes before serving.

Bread, cakes and biscuits

Sour dough yeast bread

South Africa

For colonists all over the world, the introduction of their traditional foods to the colonised territory has often been a tangible demonstration of ethnic or tribal difference and of a perceived culinary and, consequently, cultural superiority. In many cases some of the invader's foods are adopted by the invaded, and bread is an enduring example: fifty years after the French left Indo-China, baguettes and croissants remain popular in Cambodia, while Portuguese-style white bread rolls are still baked daily throughout Angola and Mozambique.

Because of the difficulty of obtaining fresh baker's yeast, fresh bread had an almost mystical symbolic value to early African colonists, and this was recognised by Lord Randolph Churchill during his visit to Rhodesia in 1891, when he wrote, 'living in England where bread is so cheap, so common, and so wastefully consumed, it is impossible to imagine what a delicious luxury it becomes on the veld to the traveller who has been without it.'. The Matabeleland prospector Frank Oates wrote in his diary in 1874, 'Brown has given me a piece of bread. I enjoy it without butter or anything else with it; it is a wonderful treat.'

The value that settlers placed on their bread is vividly shown by an anecdote related by the Rhodesian colonist Jeannie M. Boggie. She describes how, when the alarm was raised in the laager at Mangwe Fort during the Matabele Rebellion of 1896 two settlers, Mrs Greeff and Mrs Boysen, were in the middle of baking. They ran for the shelter of the fort, desperate above all else to save their bowls of warm bread dough, which each woman carried on her head.

While rusks were light, inert and portable and were a food to be carried and eaten en route—what is called in Afrikaans *padkos*, or road-food—bread dough needs time to rise and bake; yeast must be stored and used from one batch to the next; the baker must have a flat, clean surface on which to knead the dough. Bread is a food which in the process of its manufacture represents settlement and development.

Traditionally, travellers carried a yeast pot with them—a wide-mouthed pot with a close-fitting lid, protected by being wrapped in a linen bag. This pot was always used to prepare yeast from potatoes, raisins, hops or wheat flour. It was filled with warm water before use, which helped to reanimate the yeast, but never rinsed out before being put away. In fact, it was necessary for yeast spores to be preserved from batch to batch in a process of continuous regeneration and by using a pot like this, yeast spores were left dormant until the next fermentation. Further north, in Kenya, Uganda and Tanganyika, settlers developed a recipe for sourdough bread which used yeast made from hops and over-ripe banana. There, cooks were advised to save some of the sodden hops from each brew of yeast, and to use them to begin the next brew. In an emergency, the powdery white pulp inside the seed pods of the baobab tree could be used as a raising agent—either as a yeast, or combined with bicarbonate of soda to make a baking powder for a form of soda bread (hence the baobab's alternative name, the 'cream of soda tree'). Some men on the 1890 Pioneer Column which annexed Rhodesia described using African sorghum beer, with its live yeasts, as a raising agent for bread while on the march.

Mrs Zillah Carey, whose family trekked up through the Transvaal to Chipinga in Rhodesia in 1896, left interesting accounts of baking on trek. After kneading the dough, the bread pan was often wrapped in newspaper and left to rise under the blankets in a warm, just-vacated bed. Dried cow dung was the favoured fuel for heating up an ant-hill oven—it burns quickly and (surprisingly enough) fragrantly but retains heat well for a long period.

Henry Seaton, in his book *Lion in the Morning*, describes his cook on tour across Kenya in the 1920s, baking bread in a large, cast-iron cooking pot (a '*potjie*', 'Dutch oven' or 'veld oven') which he had unearthed in a Nairobi store. Sheila Macdonald, too, describes her cook baking excellent bread in a *potjie*, and tartly adds that as the cook very rarely removed the embers before lifting the lid to see if the bread were cooked, it was also full of surprises.

The instructions below give a recipe for sourdough bread, adapted from the recipe of the Cape historian C. Louis Leipoldt.

50g *ou suurdeeg* (dough left over from the last baking)
275ml warm water
1 teaspoon sugar
1 teaspoon strong white bread flour

750g strong white bread flour
2 teaspoons salt

15g butter
175g warm water

The night before you plan to bake, place your *ou suurdeeg* (a lump of uncooked dough, left over from your last batch of baking) in the bottom of the yeast pot and fill it up with 275ml of warm water.

Add the sugar and a teaspoon of fresh flour. Stir well, cover and leave overnight in a warm place to ferment.

The next morning, the liquid should be cloudy, with a foamy head and clean, sour smell. Stir it well again and leave for an hour in a warm place. Sieve the flour and salt into a bowl. Rub in the butter. Add the yeast mixture and warm water, and mix into a dough. Knead it well for 10 minutes or so to make a soft, springy dough, then shape the dough into a ball, dust with flour and place it in a clean, floured basin at least twice the size of the dough, and cover with a clean cloth or cling film before leaving in a warm place to rise for 2 hours.

Turn out the dough and knead it again for five minutes until smooth—this is known as 'knocking back' the dough. Dust with flour and place it back in a clean, floured basin in a warm place for 1 hour.

Pre-heat your oven to 210°C. Turn out the dough ball onto a floured surface and use a sharp knife to cut off a piece the size of a walnut, then divide the bulk of dough into two equal parts. Place each half in a greased baking loaf tin. Cover each tin with cling film or a clean cloth and leave in a warm place for 45 minutes to rise again. Bake for 45 minutes, and turn out on a wire rack to cool. Rinse out the yeast pot and lid with cold water and leave in the fresh air to dry thoroughly.

Roll the small piece of dough in flour. This is your *ou suurdeeg* for the next batch of loaves, and was traditionally kept lightly buried in the top of the flour bag or bin, where the surface quickly dried out and prevented it from becoming mouldy. Alternatively, you can wrap the *ou suurdeeg* in cling film and refrigerate it; it will come back to life with disconcerting swiftness once warmed up for the next batch.

This recipe can be adapted for use in a bread machine: fill the pan with dry ingredients as if making your usual white bread recipe, but omitting the yeast. Measure out the normal quantity of water called for in the recipe, add one extra tablespoon of water, and warm it to blood heat; when warm, dissolve a teaspoon of sugar in it and stir in a teaspoon of flour. Mash the *ou suurdeeg* with the warm sugar-water and pour all into the pan. Set the timer for 12 hours, and start the programme as usual. This makes dense bread that does not rise as high as white bread made with baker's yeast, but has a wonderful flavour that goes brilliantly with cheese or pâté.

RHODESIA'S FINEST
SUNGLOW
FLOUR
ASSURED BAKING SUCCESS IS
IN THE BAG
★
A WIGHTMAN PRODUCT

Sourdough yeast starter

Zimbabwe

From Mrs Winslow's bread recipe in the *Bulawayo Cookery Book and Household Guide.*

'Take 2 breakfast cups of water that potatoes have been boiled in, 1 tablespoon flour, 1 tablespoon sugar and half dessertspoon [i.e. 1 teaspoon] salt. Mix these into the potato water when cool and bottle in a well-stoppered bottle. This should have risen sufficiently in 24 hours for use.'

Mrs Winslow's recipe goes on to turn a cup of this starter into a 'sponge' with the addition of flour and water, into which after a couple of hours the flour is kneaded. This makes an excellent sourdough starter, with the potato water providing a range of complex sugars which wild yeasts thrive on; however, I add a tablespoon of chopped raisins or dates and omit the salt, which inhibits the action of the yeast. In addition, it seems strongly inadvisable to leave the yeast to rise in a stoppered bottle—the whole point of using yeast in baking is that it gives off carbon dioxide, and a stoppered bottle is quite likely to explode. Far better to use a basin, covered with a dinner plate or clean tea towel.

Ashkoek

South Africa

Ashkoek is a very traditional bread from the European tradition, dating back to the earliest period of African colonial settlement. It takes its name from the Afrikaans for ash-bread, because the dough is formed into small loaves or large bread rolls and baked in the ashes of a braai or camp fire. This recipe is great for braais or for camping. If you have a bread machine, using a pizza dough setting is a painless and quick way to make the dough, and for a genuine taste from the past you can use the sourdough recipe, although *ashkoek* is satisfying and tasty made with any bread dough.

500g strong white bread flour
1 teaspoon instant dried yeast—the type used in bread machines
1 tablespoon buttermilk or plain Greek yoghurt
25g unsalted butter, melted
1 tablespoon caster sugar
1 teaspoon salt
325ml cold water

Sift the flour into a mixing bowl and add the other dry ingredients. Make a well in the centre and add the melted butter, buttermilk and water, and stir together with a knife blade to mix. Form into a dough and knead for about 8-10 minutes or until smooth and silky. Leave the dough covered in a warm place for an hour to rise.

You cannot bake *ashkoek* until the fire has burnt down enough to leave a good bed of hot, white ashes from the firewood or charcoal. Once burnt down, remove the live coals from the centre of the fire and place them at the edge, leaving a circular bed of ash at least 40cm in diameter, surrounded by a ring of live coals. Cut off egg-sized pieces of dough and slightly flatten them into rough discs, then lay them in the ash to cook. They should be turned after about 20 minutes, and should take about 30-40 minutes in total to cook; to ascertain whether they are done, just tap with a finger and listen for a hollow sound.

Roosterkoek (or roosterkoekies)

South Africa

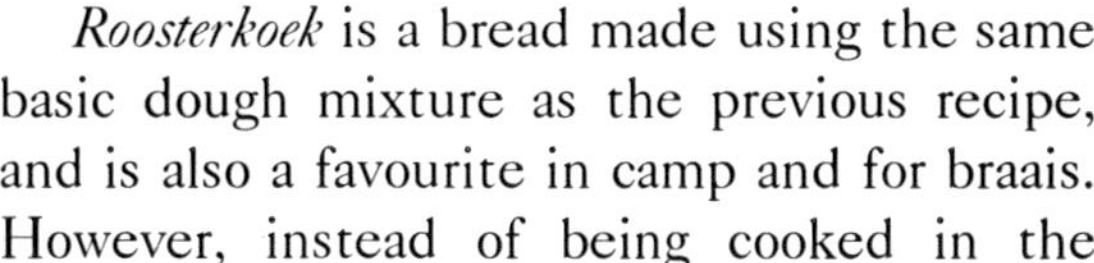

Roosterkoek is a bread made using the same basic dough mixture as the previous recipe, and is also a favourite in camp and for braais. However, instead of being cooked in the ashes, the bread is baked on a grill suspended over the hot coals. You may flatten egg-sized pieces of dough into a rough disc shape, and bake and turn the discs halfway through cooking, or split the entire batch of dough into two circular loaves which are part-cut with a sharp knife into six segments and baked. In the Boland *roosterkoek* is traditionally formed into square loaves, and each side quickly cooked before being turned. In either case, the bread should be turned over after about 20 minutes, and should take about 30-40 minutes in total to cook; to ascertain whether the loaves are done, just tap with a finger and listen for a hollow sound.

Try *roosterkoek* warm, with cold, unsalted butter and grape or apricot jam slathered over it.

Mosbrood

South Africa

Mosbrood is a sweet bread made using must—fresh grape juice—and was made almost exclusively at harvest-time, when the winelands of the Cape were awash with must. Must ferments naturally using the wild yeasts present on the skin of the grape (forming the 'bloom' that you see on many fruits). It is likely that, before the first Cape grapes were harvested, a solution of raisins soaked in warm water was used as a raising agent, much as it continued to be used in areas where baker's yeast was unavailable until the late nineteenth century.

600g white grapes
750g plain white flour
250g light brown sugar
1 teaspoon fennel seeds, caraway seeds or aniseed
30g currants

Let the grapes stand in a warm kitchen for an hour to come to room temperature. Crush the grapes to a coarse pulp using a food processor or blender, pour the juice into a basin and leave to stand for 48 hours in a very cool oven, airing cupboard or other warm place. Strain the juice through a sieve or colander lined with muslin, and squeeze all the juice out of the remaining pulp, skins and seeds. Mix the juice with one cup of the flour to form a light batter, and leave in a warm place overnight to form a 'sponge'.

The following morning, add the sponge to the remaining flour, sugar, seeds and currants, and knead the ingredients for about 8 minutes to form a light dough. Leave to rise in a warm place for 2 hours before kneading again for 3 or 4 minutes and forming the dough into rolls the size of a golf ball. Leave these on oiled baking trays to rise for 45 minutes, and then bake for 25 minutes at 180°C or until nicely golden brown.

Mosbolletjies

South Africa

Mosbolletjies are a form of rusk made from *mosbrood*.

To make them, pack the dough balls into tins as for ordinary rusks, and bake for 1 hour at 180°C. During cooking, the balls will amalgamate into a large loaf. Turn out the loaf and, while still warm, use two forks to divide the loaf into the smaller *mosbolletjies* by pulling it apart along the visible seams. Leave the *mosbolletjies* to cool on a wire rack. Once cool, preheat your oven to 110° and arrange the *mosbolletjies* on wire racks or lay them straight on the oven shelves if clean; leave them to dry overnight or for at least 8 hours, until crisp and totally dried out. Leave to cool and store in an airtight container.

Carrot and mielie meal bread

Zimbabwe

Maize, or mielies (the name given in southern Africa), was probably introduced into Africa from America by the Portuguese in the early sixteenth century. It is astonishing to see how, in a little over five hundred years, maize has almost entirely replaced millet and sorghum to become the staple grain food in many parts of the continent. This bread is delightful when served warm—moist and golden, with an interesting texture and bags of taste.

150g grated carrot
300g mielie meal (i.e. ground maize meal; it is worth trying to find mielie meal at a South African food store for this recipe—at a pinch you can use polenta meal)
1 tablespoon sunflower oil
1 tablespoon light brown sugar
½ teaspoon salt
¾ cup boiling water
2 eggs—separated

Preheat your oven to 180°C. Simmer the mielie meal with 450ml of cold water for about 20 minutes, stirring occasionally, until it forms a thick porridge, then remove from the heat and leave to cool.

Separate the egg yolks from the egg whites and beat the whites with a pinch of salt until stiff. Mix the carrot, mielie porridge, oil, sugar and salt with the boiling water. Beat the egg yolks lightly and add to the mixture. Fold in the egg whites with a metal spoon, and when amalgamated pour into a greased loaf tin. Bake for ¾ hour to 1 hour at 180°C. After taking the loaf out of the oven, leave it to cool for five minutes before turning out onto a cooling rack.

Rusks

South Africa

In most of the English-speaking world rusks are viewed as a hard biscuit given exclusively to children when teething—Farley's rusks are the best-known British brand. However, in Southern Africa rusks were originally used as a substitute for fresh bread, and they remain a popular everyday biscuit, particularly at breakfast with coffee or tea. Rusk recipes in southern Africa descend from recipes for breads made with yeast—either baker's or sour yeast, or natural must yeasts made from fermented grape juice or raisins—which are then dried into a sort of hard biscuit. It is tempting to suppose that the widespread popularity of rusks might have come about as a consequence of all early settlers' intimate familiarity with ship's biscuit, the hard, tasteless rusk carried by sailing ships as one of the staple foods of their passengers and crew.

The drying not only ensures that the breads last longer, but also by removing the water, the rusks are made much lighter and easier to transport. This was particularly desirable in the seventeenth, eighteenth and early nineteenth centuries, when the only way of travelling around South Africa was by sea, by ox-wagon, by foot or on horseback.

This recipe is the one I use; it makes about 28 rusks and is basically a scone mixture with the addition of condensed milk, baked and then dried out; it gives a creamy-tasting, not over-sweet rusk with a good brown top and off-white body. The rusks can be stored more or less indefinitely in an airtight tin. If you are planning to store them for more than a few weeks, do not substitute margarine for butter, or you will find that the oils lend a rancid taste to the rusks over time.

There is an unusual Rhodesian variation on the theme of rusks, by Mrs C. M. Parry, in the 1909 *Bulawayo Cookery Book and Household Guide.* It is based on a similar recipe, made using baking powder instead of yeast or grape must as a raising agent, but the rusks are made into rounds like scones and half-cooked before being split and dried. This recipe lies very much in the British tradition, and is an interesting addition to the variety of southern African rusk forms. Another Rhodesian pioneer, Mrs Zillah Carey, remembered her family baking rusks on trek in the 1890s: '... a favourite to eat with coffee. They were made rather like bread, but with lard added, and were cooked in the ant-heap oven and then dried in the same oven to be almost like toast.'

1 kg self-raising white flour
1 teaspoon baking powder
1 teaspoon salt
2 eggs, beaten
50g white sugar
1 tin condensed milk
180g melted butter
1 tablespoon milk

Preheat your oven to 180°C and butter two loaf tins. Sift the flour and baking powder into a large bowl and add the salt. Stir lightly to mix. In a pan, mix together the sugar, melted butter, eggs and condensed milk, and add to the dry ingredients. Stir to mix, and knead into a medium, sticky dough. Divide the dough into four and then divide the first portion into seven equal amounts. Roll each smaller piece into a ball and pack the balls side-by-side into the loaf tin (as the rusks bake, the dough will be forced to rise upwards, giving the characteristic shape of South African rusks).

Continue with the remaining dough until all is packed into the tins. Brush the tops of the rusks with milk and bake for 30 minutes or until browned. During cooking, the balls will amalgamate into a large loaf. Turn out the loaf and, while still warm, use two forks to divide the loaf into the smaller rusks by pulling it apart along the visible seams. Leave the rusks to cool on a wire rack. Once cool, preheat your oven to 110° and arrange the rusks on wire racks or lay them straight on the oven shelves if clean; leave them to dry overnight or for at least 8 hours, until crisp and totally dried out. Leave to cool and store in an airtight container.

Malay roti

South Africa

Malay roti are made in a specific style, distinct from Indian roti, using plain white flour. They are delicious, with a soft, elastic texture, and are particularly successful when used as flatbreads for wrapping curries, since their texture minimises the chances of the sauce leaking. The South African name for a roti wrap filled with curry is a salomi, and it is a very popular snack or takeaway lunch food, particularly in the Cape.

400g plain white flour
60g white self-raising flour
1 teaspoon salt
45ml vegetable oil
250ml cold water
50g melted butter or ghee

Extra flour and melted butter for rolling out
Butter or ghee for frying

Sift the white flour and self-raising flour together in a bowl and add the salt. Add the oil, and rub it into the flour to form breadcrumbs. Add the cold water, and mix to form a soft dough. Knead for about 8 minutes on a generously-floured board, adding more flour as required, to form a soft, silky dough, form into a ball and leave covered in a warm place to rest for 30 minutes.

Divide the dough into eight pieces, each of which will form a single bread. Roll out the first piece on a floured board to form a disc approx 20cm diameter. Use a pastry brush to dot five or six 'splodges' of melted butter randomly over the surface of the disc, sprinkle the surface with flour, then roll up the disc tightly and keep rolling the dough with the hands until you have a thin rope of dough about 20-25cm long lying horizontally in front of you. Starting at the left hand end of the dough, roll the dough up in a flat spiral in an anti-clockwise direction until half the rope is formed into a spiral. Then, starting at the right hand end of the remaining dough, roll it up in a flat spiral in the opposite, clockwise direction. You will end up with two joined spirals of dough forming a sort of infinity symbol ∞. Fold one side flat on the other and roll out again on a floured board to form a single flat piece of dough about 20cm across. Repeat with the other pieces of dough.

When you are ready to cook the breads, heat a heavy-bottomed frying-pan and brush it with melted butter. The rotis will need about four or five minutes each side, and should puff up and bubble during cooking—don't worry if there are burnt patches. When you remove them from the pan, gently pat them backwards and forwards between your palms to fluff them up. Stack the rotis in a warm oven until ready to serve.

Indian roti

South Africa

This is a Durban recipe for Indian roti, or griddle flatbread. The roti made by the Indian community in kwaZulu-Natal is sometimes made using mielie (maize) meal, and this ingredient quite successfully reproduces the texture of some Northern Indian flatbreads which are made using corn flour. The addition of yoghurt makes softer and more nourishing bread, and the extra ghee added during cooking makes these rotis richer than the Malay rotis. One of the delights of visiting a really top-class Indian restaurant, like the Ulundi in Durban or the Haandi in Nairobi, is the wonderful selection of different breads, each made from different ingredients or cooked using a slightly different technique.

350g plain white flour
50g mielie meal
2 tablespoons plain yoghurt
75g melted ghee or butter
210ml boiling water
A pinch of salt

Extra melted ghee and flour for rolling out
Ghee for frying

Sift together the plain flour and mielie meal, and add the boiling water and yoghurt. Stir to mix, and leave to cool to blood temperature. When cool, add the ghee and knead for about 8 minutes to form a soft, silky dough; form into a ball and leave covered in a warm place to rest for an hour. Divide the dough into six pieces, each of which will form a single bread. Roll out the first piece on a floured board to form a disc approx 20cm diameter. Use a pastry brush to brush melted ghee over the surface of the disc, sprinkle the surface with flour, then fold the disc in half. Brush the top with more ghee and sprinkle with some more flour, and fold again to form a quarter. Repeat with all six pieces of dough, and leave the breads to rest for another 30 minutes.

When you are ready to cook the breads, roll each out on a floured board to a flat, roughly circular bread about 20-25cm in diameter. Heat a heavy-bottomed frying-pan and brush it with melted butter. The rotis will need about four or five minutes each side, and should puff up and bubble during cooking—don't worry if there are burnt patches. Brush the upper side of the rotis with melted ghee during cooking and, once cooked, stack the rotis in a warm oven until ready to serve.

Vetkoek

South Africa

You can try these little deep-fried breads with either sweet or savoury fillings. They are especially popular as a rich breakfast bread, perhaps filled with jam or konfyt, but are also served with a spiced mincemeat filling. They were often made on baking days, using some of the surplus bread dough, but the batter gives a lighter and slightly more digestible result. Breads made with fried bread dough were known during the Anglo-Boer War as *stormjaers*, or 'storm troopers'.

240g plain white flour
2 teaspoons baking powder
1 tablespoon sugar
½ teaspoon salt
2 beaten eggs
120ml milk or milk-and-water

Sift the flour and baking powder together and whisk in the eggs, sugar and milk to form a stiff batter. Heat the oil—traditionally, in the Cape, oil rendered from the tails of sheep was used for frying—and when the oil is hot but not smoking, drop in a teaspoon of batter to test the temperature. The batter should immediately start cooking and float to the top of the oil, where it should brown in ten or twenty seconds.

Dip a tablespoon in the hot oil and use the spoon to drop balls of batter into the hot oil, dipping the spoon in hot oil after each one to prevent the batter from sticking to it. Fry the *vetkoekjies* in batches of five or six—any more, and the temperature of the oil will drop too low, leaving the breads soggy and oily—until deep golden brown, and drain them on kitchen paper.

Honey loaf

Mozambique

Many of the Portuguese settlers who arrived in Mozambique during the 20th century originated from the island of Madeira rather than from mainland Portugal. This rich, moist cake is still a Madeiran favourite, and you find it on the slatted wooden shelves of traditional Portuguese bakeries throughout Southern Africa—in the old days, as with so many European delicacies, it was strictly seasonal and made only around Christmas.

75g butter
300g plain flour
2 eggs
The grated zest of one lemon
100g ground almonds
½ teaspoon powdered cinnamon
2 teaspoons baking powder
200g honey
100g black treacle
A pinch of salt

Pre-heat the oven to 200°C and butter a large loaf-tin or square springform tin. Melt the butter in a pan over a very low heat, then remove from the stove and add the honey and treacle. Add the lemon zest and cinnamon and stir until amalgamated. Separate the eggs, and add the yolks to the butter mixture, stirring well to mix them, then add the ground almonds. Sift the flour and baking powder together and add to the butter mixture. Whisk the egg whites with a pinch of salt until they form soft peaks, then fold into the mixture using a metal spoon. Bake for an hour; leave the cake to cool in the tin for 5 minutes before turning out.

Cassava fairy cakes

Kenya

Cassava was often grown in East Africa because it will produce food even when other crops fail due to drought. Cassava itself is a starchy vegetable with little nutritional value, but its flour was a colonial favourite for making cakes: these little cakes are reminiscent of French madeleines, and are a useful recipe for anyone intolerant of wheat flour or gluten. Cassava flour is a white, mealy flour widely available in South Asian food stores, where it is labelled *gari*.

140g cassava flour
140g sugar
90g butter
3 eggs
The grated rind and juice of a lemon
1 teaspoon baking powder

Pre-heat your oven to 190°C and grease and flour a muffin tin or lay out paper muffin cases. Beat together the sugar and butter until light and creamy. Beat the eggs and add them to the butter mixture. It helps if you add a spoonful of flour first to prevent the butter from curdling. Add the rest of the flour and beat well before adding the baking powder, lemon juice and rind and beating to mix. Quickly fill the muffin tin or paper cases and bake for 15-20 minutes or until nicely risen and light brown in colour.

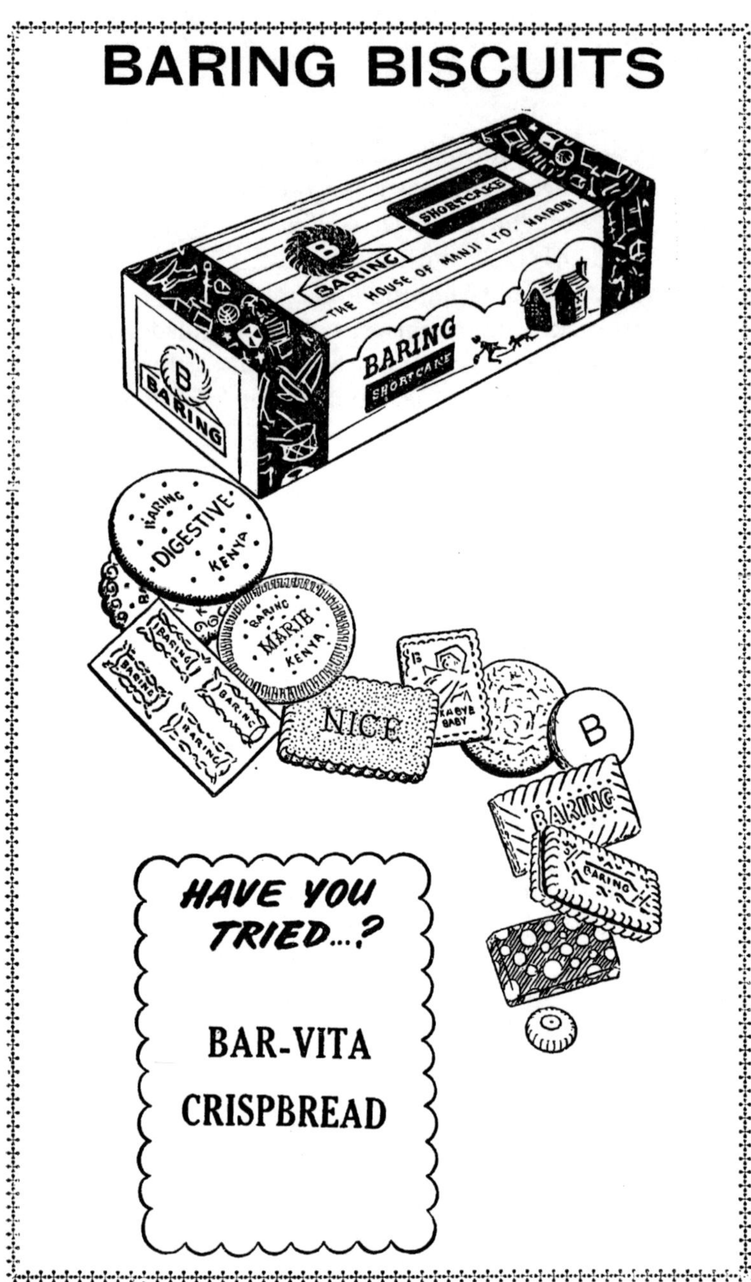
BARING BISCUITS
SHORTCAKE
BARING
THE HOUSE OF MANJI LTD. NAIROBI
BARING
SHORTCAKE
BARING
BARING DIGESTIVE KENYA
BARING MARIE KENYA
NICE
B
BARING
HAVE YOU TRIED...?
BAR-VITA
CRISPBREAD

Koeksisters

South Africa

Koesisters or koeksisters are a Batavian or Dutch delicacy, from the same tradition as doughnuts, *beignets* and Jersey *mervelles*—sweetened, fried dough finished with syrup or sugar. Koeksisters have a definite spicy edge, with cooks favouring a range of different spices including ginger, naartjie peel, cinnamon and nutmeg. You will find most koeksisters made nowadays with plaited dough, but older recipes call for the dough to be formed into sticks or balls, and in the Cape Muslim tradition, koeksisters are always oval.

Dough

550g plain flour
250ml milk
Pinch of salt
90g sugar
125g melted butter
15g dried yeast
1 egg, beaten
1 teaspoon ground ginger
1 teaspoon ground cinnamon
1 teaspoon ground naartjie peel
1 teaspoon ground mixed spice

Syrup

1 kg sugar
500ml water
A 2.5cm piece of root ginger, peeled
Grated rind and juice of a lemon

750ml vegetable oil for frying

Place all of the ingredients for the syrup in a deep pan and bring to the boil; after the sugar has dissolved, remove from the heat and leave to cool, then refrigerate. Mix the dried yeast with two tablespoons of warm water, a teaspoon of sugar and a teaspoon of flour, and leave in a warm place for ten minutes to activate. Sift the flour, salt and sugar into a mixing bowl and add the spices. When the yeast is frothy and active, pour it into the flour and add the remaining ingredients, then mix thoroughly and knead for about 8 minutes to make a firm, silky dough. Cover the basin with a cloth and leave the dough in a warm place for two hours until the dough has doubled in volume.

After rising, knead the dough again for a minute or two, and divide it into four. Divide the first quarter into quarters, and then divide those into thirds, to give you twelve pieces of dough. Each of these pieces will make a koeksister. Roll each piece of dough into a flattened pencil shape, and then, using a sharp knife, cut two parallel lines along the length of the dough, stopping short at one end. This gives you three lengths of dough, connected at one end that you can plait together. Leave the koeksisters aside to rise for 30 minutes.

Divide the cold dipping syrup between two bowls and leave one in the refrigerator. When the koeksisters have risen, fry them in hot oil until golden brown, remove them from the oil and drain them on kitchen paper. Dip them into the cold syrup while still hot, then drain on a cooling rack. It is important that the syrup is cold when the koeksisters are dipped—it helps to keep them crisp on the outside—so when the cold syrup begins to get warm, swap it with the cold bowl in the refrigerator.

You can sprinkle desiccated coconut over the koeksisters after they have cooled; koeksisters will keep very well in a refrigerator for up to two weeks.

LOURENÇO MARQUES

2 — SENSACIONAIS CORRIDAS — 2

DIAS **25** E **26** DE DEZEMBRO ÀS 16 HORAS

Dia **25** às 16 horas

1 — «CAVALEIRO» — 1

DAVID R. TELLES

2 — «MATADORES» — 2

Duas grandes estrelas no mundo taurino

JOSÉ SIMÕES

JOSÉ FALCÃO

«FORCADOS»

AMADORES DE LOURENÇO MARQUES

Chefiados pelo cabo

Machado Lourenço

12 — Bonitos e pesados Toiros — 12

DAVID R. TELLES

CARLOS EMPIS

JOSÉ SIMÕES

JOSÉ FALCÃO

Dia **26** às 16 horas

2 - «CAVALEIROS» - 2

DAVID R. TELLES

CARLOS EMPIS

1 — «MATADOR» — 1

O melhor matador português

JOSÉ FALCÃO

«FORCADOS»:

AMADORES DE VILA FRANCA DE XIRA

Chefiados pelo cabo

José Lourenço

PREÇOS:

SOMBRA DESDE **100$00**

S/SOL DESDE **80$00**

SOL DESDE **60$00**

Informações e reservas Restaurante MARIALVA — Telefone, 26220

Fruit cake

Zimbabwe

The glory of Rhodesian cookery lay not in the tired repetition of solid middle-class English dishes, many of which were totally unsuited to the climate of central Africa, but in the fervour and enthusiasm with which Rhodesians baked. Every recipe book produced in Rhodesia, whether a battered family notebook stuffed with recipe cuttings from the *Rhodesia Herald* and the Bulawayo *Chronicle*, or one of the patriotic cookbooks encouraged by the government in the years after U.D.I. ('Published in the interests of Rhodesian Home Products!'), contains dozens of recipes for cakes, biscuits, breads, pastries, pies and flans.

One of the first buildings to be erected in Salisbury was a bakery, a small red house on First Street where bread was baked in a huge anthill oven; and it is notable that the first brick-built house in Salisbury was erected by Mr Brewan, the proprietor of Brewan's Tea and Cake Shop. (Brewan is reported to have charged one customer, the Rhodesian pioneer Jack Carruthers, an outrageous 14/- for ginger beer and cakes—about £45 at today's prices—which may go some way to explaining how he could afford to build such a prestigious house!)

Northern and Southern Rhodesian recipes from before the First World War are notable for the economy with which eggs are prescribed. In stark contrast to contemporary British recipes, which airily called for four or six eggs—Mrs Beeton's standard sponge cake recipe requires eight eggs—early Rhodesian recipe books are filled with reassuring admonitions: 'made without eggs'; 'very cheap'; '1 egg (may be omitted)'.

After the First World War wheat and maize flour was cheap and plentiful; Rhodesia was often described, with some accuracy, as 'the breadbasket of central Africa'. White women were encouraged to be homemakers and housewives in the best pre-war English tradition, and that included bridge parties and baking sprees for the Women's Institute. My great-aunt, whose husband worked at the Globe and Phoenix gold mine in Que Que, used to hold afternoon tea-parties every week for the other mine wives, and it was a point of honour to provide a cake cooked to a novel recipe at every party.

The writer Philippa Berlyn suggests that the widespread adoption of baking as a social activity might to some degree have been imposed upon white Rhodesian women following the introduction of petrol rationing not long after U.D.I. in 1965. The lack of petrol circumscribed everybody's social activities, and it may be that the added difficulty in arranging travel led women to seek social and creative recreation at home.

280g plain flour
A pinch of salt
3 teaspoons mixed spice
225g butter
225g caster sugar
4 medium eggs
225g currants
225g sultanas
125g glacé cherries, halved
100g mixed citrus peel
1 tablespoon milk

Preheat your oven to 160°C. Grease a 22cm (9-inch) round cake tin and line it with greased greaseproof paper or baking parchment. If you have a springform cake tin, high-sided with a removable base, then this will be ideal for this cake.

Sift the flour, salt and mixed spice together into a large bowl. Cream the butter and sugar together until light and fluffy, and then add one tablespoon of the dry flour mix and gradually beat in one lightly beaten egg, then another tablespoon of dry flour mix and another egg, continuing until the eggs have all been added and the mixture is pale yellow and creamy. If by chance it should start to curdle, just add another tablespoon of dry flour mix and beat it vigorously with a balloon whisk or electric beater until it emulsifies again; and remember, if it refuses to amalgamate it isn't the end of the world!

Stir in the sultanas, currants, cherries and peel—if you toss them in a little flour first they won't sink to the bottom of the cake—before folding in the rest of the dry flour mixture and the milk.

Turn into the tin and smooth the top with a wet palette knife. Bake in the centre of the oven for about 2¼ hours, or until nicely brown and springy to the touch. Leave the cake to cool for 30 minutes in the tin before turning it out onto a wire rack to cool.

Glacé fruit triem

South Africa

A 'triem' is a rich, buttery cake. This recipe is based on the definitive version, by Faldela Williams. It uses the famous Cape glacé fruits, which are still made in vast quantities in the Western Cape district of Malmesbury, and exported all over the world (look on the Internet for Sugarbird brand glacé fruit—the most widely available).

550g self-raising flour
300g unsalted butter
250g mixed whole glacé fruit (figs, pineapple, orange, pear, watermelon)
160g soft brown sugar
125ml single cream
100g walnuts chopped
60g vegetable oil
50g glacé cherries
50g golden syrup
4 eggs, beaten
25g currants
25g mixed peel
25g sultanas
1 teaspoon vanilla essence
1 teaspoon salt
1 teaspoon ground mixed spice
½ teaspoon baking powder

Preheat your oven to 180°C and grease a very large, deep cake tin, preferably a springform or similar, with a removable base. Halve the cherries and chop the mixed glacé fruit. Shake the glacé fruit, cherries, nuts, mixed peel and dried fruit in a plastic bag in a couple of spoons of flour to coat them well with flour—this will help prevent them from falling to the bottom of the cake during cooking.

Cream the sugar and butter together until fluffy, and gradually whisk in the beaten eggs until pale and creamy. Add the oil, golden syrup and vanilla, and mix well. Sift together the baking powder, salt, flour and spice and add to the mixture, mixing well. Finally, fold in the fruit and nuts. Pour into the baking tin and cook for 45 minutes. At the end of that time, reduce the oven temperature down to 160°C and bake for a further 45 minutes or until a skewer slipped into the centre of the cake comes out clean. Leave to cool in the tin for 15 minutes before carefully turning out onto a wire rack to cool.

NOTICE.

THE Depôt for sale of ICE from the "Albion Ice Factory" IS REMOVED to 19, Burg-street. Orders for large or small quantities supplied at reasonable rates, in Town and Suburbs, by the undersigned.

EDW. A. CHUCK.

Gingerbread

Zimbabwe

Based on a recipe from the *Rhodesia Herald*, c1934. The addition of mixed peel and caraway seeds is typically Victorian. Like most gingerbread, this cake improves with age: I usually cut the loaf in half and store half in the cupboard, wrapped in cling film, for a week or two while we finish off the first portion—the cake becomes soft, sticky and even more intensely flavoured.

450g plain flour
½ teaspoon salt
2 tablespoons ground ginger
1 teaspoon ground cinnamon
1 teaspoon ground cloves
1 teaspoon ground, mixed spice
1 tablespoon baking powder
1 teaspoon bicarbonate of soda
60g chopped, mixed peel
1 tablespoon caraway seeds (optional)
175g unsalted butter
175g molasses or black treacle
175g golden syrup
200g soft brown sugar
1 large egg
150ml milk

Preheat your oven to 160°C and grease a 23cm-square cake tin. Sift together the flour, salt, ginger, cinnamon, cloves, spice, baking powder and bicarbonate of soda into a large mixing bowl. Stir in the caraway seeds. In a saucepan melt together over low heat the butter, sugar, treacle and golden syrup until smooth. Add to the flour mixture and stir in the beaten egg and milk, and mix thoroughly. Toss the mixed peel in a little dry flour (to prevent it sinking) and fold into the mixture, then pour into the tin and bake immediately for 1¼ hours approx or until a skewer inserted into the mixture comes out clean.

Rhodes and Founders loaf

Zimbabwe

The first Monday and Tuesday in July were, respectively, Rhodes Day and Founders Day—Rhodesian national holidays. White families would go camping over the long weekend, or settle down at home for hearty winter meals. This loaf, adapted from a 1968 *Rhodesian Woman and Home Magazine* recipe, makes excellent tea bread for family gatherings. The golden syrup gives it a rich, malted flavour, and if you make it in a food processor it takes only a few minutes to mix.

225g self-raising flour
1 teaspoon bicarbonate of soda
2 generous tablespoons golden syrup
25g butter
140ml milk

Preheat your oven to 160°C and grease a small loaf tin. Sift the flour and bicarbonate of soda into a mixing bowl. Place the syrup, milk and butter into a saucepan on low heat, and stir occasionally until the butter has just melted and the ingredients are blended. Add to the flour and bicarbonate of soda and mix well. Pour mixture into the baking tin and bake at 160°C for about 45 minutes before turning out onto a wire rack. When cool cut into slices and spread with butter.

Spiced honey loaf

South Africa

The exotic spicing of this Western Cape favourite reveals its origins in the Dutch colonial culinary tradition. In fact, it is very similar to the Dutch *ontbijtkoek* or breakfast cake, which is still a popular breakfast bread in the Netherlands: try it spread with creamy, unsalted butter with a cup of fresh coffee!

250g honey
100g white sugar
40ml brandy
350g plain flour
1 teaspoon baking powder
20g mixed peel
The grated zest of 1 lemon
1 teaspoon ground cinnamon
½ teaspoon ground cloves
½ teaspoon ground allspice

Preheat your oven to 160°C and grease and flour a small loaf tin. Place the honey in a small pan with the sugar and brandy, and bring to the boil. When it begins to foam, stir in the mixed peel, lemon zest, cinnamon, cloves and allspice, and immediately pour into a large mixing bowl to cool. Once cooled, sift in the flour and baking powder and mix to give a firm, stiff dough. If the dough is too wet, add a little more flour. Bake for 1 hour or until well risen and dark golden brown on top.

Date loaf or Boston bread

Zimbabwe

A colonial favourite—this rich fruit bread was traditionally steamed in empty oatmeal or Cadbury's Cocoa tins and turned out in cylindrical form.

250g chopped dates
1 teaspoon bicarbonate of soda
1 tablespoon butter
250ml boiling water
250g self-raising flour
150g brown sugar
Pinch of salt

Preheat your oven to 180°C. Put the dates, butter and bicarbonate of soda into a bowl and carefully add the boiling water. Leave to cool. Once cool, add the remaining ingredients and mix together before pouring into a greased loaf tin (or, I suppose, an empty cocoa tin) and baking at 180° C for 1½ hours. Leave the loaf to cool for five minutes before turning it out.

Apple cake

Zimbabwe

An unusual recipe, adapted from a 1960s recipe provided by Mrs Kalweit of Salisbury to *Rhodesian Woman and Home Magazine*. The layered effect is reminiscent of some Jewish South African recipes for farfel cake, where a rich, buttery dough is grated onto a fruit-filled base before being baked.

1 tin condensed milk—not evaporated milk
2 tablespoons melted butter
1 teaspoon powdered cinnamon
3 cloves or whole allspice
150g trifle sponges
3 medium eggs
500g cooking apples
2 tablespoons sugar
2 teaspoons lemon juice
Pinch of salt

Preheat the oven to 190° C. Peel, core and finely chop the cooking apples and cook them with the cloves or allspice, half the lemon juice and a tablespoonful of water until they are pulped and translucent. Remove the cloves and leave the pulp to cool. Either grate the trifle sponges on the coarse side of a grater or whizz them in a food processor to reduce them to cake crumbs. Mix the butter, cinnamon and half the cake crumbs, and spread the mixture on the bottom of a deep, round baking tin. Separate the eggs, and lightly beat the yolks; add the condensed milk, apple and remaining lemon juice to the yolks and mix thoroughly. Beat the whites with a pinch of salt until stiff, and fold in the apple mixture with a metal spoon. Pour this mixture into the baking tin and spread the remaining cake crumbs on top of the mixture. Bake for 45 minutes.

Soetkoekies (sweet biscuits)

South Africa

These biscuits used to be coloured with red boll—a harmless, red-brown iron oxide powder used by nineteenth-century gilders to add warm tones to gold leaf!—or port wine. Hildagonda Duckitt wrote in the 1890s that instead of decorating soetkoekies with pink dough, 'the old Dutch people put a small piece of citron preserve in the centre of each little cake.' You can try this—either with citron preserve or with pieces of mixed peel.

250g butter
100ml oil
350g soft brown sugar
1 teaspoon ground cloves
1 teaspoon ground ginger
1 teaspoon ground allspice
1 teaspoon ground mixed spice
1 egg
100g ground almonds
500g plain white flour
5ml bicarbonate of soda
½ teaspoon approx red food colouring

Preheat your oven to 200°C. Cream butter and sugar together, and gradually add the oil until blended. Stir in the spices, the beaten egg and the almonds, and add the sifted flour and bicarbonate of soda, stirring together to make a stiff dough. Separate one-fifth of the dough and keep it aside; knead it well with the red food colouring to give it a reddish-pink colour. Roll out the rest of the dough on a floured board, and cut into circles or shapes with a cutter. Roll the red dough into a thin sausage of approximately 1.5cm diameter, and slice the sausage into discs; decorate each biscuit with a disc of pink dough or a piece of preserved lemon or orange peel. Bake for 10-15 minutes or until golden.

Krapkoekies

South Africa

A lovely biscuit: the ground naartjie peel and cardamom give an absolutely unique blend of flavours that cannot be replicated. (No need for alarm: *krap* simply means scrape in Afrikaans.)

200g butter
1 tablespoon sunflower oil
100g caster sugar
100g soft brown sugar
1 egg, beaten
500g flour
1 teaspoon baking powder
2 teaspoons ground cardamom seeds
2 teaspoons ground dried naartjie peel
1 teaspoon orange flower water
200g desiccated coconut
100g mixed peel or glace orange slices, cut into 1.5 cm pieces

Preheat your oven to 190°C. Cream together the butter, oil and sugar until soft. Add the egg, and sift in the flour, baking powder, cardamom and naartjie peel. Stir to mix, and add the coconut and orange flower water. Mix to form a stiff dough. Roll out to about 6mm thick on a floured board, and cut into circles with a biscuit cutter. Decorate each of the biscuits with a piece of mixed peel or glace orange, and bake for 10-15 minutes, or until golden.

Orange and almond cake

Mozambique

This recipe uses the egg whites to make the cake light and airy—a typical Spanish or Portuguese cookery method. The lack of wheat flour makes this a useful recipe for anyone who is intolerant of gluten.

6 eggs, separated into whites and yolks
70g caster sugar
50g ground almonds
Juice and rind of two oranges
1 tablespoon cornflour
150g icing sugar

Preheat your oven to 180°C. Beat the egg yolks and caster sugar until the mixture is pale and frothy. Fold in the almonds and half the orange juice, spoon by spoon, working alternately, until you have a fairly stiff batter. Stir in the cornflour and orange rind and then with a spoon fold in the egg whites, beaten to stiff peaks. Bake immediately for 40 minutes, and allow the cake to cool in the tin for fifteen minutes before turning out onto a wire rack. To ice the cake, mix together the remaining orange juice and the icing sugar and pour over the cake while it is still on the cooling rack—remember to place a dinner plate under the cake to catch the drips.

Boer meal biscuits

Zimbabwe

This is a recipe from the Victorian settler Mrs Norman Chataway, whose son later became the Rhodesian High Commissioner to South Africa. The original recipe calls for four ounces of 'Boer meal'—coarsely-ground wheat flour. Using wholemeal flour gives a delightful, nutty biscuit rather like a digestive biscuit.

125g plain wholemeal flour
60g plain flour
1 egg
½ teaspoon baking powder
50g butter
50g sugar
2 teaspoons golden syrup
Pinch of salt

Preheat your oven to 200°C. Sieve together the flour and baking powder and add the sugar. Make a hole in the centre and break in the egg, then pour in the syrup before mixing the ingredients together into a fairly moist pastry. Roll the pastry out to about 1cm depth, prick all over with a fork, and stamp out into rounds with a pastry-cutter. Bake on a greased baking sheet for 12-15 minutes or until lightly golden at the edges, and arrange on a wire rack to cool.

Honey biscuits

Angola

You need a robustly-flavoured honey for this recipe—look in Waitrose or health food shops for the fairly-traded African honey imported by Tropical Forest.[1]

2 eggs
3 tablespoons clear honey
1 tablespoon ground allspice
1 tablespoon soft brown sugar
350g plain flour
1 teaspoon baking powder

Beat together the eggs and the sugar. Slightly warm the honey on a very gentle heat, and when runny, add to the egg mixture and whisk together thoroughly. Add the rest of the ingredients and knead lightly to a soft dough. Leave the dough to stand in a cool place for an hour before preheating your oven to 190°. Roll out the dough thinly and cut out fairly small biscuits. Place them on an ungreased tin lined with baking parchment and bake for 10-15 minutes or until they change colour.

---

[1] See www.tropicalforest.com for a list of products and stockists

Traditionally these are iced with a thin glacé icing made with icing sugar and rose water.

THE ZEEDERBERG GRILL

For a quick meal that won't take a bite out of the budget!

Snappy service, imaginative light meals, and amazingly reasonable prices make the Zeederberg Grill the ideal place for that quick, inexpensive meal, lunch or supper.

THERE'S AN EXCITING NEW MENU

Spare-ribs, Ploughman's lunch and special salads – just to mention a few ... all with the good old pioneering flavour!

MEET AT THE ZEEDERBERG GRILL

THE SOUTHERN SUN HOTEL, BULAWAYO. L★★★

Chocolate cakes

South Africa

A wonderful, rich Victorian recipe from Hildegonda Duckitt, who writes that she received the recipe from a Miss van Renen. The original recipe calls for a whopping half pound of butter, but so much butter makes the cakes greasy and prevents them from rising.

125g butter
125g white sugar
3 eggs, beaten
125g dark chocolate, melted
65g ground almonds
85g plain flour
½ teaspoon baking powder

Preheat your oven to 200°C and set out a dozen paper muffin cases on a flat baking sheet. Beat together the eggs and the sugar. Cream in the beaten eggs, and then beat in the almonds, flour, melted chocolate and baking powder. Fill the cases one-third full and bake for 10-15 minutes. You can ice these cakes with vanilla or chocolate icing, but I prefer them plain.

Herzoggies or Herzog cookies

South Africa

These delightful little biscuits are said to have been named after General J.B.M Herzog, Anglo-Boer War hero and South African Prime Minister from 1924 to 1939.

125g self-raising flour
125g plain flour
2 tablespoons caster sugar
50g butter
1 egg yolk
1 teaspoon vanilla essence
A pinch of salt

Filling

Apricot jam
100g caster sugar
75g desiccated coconut
1 egg white

Butter a bun tin and pre-heat the oven to 180°. In a mixing bowl cream together the butter and sugar until fluffy. Gradually add the egg yolk and vanilla essence and mix until creamy, then stir in the flour and salt to make a stiff dough. Roll out the dough and cut into rounds or stars with a pastry cutter, and place one round in each compartment in the bun tin. To make the coconut filling, whisk the egg white and sugar until stiff, and fold in the desiccated coconut. In the middle of each pastry piece place a teaspoonful of jam, and top it with two teaspoons of coconut filling, which should cover the jam. Bake for 12-15 minutes or until golden.

Teiglach

South Africa

Most South African Jews are descended from Lithuanian emigrants who arrived in Africa before the First World War, although Jewish emigration from Lithuania to South Africa continued steadily until the start of the Second World War. The single dish that is most closely associated with this community is the sweet called *teiglach*—crumbly little pastry pieces cooked in a honey or sugar syrup, often cooked at the end of September to celebrate Rosh Hashanah, the start of the Jewish New Year.

The only place outside South Africa that I have seen *teiglach* was in a very fancy deli in New York, almost opposite the Lincoln Centre, but there the pieces of pastry were much fatter and fluffier, and the whole affair was closer to a syrupy doughnut.

Dough

3 eggs
1 tablespoon oil
A pinch of salt
1 teaspoon baking powder
300g plain flour

Syrup

500g honey
Grated zest of a lemon
1 teaspoon ground ginger

Beat the eggs with the oil, salt and baking powder, then the flour to make a soft dough that holds together, mixing it in with a fork, then working it in with your hand. Knead for ten minutes, until smooth and elastic, adding a little flour if the dough is sticky. Wrap the dough in cling film and leave it in the refrigerator for 30 minutes.

With floured hands, roll the dough between your palms into ropes about 1.25cm thick—a little thicker than a pencil. Lay the ropes on a floured board and cut them into 1.25cm lengths with a sharp knife.

Bring the honey to the boil in a pan and add the lemon and ginger. Put in the *teiglach*, adding them one-by-one so that they do not stick together. Simmer the pieces for about 15 minutes until a dark golden brown, then drain and turn into an oiled dish and sprinkle with chopped almonds or hazelnuts. If the honey thickens and becomes sticky, pour in a little cold water and bring back to the boil.

Butter biscuits

Zimbabwe

My great-aunt Iris brought this recipe back from Zimbabwe, where her husband was an engineer in the 1950s. She used it until she died, and always gave me tins of these rich little biscuits to carry back from South Africa for the family in England.

500g plain flour
250g chilled, unsalted butter
A pinch of salt
375g caster sugar
2 eggs, lightly beaten

Preheat the oven to 190°C. Rub the cold butter into the flour, then stir in the sugar. Add the eggs and stir together with a knife. Make a dough without too much handling, and roll it out to about 1.5cm thick before cutting into biscuit shapes with pastry cutters. Lay the biscuits on a greased baking tray and bake for 15-20 minutes or until golden. Leave to cool on the baking sheet for five minutes before transferring to a cooling stand.

Banana loaf

Zimbabwe

An excellent way to make use of soft bananas—the flavour becomes stronger with age, so that the older and squishier the bananas, the better the flavour of your loaf.

3 large bananas, mashed
125g butter
175g soft brown sugar
2 beaten medium eggs
250g plain flour
1 teaspoon bicarbonate of soda
¾ teaspoon salt
3 tablespoons sour milk or plain yoghurt

Pre-heat your oven to 180°C. Cream the butter and sugar, and then gradually beat in the eggs. Sieve the flour with the soda and salt, and add it spoon-by-spoon to the egg mixture alternately with the sour milk and bananas, stirring well to mix. Turn the mixture into a greased loaf tin and bake for 1 hour. Leave the loaf to cool for 5 minutes in the tin before turning out.

Saboera biscuits

South Africa

Another old biscuit recipe from the Cape; the name saboera derives from the Malay word *buah*, meaning fruit, and refers to the currants with which these biscuits are invariably decorated.

200g butter
1 tablespoon sunflower oil
210g caster sugar
500g plain white flour
1 teaspoon baking powder
A pinch of salt
1 tablespoon rosewater
50g currants for decoration
Caster sugar for decoration

Preheat your oven to 190°C. Cream together the oil, butter and sugar until fluffy. Sift in the flour, baking powder and salt. Add the rosewater and mix to form a fairly stiff dough. Roll out on a floured board and cut into ovals of about 7cm x 4cm. Scatter some caster sugar in a dish, and place each biscuit face-down into the sugar in order to coat the top with sugar, then decorate the top with three currants pressed in a row along the length of the oval biscuit. Bake for about 15 minutes or until golden.

Preserves, confectionery and drinks

Tablet

South Africa

This recipe for the brittle, creamy Scottish fudge known as tablet is from my great-great-grandmother, who as a seven-year-old in 1868 arrived aboard the *Natal Star* in Durban, where her father was to take up an appointment as the manager of the Woodville coffee plantation in what is now the Durban suburb of Wentworth

1lb (450g) tin of sweetened, condensed milk
1lb (450g) white sugar
2oz (50g) unsalted butter.
1 teaspoon vanilla essence
2 tablespoons fresh milk

Butter a shallow baking tray or Swiss roll tin. Stir together the condensed milk, milk, sugar and butter over a gentle heat until the sugar is fully dissolved, then bring to the boil. Take out a teaspoonful of the mixture and put it on a saucer so that you can compare the colour as it changes. Keep boiling and stirring until the mixture darkens to a golden colour, crystals begin to form around the edge of the pan and when you tilt the pan the mixture bubbles and tumbles down the bottom of the pan instead of just running clear like a liquid. At this stage drop a teaspoon of the mixture into a glass of cold water. If it forms a soft ball the mixture is cooked. (If you have a sugar thermometer, the key temperature is 115°C).

Remove the pan from the heat, carefully add the vanilla essence (the mixture will sputter up as you add it) and beat the mixture with a wooden spoon until it begins to thicken, then pour out into the buttered tin and leave to cool and harden before cutting into squares.

Do not be tempted to use margarine for this recipe! Margarine gives a curdled, fatty taste to the finished sweet.

Pineapple fudge

Zimbabwe

The description of this sweetmeat as fudge is a misnomer—it is more like a slab of crystallised fruit. This keeps very well and makes a wonderful addition to a tray of *petits fours* with coffee.

1 large pineapple
500g sugar

Butter a shallow baking tray or Swiss roll tin. Top and tail and peel the pineapple. Cut it into quarters, slice out the hard centre of the core and grate the flesh coarsely. Place into a saucepan and add the sugar, and cook on a medium heat until the sugar is dissolved; then increase the heat and keep boiling until the sugar is on the verge of caramelising and forms long threads when dropped into water. (If you have a sugar thermometer, the key temperature is about 130°-135°C). Immediately remove the pan from the heat and beat the contents with a wooden spoon or whisk; the aim is to cool the mixture quickly and break up the sugar crystals while it cools. Beat for five minutes, and then turn the mixture into the prepared tin and leave to cool. Cut it into squares before it is totally cool.

Banana jam

Uganda

I made this for friends as a Christmas present a couple of years ago, and it seems to have been received well. It doesn't keep terribly well once opened, so it is a good idea to bottle it in reasonably small quantities.

900g sugar
The juice of six lemons
The grated zest of two limes
15 bananas

Make sure the bananas are unbruised; they should be ripe but still very firm. Peel them and cut into 2.5cm pieces. Mix together the sugar, lemon juice and lime zest in a large stainless steel or china bowl, add the chopped bananas, stir and leave to marinade for an hour.

Tip the banana mixture into a large, shallow saucepan or preserving pan, and cook on a low heat for five minutes to dissolve the sugar, stirring continuously, before bringing to the boil. (If you lightly grease the pan with a touch of unsalted butter beforehand you will find it easier to clean afterwards.) Boil the jam, stirring occasionally, until the sugars start to caramelise to a deep gold colour. You can test to see if the jam is ready by ladling a teaspoonful onto a cold plate, and leaving it for three minutes before gently touching the surface of the cool jam. If the surface wrinkles, the jam is ready to bottle.

Ensure that you have four sparkling-clean, empty jam-jars and covers. I use French *Le Parfait* jars, with clip-on lids and orange rubber seals. You need to sterilise the jars, and the easiest way is to keep a large pan of boiling water bubbling on the stove. A couple of minutes before you are ready to fill the jars, place the first jar in the pan, ensuring that it is fully covered by boiling water. Take it out with metal tongs or a slotted spoon and allow the surplus water to drip off or evaporate.

Place a new jar in the pan of water, and keep replacing the jars as you fill the sterilised ones with jam. They will still be very hot, so take care, and ensure that you do not touch the inside of the jar or its lid. Fill the jar with hot jam until almost full, and wipe off any drips with a piece of kitchen towel. Clip the cover closed, and leave to cool before labelling.

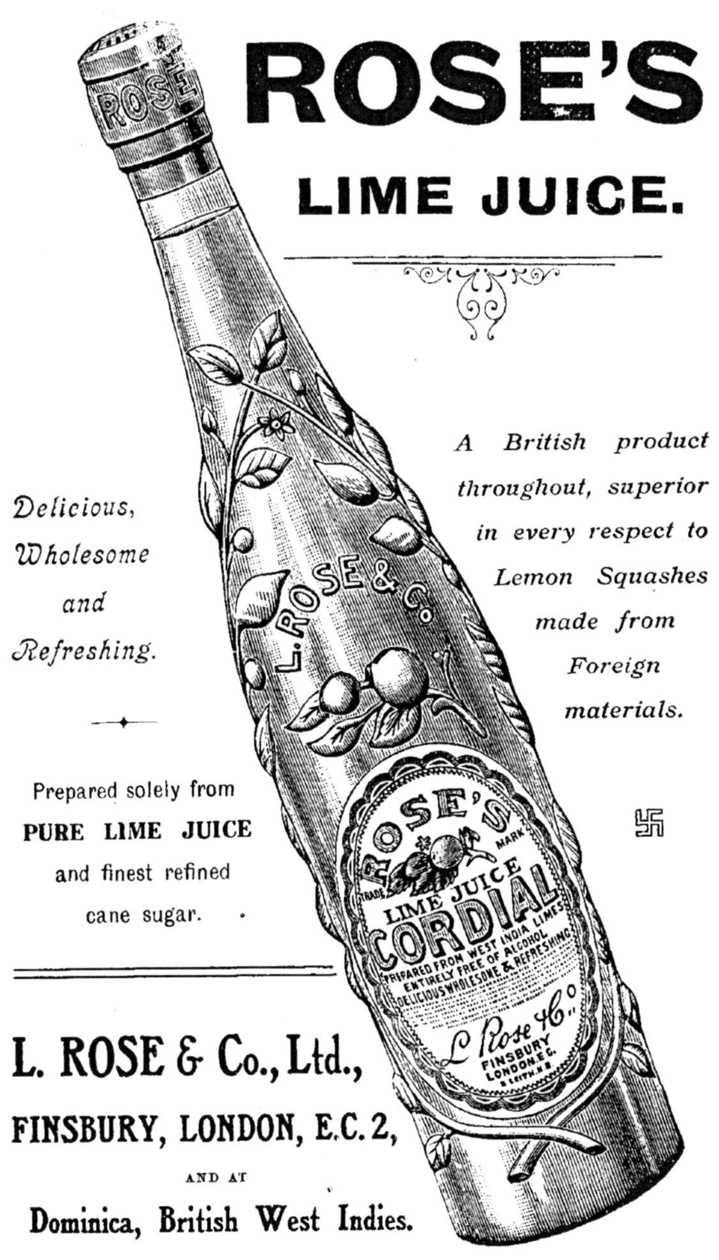

Pawpaw jam

Nigeria

You can use the large pawpaws found in West Indian and South Asian markets or grocers' shops for this jam; alternatively, use two small pawpaws from a supermarket. The important thing is that the fruit should be somewhat under-ripe and only just beginning to turn yellow.

For instructions on how to sterilise jars for preserves or fruit, and how to bottle, see the preceding recipe for Ugandan banana jam.

1 large pawpaw or two small ones
200ml cold water
A 2.5cm piece of fresh ginger
400g sugar
The juice of one lemon and a teaspoon of the grated zest
1 teaspoon butter

Grease a large preserving pan or saucepan with a little butter (this helps prevent the jam from burning). Peel the pawpaw, cut in half and remove the seeds, then cut into small dice. Place the fruit into a large pan with the ginger, sugar and water and cook for about 90 minutes, stirring occasionally. At the end of that time, add the lemon juice and zest and cook for another 25 minutes. Test to see if the jam is ready by ladling a teaspoonful onto a cold plate, and leaving it for three minutes before gently touching the surface of the cool jam. If the surface wrinkles, the jam is ready to bottle.

Naartjie preserve

South Africa

Naartjies are clementines or mandarin oranges: small and juicy, with an aromatic skin that is traditionally saved, dried and used to flavour liqueurs, cakes and biscuits. You may be surprised to discover just how easy it is to make this simple whole fruit preserve (what is called in South Africa a *stukkonfyt*); it is ideal for Christmas, when the fruit is economically priced and easily available. This recipe is based on Hildegonda Duckitt's nineteenth-century recipe which she describes as being from her grandmother's Dutch recipe book. Typically for Victorian instructions, the recipe takes four days to preserve the fruit; however, it requires only an hour's cooking each day.

For instructions on how to sterilise jars for preserves or fruit, see the recipe for Ugandan banana jam.

2 kg naartjies (clementines or mandarin oranges—choose clean, flawless ones with tight skins)
3 kg granulated sugar
Water

Scrub the naartjies well and rasp each one a couple of times with a blunt knife—this helps to flavour the syrup. With a sharp knife, make a deep, X-shaped cut approx 2.5cm square on the rounded base of each naartjie, and use a table knife to squeeze out any pips through the cut. Lay the naartjies to soak in cold, clean water for 48 hours, replacing the water with fresh water each day; you may need to place a weighted plate on top of the fruit in order to keep them under the surface of the water—a basin of cold water is ideal as a weight.

After two days' soaking, drain the naartjies, reserving the soaking water, and put the naartjies in a large saucepan or preserving pan. Measure out in a saucepan 4 litres of the soaking water and add the sugar. If you do not have enough soaking water, just make up the quantity with fresh water. Boil the sugar and water together, removing from the heat when the sugar is fully dissolved. Leave this syrup to become cool, and once cool pour it over the naartjies. Cover the pan and leave the fruit to soak in the syrup overnight.

The following day, bring the fruit mixture to the boil before reducing the heat and simmering for one hour. At the end of that time, remove the pan from the heat and leave the pan to cool overnight.

On the final day, bring the pan to the boil again and reduce the heat and simmer for 20 minutes, then spoon the naartjies into hot, sterilised jars and top up with syrup before sealing.

Quince preserve

South Africa

Quinces are becoming popular again: perhaps because of a general sense of adventurousness in eating, and a willingness to look again at the sort of fruit and vegetables that our grandparents enjoyed, or maybe because foreign trips and holiday homes have exposed more of us to the delights of the quince.

The quince looks like a large, iron-hard yellow pear and is no fun raw, but ambrosial when cooked; quinces grow readily in the United Kingdom—unfortunately you rarely see them for sale in British supermarkets, but my local Turkish grocer has them all through the winter. Quinces were one of the first fruit trees to be transplanted to the Cape of Good Hope by Jan van Riebeeck, and cultivation crept northwards with European settlers: the Rev. Charles Helm brought quince cuttings with him to Hope Fountain Mission in Matabeleland in Rhodesia in 1874.

This recipe is adapted from the recipe given by Hilda Gerber in *Traditional Cookery of the Cape Malays*. It gives an aromatic, garnet-coloured konfyt with a rich, spicy taste—wonderful spooned over rice pudding or ice cream.

For instructions on how to sterilise jars for preserves or fruit, see the recipe for Ugandan banana jam.

6 large quinces
700g sugar
6 cloves
3 whole allspice
A 2.5cm piece of fresh ginger
A 2.5cm piece of pounded mace
1 tbsp salt

Peel, quarter and core the quinces and cut them into 2cm slices. Sprinkle the slices with salt and leave them to soak, covered in cold water, for 30 minutes. In the meantime, mix the sugar and spices with

1.5 litres cold water. Bring the solution to the boil and boil for about five minutes before turning the temperature down to a medium heat. Place the quince pieces in the syrup one by one, ensuring that the syrup boils very gently but continuously, and simmer gently for approximately 1¼ hours, stirring every five minutes. If the syrup becomes thick and treacly as the moisture evaporates, add a little more water. Watch out while boiling the fruit, since quince syrup stains a rust-red colour it if splashes on your clothes,. After an hour's boiling drop a little of the syrup on a chilled saucer and tilt the plate. If the syrup forms a skin and appears thick, the fruit is ready to bottle; otherwise, simmer for another fifteen minutes. Spoon the quince pieces into hot, sterilised jars and top up with syrup before sealing.

Green fig preserve

South Africa

Although fig trees grow readily where I live in London, the fruit tends not to ripen fully. In South Africa one of the most popular preserves is made from green figs, and this is a wonderful way to turn unripe figs into an intensely perfumed, translucent conserve. In South Africa the fruit is traditionally left overnight to soak in limewater—a solution of calcium hydroxide or 'slaked lime'. In the United Kingdom the only place I have ever seen slaked lime for sale is at specialist builders' merchants, and regrettably we are forced to substitute bicarbonate of soda or salt water for the limewater.

For instructions on how to sterilise jars for preserves or fruit, see the recipe for Ugandan banana jam.

1kg unripe, green figs—try to keep the stalks intact when you pick them

2 tablespoons slaked lime, salt, or bicarbonate of soda

2.5 litres cold water

1.5kg granulated sugar

20ml lemon juice

Five cloves

A 5cm piece of ginger root, peeled

3 small fig leaves—about 10cm diameter

1 teaspoon rose water

Scrub the figs briskly with a very stiff brush to remove the downy hairs on their skin. Do not cut off the stalk—this will cause a sticky, white sap to be exuded, coating your fingers and leaving a sticky deposit on everything it touches. With a sharp knife cut an X-shaped cross approx 2.5cm square on the rounded base of each fig. Dissolve the lime, salt or bicarbonate of soda in the 2.5 litres of cold water and leave the figs to soak in it for 24 hours. You will need to place a weighted plate on top of the figs in order to keep them under the surface of the water—a basin of cold water is ideal as a weight.

After 24 hours rinse the figs and leave them to soak in fresh water. After 15 minutes drain them. Bring 2.5 litres fresh water to the boil in a large pan, add the figs and boil for 12-15 minutes, or until the skin is tender. Drain the figs and reserve the cooking water. Measure out in a large pan 2 litres of the cooking water and add 1.5kg sugar. Add the lemon juice, ginger, cloves and the rinsed fig leaves—they add colour and a characteristic, aromatic taste to the preserve—and bring the syrup to the boil. Place the figs in the syrup one by one, ensuring that the syrup boils continuously, and boil gently for approximately an hour, stirring every five minutes. After an hour the figs should be a translucent dark green, and the syrup will be perfumed and fragrant. Remove the fig leaves, cloves and ginger, and leave the figs to cool overnight in the syrup. The following day add a teaspoon of rosewater to the syrup; bring it back to the boil and boil the figs for five minutes, then spoon the figs into hot, sterilised jars and top up with syrup before sealing.

Citron preserve

South Africa

Another traditional Cape preserve, using the citron or etrog, which can be found in some supermarkets or South Asian greengrocers around October. With this preserve and the recipe for whole orange preserve which follows it, it really is important to remove the very top layer of zest, otherwise your preserve will have an unpleasant, bitter aftertaste.

For instructions on how to sterilise jars for preserves or fruit, see the recipe for Ugandan banana jam.

1kg green citrons
2 tablespoons slaked lime, salt, or bicarbonate of soda
1.5 litres water
The weight of the prepared citrons in granulated sugar—usually about 750g

Thinly grate the very outer layer of the citron fruits, removing the top layer of zest, which is where the bitter oil is located—a wire brush does the trick with ease. Cut the citrons into quarters and with a sharp knife or sharp-edged spoon cut out the flesh inside, leaving the thick rinds intact. Dissolve the lime, salt or bicarbonate of soda in cold water and leave the citrons to soak in it for 24 hours. You will need to place a weighted plate on top of the fruit in order to keep them under the surface of the water—a basin of cold water is ideal as a weight.

After 24 hours rinse the citrons, discard the water, weigh the fruit and make a note of the weight—you will need an equal weight of granulated sugar to make the syrup. In other words, if the citrons weigh 774g, the recipe will require 774g of granulated sugar. Leave the citrons to soak in fresh water for 15 minutes before draining them, just to get rid of any remaining lime or salt.

Bring 1.5 litres of fresh water to the boil in a large pan, add the citron pieces one by one and gently boil for 12-15 minutes, or until the skin is tender enough to be pierced with a matchstick. Drain the fruit and reserve the cooking water. Strain the cooking water into a large pan through a sieve or colander lined with muslin, and add a weight of granulated sugar equivalent to the weight of the citrons. Bring the solution to the boil and boil for about five minutes before turning the temperature down to a medium heat. Place the citron pieces in the syrup one by one, ensuring that the syrup boils very gently but continuously, and simmer for approximately an hour, stirring every five minutes. If the syrup becomes thick and treacly as the moisture evaporates, add a little more water. After 45 minutes drop a little of the syrup on a chilled saucer and tilt the plate. If the syrup forms a skin and appears thick, the fruit is ready to bottle; otherwise, simmer for another fifteen minutes. Spoon the citron pieces into hot, sterilised jars and top up with syrup before sealing.

Orange preserve

South Africa

Another fruit *stukkonfyt* recipe from the Cape.

1kg oranges
2 tablespoons salt
2.5 litres cold water
1.25kg granulated sugar
20ml lemon juice
Five cloves
A 5cm piece of ginger root, peeled
Peel of half a naartjie or tangerine

Thinly grate the very outer layer of the oranges with a fine grater, removing the top layer of zest, which is where the bitter oil is located, and then rub the oranges all over with salt.

Leave the oranges to stand for 30 minutes, and then pour boiling water over them. Leave them to cool, then rinse again with fresh water and leave to stand overnight to soak in fresh cold water. You will need to place a weighted plate on top of the fruit in order to keep them under the surface of the water—a basin of cold water is ideal as a weight.

The next day, discard the water and remove the orange pips by cutting a very deep X-shaped cross at the base of each orange—the cut must be deep enough to extend at least halfway up inside the orange. Roll the fruit between your palms until the pips drop out. Bring a large pan of water to the boil and boil the oranges for about 15-20 minutes or until the skin is tender enough to be pierced with a matchstick. Discard the water and leave the oranges to cool, and then cut them into quarters and remove any remaining seeds.

In a large pan bring 2.5 litres of water to the boil with the lemon juice, naartjie peel, ginger and cloves; add the sugar, and gently boil until the sugar is fully dissolved. Place the orange pieces in the syrup one by one, ensuring that the syrup boils continuously, and boil gently for approximately an hour, stirring every five minutes. If the syrup becomes thick and treacly as the moisture evaporates, add a little more water. After 45 minutes to an hour the oranges should be translucent; drop a little of the syrup on a chilled saucer and tilt the plate. If the syrup forms a skin and appears thick, the fruit is ready to bottle; otherwise, simmer for another fifteen minutes. Remove the naartjie peel and spices, then spoon the oranges into hot, sterilised jars and top up with syrup before sealing.

Marula jelly

Zimbabwe

The marula is an attractive, medium-sized tree, found right across southern Africa. The fruit is slightly smaller than an apricot and is a golden-yellow in colour, with a sweet, aromatic smell.

Although the fruit is fairly tart, animals love it, and once the season begins

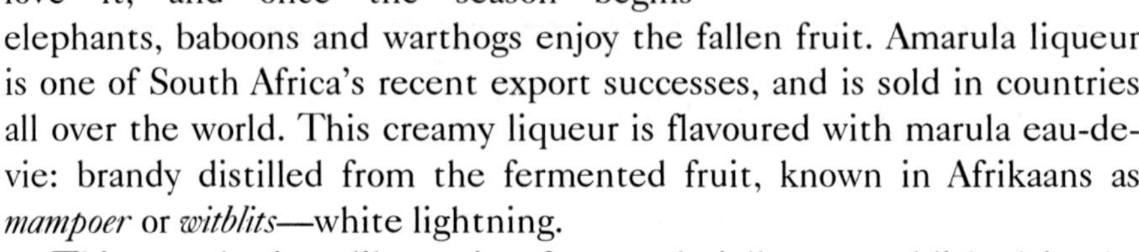

elephants, baboons and warthogs enjoy the fallen fruit. Amarula liqueur is one of South Africa's recent export successes, and is sold in countries all over the world. This creamy liqueur is flavoured with marula eau-de-vie: brandy distilled from the fermented fruit, known in Afrikaans as *mampoer* or *witblits*—white lightning.

This very businesslike recipe for marula jelly was published in the *Rhodesia Herald* in the early 1950s.

2kg ripe marula fruit

White sugar (usually about 3.5kg, but the precise amount depends on the amount of juice from the fruit)

Water

Take the fruit, wash and make an incision right around the centre of the fruit. Put into a preserving pan and cover with water to 5cm above the level of the fruit. Boil fairly rapidly until the liquid is reduced to one-third. Now place in a cotton muslin jelly bag and leave to drain overnight. The following day take the juice, and for every cup of pulp add 1¾ cups of white sugar. Boil rapidly for 15 minutes, and then test for jellying . Bottle when ready.

Brandy and ginger

Ghana

A favourite hangover cure on the 'monkey-boat', as the passenger vessels were called that travelled on the route between Liverpool and British West Africa.

In a wine glass mix together a tot of brandy and a tot of green ginger wine. Sip slowly.

Van der Hum

South Africa

Van der Hum was South Africa's first indigenous liqueur, although Amarula is probably more widely known nowadays. Van der Hum is named after Admiral van der Hum of the Dutch East India Company fleet, and is a delightful seventeenth century combination of spiced spirits with the clean, fresh taste of naartjies. Make sure to scrub the naartjies or mandarins first with hot water to remove any wax on the surface.

750ml brandy
100ml dark rum
6 cloves
2 tablespoons grated naartjie or mandarin orange peel
1 tablespoon orange-flower water (optional)
1 cardamom pod
1 stick cinnamon
Half a fresh, whole nutmeg

250g white sugar
125ml water

Tie up the spices and peel in a piece of muslin and gently bruise with a pestle or rolling pin. Place in the bottom of a wide-mouthed jar and top up with the brandy and rum. Leave in a dark place to infuse for a month, shaking every day. After a month, discard the spices and strain the liquid through muslin until perfectly clear. Boil together the sugar and water until dissolved and leave to cool. Once cool, combine the strained liquid with the sugar syrup and decant into bottles. Store in a cool, dry place.

Mozambican lime drink

Mozambique

A favourite from the British-owned Savoy Hotel in the Mozambican coastal town of Beira, where the Zambian pioneer Winifred Tapson recorded that it was served at 1/9 a glass in the early 1900s.

4 large limes
130g caster sugar
2 litres cold water or chilled mineral water

Scrub one of the limes under hot water to remove the wax, halve it crossways and set one half aside for garnish. Halve and juice the remaining limes, and dissolve the sugar in the juice, in a large jug. Top up with 2 litres of cold water or sparkling mineral water, and garnish with the remaining half lime, sliced into thin rounds.

Advokaat

South Africa

Nowadays advokaat (described by the comedian Billy Connolly as 'the alcoholic's omelette') is known mainly as a Christmas drink and as one of the ingredients of the Snowball cocktail. It is one of a variety of sweet, winter drinks, fortified with spirits and flavoured with spices, recorded in Europe from medieval times onwards and represented in the present day by mulled wine and egg-nog.

The recipe below is based on the instructions given by Mrs E. J. Dijkman in 1890.

750ml brandy
6 large eggs, separated
1 fresh nutmeg, grated
1 tsp ground cinnamon
250g caster sugar

Beat the egg whites until stiff. Whisk the egg yolks in a large bowl until pale, add the sugar, nutmeg and cinnamon and continue to whisk until the sugar is dissolved. Add the brandy and stir to mix.

Add the egg whites and mix thoroughly, tasting to ensure that the advokaat is sweet enough. Refrigerate for at least 3 hours before serving.

Dom Pedro

South Africa

A modern South African classic!

2 scoops vanilla ice cream
1 tablespoon single cream
1 tablespoon Irish whiskey
1 tablespoon Baileys Irish Cream

Blend together and serve with a straw.

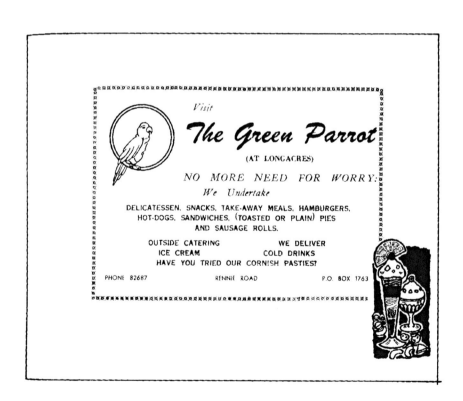

Amarula Pedro

South Africa

A wonderful after-dinner drink made using Amarula liqueur.

2 scoops vanilla ice cream
1 tablespoon single cream
2 tablespoons Amarula liqueur

Blend together and serve with a straw.

The Zambezi cocktail

Zimbabwe

Nowadays a 'Zambezi cocktail' is the fancy name given in Zimbabwean bars to a glass of cold water, but the original version was invented by Mr H. de Laessoe in Bulawayo in the early 1900s . A refreshing, long, summer drink best served in a tall glass with lots of ice.

Fill a one-pint glass jug one-third full with ice. Add three generous tablespoons of London dry gin, along with a tablespoon of Rose's lime-juice cordial and a teaspoon of Angostura bitters. Top up with soda water and decorate with a slice of lime.

MalaMala

South Africa

The eponymous speciality of the bar at the MalaMala game reserve, bordering the Kruger National Park in South Africa.

125 ml vanilla ice-cream
25 ml Amarula Cream Liqueur
25 ml Brandy

Blend together and serve in a tall glass with a straw.

Malawi shandy

Zimbabwe

Shandy, the refreshing mixture of cold beer and lemonade or ginger beer, tends in most of Africa to be made with ginger beer—what used to be called in Britain a shandy-gaff. The Malawi shandy is non-alcoholic and demonstrates a further refinement:

Half-fill a half-pint glass with ice cubes and shake in a couple of drops of Angostura bitters. Half-fill the glass with cold ginger ale and top up with lemonade.

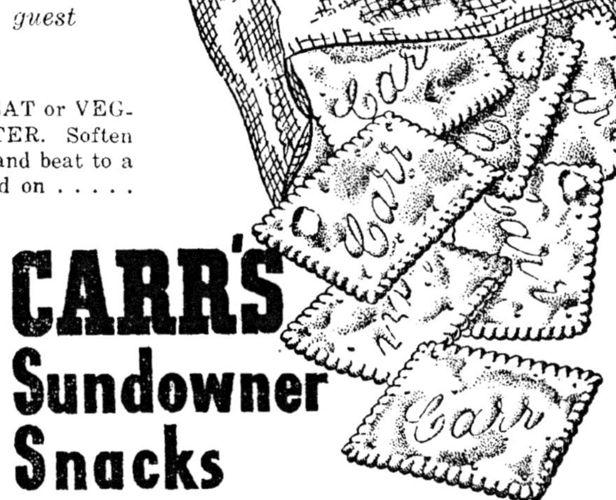

Club special shandy

Zimbabwe

Half-fill a half-pint glass with ice cubes and add one teaspoon of orange squash—for the true Zimbabwean taste you need to use Mazoe Orange Crush—and half-fill with ginger ale before topping up with soda water.

The best club special shandy I have tasted in Zimbabwe was at the Ilala Lodge Hotel in Victoria Falls, where you can see from the bar terrace great plumes of white spray from the Falls rising several hundred feet into the brilliantly blue sky, and where there is a constant faint, dull roar in the background from the water thundering over the Falls.

Mint lemonade

Zimbabwe

A favourite Rhodesian summer drink.

6 lemons
100g caster sugar
A handful of stalks of fresh mint
Ginger ale

In a large (1.5 litre) jug, squeeze the juice of the lemons over the sugar and leave to dissolve. When the sugar is mostly dissolved, put into the jug five or six stalks and leaves of fresh mint, first using the back of a wooden spoon to crush them gently to release their fragrance. Add 500ml iced water or chilled, still mineral water, and stir to help dissolve the remaining grains of sugar.

Top up with cold ginger ale and serve over ice with a sprig of mint in each glass.

Lemonade

South Africa

1.2 litres hot water
Four or five white sugar cubes
450g caster sugar
3 large unwaxed lemons

Lightly scrub the lemons under the hot tap and dry thoroughly. Rub them hard all over with the sugar cubes in order to impregnate them with lemon oil from the peel—the cubes will gradually turn yellow if you rub them hard enough. Place the cubes in a large (1.5 litre) jug with the caster sugar and top up with the hot water; stir until the sugar is dissolved. Halve the lemons and squeeze five of the six half pieces, then stir the juice into the sugar solution. Cover the jug and leave the lemonade to cool before refrigerating. Just before serving, thinly slice the remaining half lemon into rounds, and add it to the lemonade as a garnish.

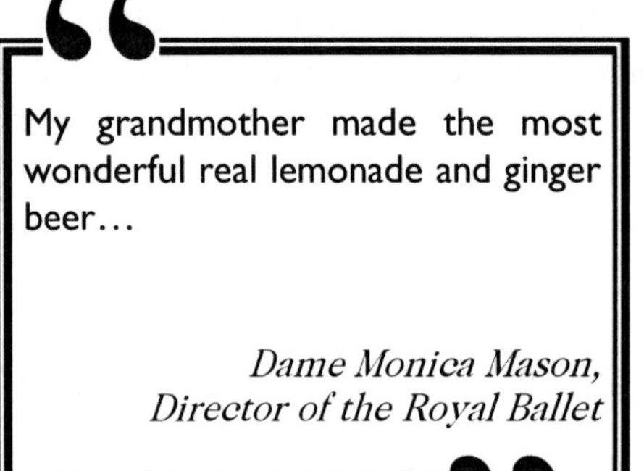

“My grandmother made the most wonderful real lemonade and ginger beer...

Dame Monica Mason,
Director of the Royal Ballet”

Pink gin

Nigeria

Not just found in West Africa, but one of the staple pre-dinner drinks across the British Empire; its popularity in British West Africa probably stems from the long connection that the Royal Navy had with the region—pink gin is a longstanding Navy favourite.

Three or four dashes of Angostura bitters
A generous tot of gin

Shake some Angostura bitters into a heavy tumbler and tilt the glass in all directions to coat the inside of the tumbler with bitters. Discard any remaining bitters and pour a tot of gin into the glass.

Pink gin is traditionally enjoyed without ice. Rather than dilute the gin with ice, if you prefer a cold version it is better to store the gin bottle in the freezer.

Dawa

Kenya

Dawa is Swahili for medicine; it is also a great Kenyan cocktail, one of the specialities of the famous Carnivore Restaurant in Nairobi. This version uses honey to sweeten it.

25ml vodka
25ml white rum
Half a lime, cut into two quarters
Crushed ice
A swizzle stick, teaspoon or twig
1 tablespoon clear honey

Lightly squeeze the two lime quarters into the glass and leave the quarters in the bottom of the glass. Half-fill the glass with crushed ice, and pour in the vodka and white rum. Dip the swizzle stick, teaspoon or twig into the clear honey and drop the stick or spoon into the drink so that the honey forms a ball on the stick—you can then use the spoon or swizzle stick to sweeten the cocktail and to squeeze the rest of the juice out of the lime quarters.

Coconut lassi

Kenya

A deliciously refreshing drink, perfect for enjoying with an East African curry.

The liquid and flesh of one large coconut
OR
300ml tinned coconut milk
75ml sugar syrup (sometimes known as gomme syrup—or simply make your own by boiling together 100g granulated sugar and 50ml water until dissolved, and then leaving to stand until cold)
300ml plain yoghurt

If you decide to use a fresh coconut, choose a heavy nut; the liquid should be removed by boring through two of the 'eyes' with a skewer and then letting the clear watery liquid contained inside run out of one of the eyes. Once the nut is empty, place it in a very hot oven for three minutes, then remove it, wrap it in a clean tea towel and give it a thump with a hammer. The nut should break open cleanly, and you can then remove the white flesh inside and pare off the brown lining.

Place all the ingredients in a refrigerator to get properly chilled. When cold, place all ingredients in a food processor with a handful of ice cubes and blend until perfectly smooth.

Ginger tea

Tanzania

An infusion of ginger and other spices, known in Swahili as *chai yatangawizi*. Ginger tea is particularly good to drink after a rich or heavy meal, and is popular along the Indian Ocean coast.

2 litres water
A 2" piece of root ginger, crushed with a hammer or rolling pin
A 2" quill of cinnamon
2 cardamom pods
2 allspice berries
Sugar to taste

Place all the ingredients in a large saucepan and bring the water to the boil. Turn down the heat and simmer for five minutes before serving—pour the tea carefully through a sieve or tea strainer.

Iced makoni tea

Zimbabwe

A great summer drink made from makoni, an indigenous Zimbabwean tea which is available from some health food and southern African food shops.

1 teaspoon of leaf makoni or
1 makoni tea bag per person
1½ mugs boiling water per person
Sugar to taste
One whole, unwaxed lemon

Halve the lemon and cut one half into rings; reserve these. Squeeze the juice from the other half into a jug. Add the makoni leaves or tea bags and pour on boiling water. Add sugar to taste and leave to cool. Once cold, strain through a fine sieve or tea strainer, and chill in the fridge before serving. Immediately before serving, add a few ice cubes and the remaining sliced lemon rings.

Rooibos tea

South Africa

One of the few foodstuffs of the indigenous Khoikhoi and San people that European colonists adopted with any enthusiasm was a tea made from the dried, fermented leaf tips of a scrubby bushveld plant, *Aspalathus linearis*, known as redbush or *rooibos*. The trade in rooibos is centred around the town of Clanwilliam in the Cape, and was developed by a Rhodes Scholar, Peter Nortier, who moved to Clanwilliam to practise as a doctor immediately after the First World War.

Dr Nortier had difficulty finding rooibos seed, and ended up offering local people a shilling for a matchbox-full. The only person who regularly responded was an elderly Khoikhoi woman: eventually Dr Nortier discovered that she was obtaining the seed from anthills, digging into each mound until she found a chamber where the ant colony had collected thousands of the tiny seeds.

Few people outside Southern Africa know how to brew rooibos properly—it is one of the few teas that can be boiled up without becoming unpalatably tannic and strong; instead, rooibos gains sweetness and flavour the longer it is infused. Mrs Barnes suggested in 1890 that rooibos (or, as she called it, Cape bush tea) should be made in an earthenware teapot—presumably because pottery retains heat better than metal—and suggested that a little of it could be added to other teas to flavour them with its distinctive, sweet aroma.

1 teaspoon of leaf rooibos or
1 tea bag per person
1½ mugs cold water per person
Milk and sugar to taste

Place the rooibos leaves or tea bags in a stainless steel saucepan and add the water. Bring to the boil and simmer for at least ten minutes before serving with milk and sugar, as for Indian tea.

Iced spiced rooibos tea

South Africa

A lovely summer drink with an unusual, red-orange colour.

1 teaspoon of leaf rooibos or
1 tea bag per person
1½ mugs cold water per person
2 cinnamon sticks
2 whole allspice
1 clove
Sugar to taste
Slices of orange for garnish

Place the rooibos leaves or tea bags and whole spices in a stainless steel saucepan and add the water. Bring to the boil and simmer for at least ten minutes. Add sugar to taste and leave to cool.

Once cold, strain through a fine sieve or tea strainer, and chill in the fridge before serving, garnished with a slice of orange.

THE
Bird and Bottle
LUXURY
GRILL ROOM
& BAR
AT THE
AMBASSADOR HOTEL
P.O. BOX 872 SALISBURY PHONE 61052

Vanilla rooibos tea

South Africa

Vanilla's rich, sweet perfume beautifully complements rooibos—sometimes I add vanilla sugar to a cup of rooibos tea to scent it quickly and conveniently.

1 teaspoon of leaf rooibos or
1 tea bag per person
1½ mugs cold water per person
½ tsp vanilla essence

Place the rooibos leaves or tea bags and whole spices in a stainless steel saucepan and add the water. Bring to the boil and simmer for at least ten minutes. Add vanilla essence to the pan and stir to mix before serving with milk and sugar, as for Indian tea.

Kupper
KupperBeer
Kupper Beer
Beer
SOLE AGENTS
SMITH, MACKENZIE & Co
MOMBASA, ZANZIBAR,
DAR-ES-SALAAM ETC...

Braaivleis and barbecues

Braaivleis simply means barbeque (in the Afrikaans language, *braai vleis* translates literally as grill-meat). Braai-ing is a large part of white African society, and one of the only cultural aspects to have been re-imported by Britain—one theory is that barbecuing in Britain only really caught on when 90,000 white Rhodesians returned to the UK following Zimbabwe's independence in 1980, bringing the southern African braai culture with them. Certainly I remember my father braai-ing in the back garden of our semi-detached suburban house in South Norwood in South London in the early 1970s, and our astonished neighbours peering over the fence with puzzled looks: "You're going to cook... *outside*?"

Many Namibian, South African, Kenyan and Zimbabwean homes have a brick braaivleis built in the garden; visit any National Park or beach in southern Africa and you will observe a number of braais available for use by visitors. Sometimes these are simple charcoal braais for which the visitors must remember to bring a bag of charcoal, but parks are increasingly encouraging the use of gas braais, for which gas bottles can be bought in the park. National Parks in some countries also work with local residents to arrange a sustainable supply of firewood for their visitors' braais.

Successful braai-ing can be done over a gas, wood or charcoal barbeque. Coal is unsuitable for direct cooking because the oily gases given off during combustion taint the meat or fish with a distinct flavour of tar. If using a wood or charcoal barbeque the key point to remember is not to cook until all the fuel has been reduced to hot, glowing coals with a healthy covering of white ash. If there is unburnt wood or charcoal still burning during the cooking, the food will taste unpleasantly resinous and smoky.

If using a communal braai, always leave the grill as close to the coals as possible for a few minutes—lying on them, if possible—to burn off any remnants of food or fat from the previous user.

There are a number of good braai recipes in this book, including:

Grilled guinea fowl with orange
L.M. prawns
Peri-peri chicken
Sosaties
Boerewors
Vlermuis
Ashkoek
Rooster-koekies

In addition, peri-peri sauce and the marinades used in the curry recipes, as well as Leipoldt's curry sauce, can all be used as pre-braai marinades for raw meat or fish. Simply lay the fish or meat in the sauce, rubbing it in well, for at least an hour, and then shake off the excess marinade and grill the meat or fish until cooked.

Vegetarians may sometimes appear hard done-by at braais, but in fact there are loads of great African dishes that can be prepared for vegetarians. Any of the marinades, curry sauce or peri-peri sauce can be used to coat slices of aubergine, butternut or sweet potato for grilling (butternut and sweet potato slices will need about 40 minutes total grilling time, aubergine about 30 minutes). Even fruit can be braai-ed—what about making fruit kebabs with pineapple, peach and banana chunks on bamboo satay skewers, grilled until the fruit begins to caramelise, and serving them with crème fraîche or ice cream?

When we braai, I wrap chunks of butternut, pre-seasoned with salt, pepper and nutmeg, in aluminium foil and bake them in the ashes while the meat and fish is grilling. Other useful vegetables for ash baking include potato, sweet potato, aubergine, courgette and all the squash varieties—gemsquash, pattypan and pumpkin are the most common in Africa. Part-baked garlic bread is perfect wrapped in foil and baked in ashes instead of in an oven—or try ashkoek or rooster-koekies split open and served with a garlic butter filling.

It sounds obvious, but always take care when braai-ing. Never put grass, paper or cardboard on the braai—hot embers and sparks can float up and set light to a patch of dry grass or a thatched roof with equal facility.

THE

HIGH CHAPERRAL

Presents its very popular 3-Course Sunday Luncheon for only

– $1,95 –

Creamed Mushroom on Toast

OR

Avocado Salad

* * *

Large Tender Rump Steak with Onion Rings

OR

Roast Duckling and Apple Sauce

OR

Grilled T-Bone, Egg and French Fries

OR

Fillet Steak (slightly peppered)

* * *

Apple Pie and Cream

PHONE 35789 FOR BOOKINGS

cp-62921-Y-10

Names

The names and spellings of many countries, towns and cities in British colonial Africa changed following independence, and since the 1960s there has been a continual process of renaming as African governments have sought to commemorate heroes or erase the memory of their former conquerors. Throughout this book I have tried to keep historical names of towns, cities and peoples consistent with the period to which a specific passage refers.

Some countries, towns and districts that have changed name or that have become part of a new, independent nation, are shown below:

Former name	Now known as
British East Africa	Kenya
Eastern Transvaal	Mpumalanga
Enkeldoorn	Chivhu
German East Africa	part of Tanzania
Marandellas	Marondera
Mazoe	Mazowe
Melsetter	Chimanimani
Northern Province, South Africa	Limpopo Province
Northern Rhodesia	Zambia
Nyasaland	Malawi
Portuguese East Africa	Mozambique
Que Que	Kwe Kwe
Rhodesia (from 1965)	Zimbabwe
Salisbury	Harare
Southern Rhodesia	Zimbabwe
South-West Africa	Namibia
Tanganyika	part of Tanzania
Zanzibar	part of Tanzania

Mrs. Slade
SOUTH AFRICA'S
foremost
cookery expert
RECOMMENDS

"Bonny Boy"

SOUTH AFRICA'S
foremost
BREAKFAST OATS

APART from outstanding qualities which have established Bonny Boy Breakfast Oats as South Africa's first choice in Breakfast Food, Mrs. Slade has devised recipes for the preparation of many delightful dishes with "Bonny Boy" Oats—including a gruel for infants.

Write to "Bonny Boy" Mills, Johannesburg, for a free copy of Mrs. Slade's Bonny Boy Recipe Booklet.

Food suppliers

Most of the recipes in this book do not call for specific, hard-to-find ingredients; in fact, depending on the season, one could buy practically all the ingredients for all the recipes in one large supermarket. I tend to use Waitrose for my shopping: partly because of their ethical approach to sourcing and supply both in the UK and abroad, and partly because they stock a wider and more unusual selection of fruits and vegetables than the other high street supermarkets.

However, there are some items that you will not be able to find in most supermarkets. Luckily there is a range of companies supplying African food and drink either through specialist shops, by mail order or through the Internet, and here is a list of some of the best:

St Marcus Fine Foods

1 Rockingham Close, Priory Lane, Off Upper Richmond Rd West, Roehampton, London SW15 5RW. Open Mon-Sun, 9.00-6.00.

Tel: 020 8878 1898

www.biltongstmarcus.co.uk

A wide selection of South African produce, their traditionally cured meats and sausages are particularly good. Their stock holdings are variable, so it is always a good idea to call before making a special journey.

Osgrow

7b Boyce's Avenue, Clifton, Bristol, BS8 4AA. (Delivery only)

Tel: (0870) 165 1408

www.osgrow.com

A brilliant selection of imported and domestic exotic meats including crocodile, wildebeest, impala, springbok, eland, kudu, zebra and ostrich. Their meat hampers are delivered to your door and offer particularly good value.

Zambezi Foods

76 Hightown Road, Luton, Bedfordshire, LU2 0BW. Open Mon-Sat, 10.30-5.30.

Tel: (01582) 419284

www.zambezifoods.com

A good selection of foodstuffs from Zimbabwe, Zambia and Malawi, including Tanganda Tea, Lion lager and marula jelly. Opening times can be variable, so don't be afraid to telephone.

Bokke Foods

Bishop's Waltham, Southampton. (Online only)

Tel: (01489) 899123

www.bokkefoods.com

The largest online supplier of South African foodstuffs in the United Kingdom, with a wide range and good availability. Quick service, too!

The Savanna

Seven shops across London, in South London and at London Bridge, Victoria and Liverpool Street railway stations

Tel: (020) 8971 9177

www.thesavanna.co.uk

A chain of London shops offering South African and Zimbabwean foods, beer and wine.

The Borough Market

8 Southwark Street, London Bridge, London SE1 1TL. Open Fri, 12.00-6.00; Sat, 9.00-4.00

Tel: (020) 7407 1002

www.boroughmarket.org.uk

London's best retail food market, with an unsurpassed range of organic meats, and brilliant fruit and vegetable stalls. One of the few places in London where you can find raw L.M. prawns. In addition, some of the traders (Elsey & Bent deserve a particular mention) buy wonderful African fruit, so that you sometimes find, for example, pawpaws from West Africa, granadillas and avocados from Swaziland and pineapples from South Africa.

Ealing Road

Alperton, London HA0

Ealing Road runs between Alperton and Wembley Central underground stations and includes parades of shops selling fresh fruit and vegetables and other groceries, as well as saris and Indian gold jewellery. This is an excellent street in which to buy fresh spices and ingredients such as rosewater; in addition, the longstanding links and routes between East Africa and India mean that this is a good place to look for produce such as Kenyan tea and the tiny, tree-ripened Ugandan 'apple' bananas.

Green Street

Ilford, East London E7

Green Street is one of the main shopping streets for East London's South Asian communities. You will find a variety of unusual fresh fruit and vegetables as well as superb freshly-cooked snacks like samoosas and pakoras. A Danish entrepreneur now runs weekly coach trips from Copenhagen to Ilford so that Danish Asians can stock up in Green Street!

Ridley Road Market

Ridley Road, Dalston, London E8

An large, friendly, chaotic market, with stalls selling African wax-cloth, kapenta, goat meat and West African and Caribbean fruit and vegetables. Best days to go are probably Tuesday and Thursday, or before about 9.30am on Saturday—it gets very busy later on Saturday.

Restaurants and cafes

Apart from Ethiopian and Moroccan restaurants, consistently good African eating-places are few and far between. Here are two of the best, one in London and one in New York City.

1860

28 South End, Croydon, Surrey, CR0 1DN. Open Tues-Sat, 11am-2pm; 5.30pm-11pm.

Tel: (020) 8688 3839

www.eighteensixty.co.uk

1860 offers South African Indian cuisine (the restaurant's name derives from the year that groups of indentured labourers first arrived in Natal from India) and is run by a brother and sister from kwaZulu-Natal. As one would expect, brilliant curries and flatbreads.

Madiba

195 Dekalb Avenue, Brooklyn, NY 11205, United States of America. Open for brunch/lunch Mon-Fri, 10am-4pm; Sat and Sun 10.30am-4pm. Open for dinner/bar snacks Sun-Thurs 4pm-midnight; Fri and Sat 4pm-1am.

Tel: (718) 855-9190

www.madibarestaurant.com

Relaxed and atmospheric, with an impressive wine list.

Illustrations

Every effort has been made to trace the source of illustrations used in this work. Illustrations throughout are taken from a number of sources and are reproduced, where copyright still exists, by kind permission of the copyright holder.

Fabrica Portugueza de Refrigerantes,

Ice and Aerated Water Factory.

PROPRIETORS - BARRETO, FERNANDES & CO.

Valsassina Street, Beira.

SODA. LEMONADE. GINGER ALE.

GINGER BEER. ICE.

All our Aerated Waters are much recommended for their purity.

LARGE DISCOUNT TO WHOLESALE BUYERS.

Meat, Fish, Fruit, etc., received and Stored in the Cold Room.

UP-COUNTRY ORDERS PROMPTLY EXECUTED.

Bibliography

There are a number of excellent books on indigenous African cookery; for a good overview I recommend *Best of Regional African Cooking*, by Harva Hachten, published by Hippocrene Books.

"A.R.B" (Mrs A. R. Barnes), 1890. *The Colonial Household Guide*, Darter Brothers and Walton, Cape Town, South Africa.

Anon., 1925. *The Uganda Cookery Book, Containing 142 Recipes in English and Luganda*, Uganda Bookshop, Kampala, Uganda.

Anthony, J., undated but c.1955. *Lourenço Marques—A Guide*, publisher unknown.

Army & Navy Co-operative Stores, 1907. *Rules of the Society and Price List of Articles Sold at the Stores*, reprinted (1969) as *Yesterday's Shopping*, David & Charles, Newton Abbot, Devon, United Kingdom.

Barretto Miranda, José Francisco, 1902. *Manica—Sofala: Guide to the Mozambique Company's Territory*, Barretto Miranda, London, United Kingdom.

Baxter, T.W., and Turner, R.W.S., 1968. *Rhodesian Epic*, Howard Timmins, Cape Town, South Africa.

Beech, Joan, 2005. *Follow the Red Dirt Road*, published online at http://dpicg.com/joan_beech/index.html

Beeton, Isabella (ed.), 1998. *Beeton's Book of Household Management*, reprinted Southover Press, Lewes, Sussex, United Kingdom.

Berlyn, Philippa, 1967. *Rhodesia—Beleaguered Country*, The Mitre Press, London, United Kingdom.

Blixen, Karen, ('Isak Dinesen'), 1937. *Out of Africa*, Putnam and Co Ltd, London, United Kingdom.

Boggie, Mrs Jeannie M., 1940. *First Steps in Civilising Rhodesia*, Philpott and Collins, Bulawayo, Southern Rhodesia.

Boyd, Andrew, and van Rensburg, Patrick, 1965. *An Atlas of African Affairs*, Methuen, London, United Kingdom.

Boyle, Laura, 1968. *Diary of a Colonial Officer's Wife*, Alden Press, Oxford, United Kingdom.

Bridger, P., House, M., and others, 1973. *Encyclopaedia Rhodesia*, College Press, Salisbury, Rhodesia.

Brown, G. Gordon, various years. *The South and East African Year Book and Guide*, Sampson Low, Marston & Company, Ltd., London, United Kingdom.

________________ various years. *The Year Book and Guide to Southern Africa*, Sampson Low, Marston & Company, Ltd., London, United Kingdom.

Bulawayo Bowling Club, 1923. *List of Officials, Fixtures, By-Laws etc*, Bulawayo Bowling Club, Bulawayo, Southern Rhodesia.

Chataway, Mrs N (compiler), 1909. *Bulawayo Cookery Book and Household Guide*, Building Fund of the New English Church, Bulawayo, Southern Rhodesia.

The Chronicle, Bulawayo, Zimbabwe.

Clark, P. M., 1936. *The Autobiography of an Old Drifter*, George G. Harrap & Co., Ltd, London, United Kingdom.

Colonial Office, 1935. *Information as to the Conditions and Cost of Living in the Colonial Empire*, His Majesty's Stationery Office, London, United Kingdom.

Coupland, R., 1935. *The Empire in These Days*, Macmillan & Co., London, United Kingdom.

Coetzee, Renata, 1977. *The South African Culinary Tradition*, C. Struik Publishers, Cape Town, South Africa.

Davidson, Ann M., 1993. *The Real Paradise: Memories of Africa 1950-1963*, Pentland Press, Durham, United Kingdom.

Davis, Alexander, 1895. *Directory of Bulawayo and Handbook of Matabeleland, 1895-96*, published by Alexander Davis, Bulawayo, Rhodesia.

Delap-Hilton, E., 1926. *Snips Without Snaps of Kenya (Without Prejudice)*, Arthur H. Stockwell Ltd, London, United Kingdom.

Desmond, Judy, undated but c.1960. *Traditional Cookery in Southern Africa*, Books of Africa, Cape Town, South Africa.

Diamond, Jared, 1998. *Guns, Germs and Steel*, Chatto and Windus, London, United Kingdom.

Dijkman, Mrs E. J., 1890. *Die Suid-Afrikaanse Kook-, Koek-, en Resepte Boek*, Paarlse Drukpers, Paarl, South Africa.

Duckitt, Hildagonda, 1902. *Hilda's Diary of a Cape Housekeeper*, Chapman and Hall, London, United Kingdom. Reprinted in facsimile 1978 by Macmillan South Africa, Johannesburg, South Africa.

________________ 1891. *Traditional South African Cookery*, Maskew Miller Ltd, Cape Town, South Africa.

Duke University Press, *Transition*, Duke University Press, Durham, NC, USA.

East Africa Annual, 1946-1966. East African Standard Ltd, Nairobi, Kenya.

East Africa and Rhodesia, London, United Kingdom.

East African Wild Life Society. *Africana*, Journal of the East African Wild Life Society, Nairobi, Kenya.

East African Standard, *Handbook for East Africa, Uganda and Zanzibar, 1906.* East African Standard, Mombasa, British East Africa.

Eaton, W. G., 1996. *A Chronicle of Modern Sunlight*, InnoVision, Rohnert Park, California, United States of America.

Eldon, Kathy, 1985. *Specialities of the House*, Kenway Publications Ltd, Nairobi, Kenya.

Fairbridge, Kingsley, 1927. *The Autobiography of Kingsley Fairbridge*, OUP, Oxford, United Kingdom.

Farson, Negley, 1940. *Behind God's Back*, Victor Gollancz, London, United Kingdom.

Ferguson, Niall, 2003. *Empire—How Britain Made the Modern World*, Allan Lane, London, United Kingdom.

Ferris, N. S., (ed) 1956. *Know Your Rhodesia and Know Nyasaland*, Rhodesian Printing and Publishing Co. Ltd, Salisbury, Southern Rhodesia.

Field, Alan, 1906. *"VERB. SAP." on going to West Africa*, Bale, Sons and Danielsson, London, United Kingdom.

Finney, Thomas B., 1922. *Handy Guide for Pork Butchers*, T. B. Finney & Co., Cornbrook, Manchester, United Kingdom.

Gann, L.H., and Duignan, P., 1962. *White Settlers in Tropical Africa*, Penguin African Series, London, United Kingdom.

Gerber, Hilda, undated but c.1950. *Cape Cookery Old and New*, Howard B Timmins for Hodder and Stoughton, Cape Town, South Africa.

____________ 1958. *Traditional Cookery of the Cape Malays*, A. A. Balkema, Cape Town, South Africa.

Gillett, M., 1986. *Tribute to Pioneers—an index of many of the pioneers of East Africa*, J. M. Considine, Headington, Oxford, United Kingdom.

Goldberg, David Theo, 2002. *The Racial State*, Blackwell Publishers Ltd, Oxford, United Kingdom.

Gordon-Brown, A., 1967 (ed). *Guide to Southern Africa*, Robert Hale Ltd, London, United Kingdom.

Green, Lawrence, 1952. *In the Land of Afternoon*, Howard Timmins, Cape Town, South Africa.

Hachten, Harva, 1998. *Best of Regional African Cooking*, Hippocrene Books, New York, NY, United States of America.

Hamilton, Cherie Y., 2001. *Cuisines of Portuguese Encounters*, Hippocrene Books, New York, NY, United States of America.

Harden, Blaine, 1990. *Africa: Dispatches from a Fragile Continent*, W.W. Norton and Co., Inc., New York, NY, United States of America.

Hartley, Aidan 2003. *The Zanzibar Chest*, HarperCollins, London, United Kingdom.

Hennings, R. O., 1951. *African Morning*, Chatto and Windus, London, United Kingdom.

The Herald, Salisbury, Rhodesia.

Higham, Mary, 1919. *Household Cookery for South Africa*, Specialty Press of S.A. Ltd, Johannesburg and Cape Town, South Africa.

Historical Society of Zimbabwe, *Heritage of Zimbabwe*, Journal of the Historical Society of Zimbabwe, Harare, Zimbabwe.

Howe, Robin, 1958. *Cooking from the Commonwealth*, Andre Deutsch London, United Kingdom.

Hunter, J.A., and Mannix, Dan, 1954. *African Bush Adventures*, Hamish Hamilton, London, United Kingdom

Hurst, Una, 1997. *Memories of Africa*, published by the author, printed by Arthur H. Stockwell Ltd, Devon, United Kingdom.

Jollie, Ethel Tawse, 1924. *The Real Rhodesia*, Hutchinson, London, United Kingdom (reprinted 1971 by Books of Rhodesia, Bulawayo, Rhodesia).

Johnson, Frederick, 1942. *A Standard English-Swahili Dictionary*, Oxford University Press, Oxford, United Kingdom.

Jones, Neville, 1953. *Rhodesian Genesis*, Rhodesian Pioneers' and Early Settlers' Society, Bulawayo, Southern Rhodesia.

Kennedy, Dane, 1987. *Islands of White*, Duke University Press, Durham, NC, USA.

Kenya and Uganda Railways and Harbours, 1937. *The Travellers' Guide to Kenya and Uganda, 1937 – No.* 7, Kenya and Uganda Railways and Harbours, Nairobi, Kenya.

The Kenya Association (1932), undated. *Kenya, Britain's Most Attractive Colony*, The Kenya Association (1932), Nairobi, Kenya.

The Knobkerrie, published by W. H. Schroeder, St George's Street, Cape Town, South Africa.

Leipoldt, C. Louis, 1976. *Leipoldt's Cape Cookery*, Fleesch and Partners, Cape Town, South Africa.

Lessing, Doris, 1992. *African Laughter*, HarperCollins, London, United Kingdom.

Levin, L. S., (ed), undated but c.1959. *East Africa Airways Guide to East Africa*, A. J. Levin, Salisbury, Southern Rhodesia.

Lovemore, Mrs Jessie, 'Journey Towards Lobengula: Recollections of Mrs Jessie Lovemore', printed in *Rhodesians Worldwide Magazine* 2004, RWW, Arizona, United States of America.

Lusaka Women's Zionist Society, no date but c.1963, *Home Cooking for Everyday and Festive Occasions*, Lusaka Women's Zionist Society, Lusaka, Northern Rhodesia.

Macdonald, Sheila, 1928. *Sally in Rhodesia*, reprinted by Books of Rhodesia 1969, Bulawayo, Rhodesia.
Macdonald, Sheila, 2003. *Winter Cricket—the Spirit of Wedza*, Sheila Macdonald, Harare, Zimbabwe.
Manning, S. (ed), 1958. *The Rhodesian and Central African Annual* 1958, Stuart Manning, Bulawayo, Southern Rhodesia.
Mesthrie, Rajend (ed), 2002. *Language in South Africa*, Cambridge University Press, Cambridge, United Kingdom.
Musiker, N. and R., 1999. *A Concise Historical Dictionary of Greater Johannesburg*, Francolin Publishers, Cape Town, South Africa.
Mutasa, Joina, 1986. *Cookery Recipes for Zimbabwean Secondary Schools*, Longman Zimbabwe, Harare, Zimbabwe.
Nairobi Handbook, published by the Nairobi Publicity Association, Nairobi, Kenya.
Nealon, Barbara, 1947. *Dinner Party Menus with their Recipes*, Central News Agency, Johannesburg, South Africa.
Nel, G.L., 1945. *Simple Zulu with Household Phrases*, Knox Publishing Company, Durban, South Africa
Newland, Captain H. Osman, 1922. *West Africa: a handbook of practical information for the official, planter, miner, financier and trader*, Daniel O'Connor, London, United Kingdom.
Nicholls, Horace W., 1896. *Stirring Events in Johannesburg 1896—A Collection of Eighteen Photographs*, Horace W. Nicholls, Johannesburg, South African Republic.
Nobbs, E. A., 1924. *Guide to the Matopos*, T. Maskew Miller, Cape Town, South Africa.
Northcote, Edith J. M. (ed), 1933. *The Gold Coast Cookery Book*, Nestlé & Anglo-Swiss Condensed Milk Co., Accra, Gold Coast.
Nyasaland Council of Women, 1947. *Nyasaland Cookery Book and Household Guide*, Nyasaland Council of Women, Blantyre, Nyasaland.
Office for National Statistics website, URL: www.statistics.gov.uk
Packer, Joy, 1953. *Apes and Ivory*, Eyre and Spottiswood, London, United Kingdom.
Parsons, Allan and Bargery, Rev. G. P., 1924. *A Hausa Phrase Book*, Humphrey Milford, Oxford University Press, Oxford, United Kingdom.
Pearse, R. S. (ed), no date, but c. 1970. *This is Mozambique*, Portuguese-South Africa Enterprise, Lourenço Marques, Mozambique.
People's Dispensary for Sick Animals (Johannesburg Branch), c1965. *PDSA Cookery Book*, PDSA Johannesburg, South Africa.

Pickering, Marie L., 1936. *Tropical Cookery*, Faber and Faber Ltd, London, United Kingdom.

Preston, H., 1967. *Ukupheka okuhle*, Mambo Press, Gwelo, Rhodesia.

Purvis, J.B., 1900. *Handbook to British East Africa and Uganda*, Swan Sonnenschein & Co., London, United Kingdom.

Reader's Digest 1985. *South African Cookbook*, Reader's Digest Association South Africa (Pty), Cape Town, South Africa.

Joyce, Peter (ed.), 1985. *South Africa's Yesterdays*, Reader's Digest Association South Africa (Pty), Cape Town, South Africa.

Rasmussen, R. K., and Rubert, S. C., 1990. *A Historical Dictionary of Zimbabwe*, Scarecrow Press, Inc., Metuchen, NJ, United States of America.

Rhodesia Calls, Rhodesia National Tourist Board, Salisbury, Rhodesia.

Rhodesian Woman and Home Publications 1968. *Rhodesian Home Cooking*, Salisbury, Rhodesia.

Richards, W. E. (John), 1975. *Life on the Farm 1929-1933, by a Young Rhodesian Farmer*, W. E. Richards, Fort Victoria, Rhodesia.

Roden, Claudia, 1997. *The Book of Jewish Food*, Viking, London, United Kingdom.

Ross, R., 1999. *A Concise History of South Africa*, Cambridge University Press, Cambridge, United Kingdom.

The Royal African Society. *Journal of the Royal African Society*, The Royal African Society, London, United Kingdom.

Saben, G.P., 1959. *Saben's Commercial Directory and Handbook of Uganda*, 1960-61, Saben's Directories, Kampala, Uganda.

St Andrew's Church Woman's Guild, no date but c1953. *Kenya Cookery Book and Household Guide*, eleventh edition, Church of Scotland Women's Guild, Nairobi, Kenya.

St Giles Rehabilitation Centre, no date but c1970. *Fun with Food*, St Giles Rehabilitation Centre, Salisbury, Rhodesia.

Salisbury Publicity Association, 1976. *Tourist Guide to Salisbury*, Salisbury, Rhodesia.

The S. A. Merry-Go-Round, Johannesburg, South Africa.

Seaton, Henry, 1963. *Lion in the Morning*, John Murray, London, United Kingdom.

Sellick, W. S. J., 1904. *Uitenhage, Past and Present: Souvenir of the Centenary*, W. S. J. Sellick, Uitenhage, Cape Colony.

Sharwood-Smith, Joan, 1992. *Diary of a Colonial Wife*, Radcliffe Press, London, United Kingdom.

Stabb, Henry, 1875. *To the Victoria Falls via Matabeleland: The Diary of Major Henry Stabb*. C. Struik, Cape Town, South Africa.

Tapson, Winifred, 1957. *Old Timer*, Howard Timmins, London, United Kingdom.

Tew, M. R., 1920. *Cooking in West Africa Made Easier*, printed by C. Tinling and Co, Liverpool, United Kingdom.

Trowell, Margaret, 1967. *African Tapestry*, Faber and Faber, London, United Kingdom.

Tulleken, S. van H., 1947. *The Practical Cookery Book for South Africa* (22nd Edition), S. van H. Tulleken, Holmdene, Transvaal, South Africa.

Union Steam Ship Company Ltd, 1880. *South African Gold Fields Emigrants Guide*, Union Steam Ship Company Ltd, London, United Kingdom.

Van Wyk, Ben-Erik, and Gericke, Nigel, 2000. *People's Plants*, Briza Publications, Pretoria, South Africa.

Ward, H. F., and Milligan, J. W. (eds), 1912. *Handbook of British East Africa*, Caxton (B.E.A.) Printing and Publishing Co., Ltd., Nairobi, B. E. A.

Wesleyan Church, Potchefstroom, 1911. *Ye Booke of Owre Onne hundred & tenne Wayes of Feastynge*, Wesleyan Church of Potcheftstroom, Potchefstroom, South Africa.

Westbeech, George, 1963. *Trade and Travel in Early Barotseland: The Diary of George Westbeech*, Chatto and Windus, London, United Kingdom.

Williams, Faldela, 1993. *The Cape Malay Cookbook*, Struik Publishers, Cape Town, South Africa.

Wills, Walter (ed), 1907. *The Anglo-African Who's Who and Biographical Sketch-Book*, L. Upcott Gill, London, United Kingdom.

Wilson, D. G., and Reynolds, L. H. (eds), undated but c.1973. *Jumbo Guide to Rhodesia*, Wilrey Publications, Salisbury, Rhodesia.

Wilson, Peter, M., 2001. *Bwana Shamba*, Pentland Publications, Durham, United Kingdom.

Women's Association of St Andrew's Methodist Church, 1951. *Well Tried Recipes*, Umtali, Southern Rhodesia.

Women's Voluntary Services of Rhodesia, no date but c.1966. *Our Cookery Book—a collection of basic recipes, suited to Rhodesian conditions, in English, Chishona and Ndebele*, Brickhill Promotions, Salisbury, Rhodesia.

Wootton and Gibson Ltd (eds), 1962. *Who's Who of Southern Africa, Incorporating South African Who's Who and the Who's Who of the Federation of Rhodesia and Nyasaland, Central and East Africa*, Wootton and Gibson, Johannesburg, South Africa.

Wylie, D., 2001. *Starving on a Full Stomach: Hunger and the Triumph of Cultural Racism in Modern South Africa*, University of Virginia Press, Charlottesville, VA., United States of America.

Acknowledgements

Grateful thanks to everyone who generously agreed to share their memories and experiences of food in Africa, and to those individuals and companies who have allowed me to reproduce illustrations and advertisements.

Yvonne and David Anderson-Bassey
Joan Beech
Helen Burt and the Commission for Racial Equality
Dr Mangosuthu Buthelezi
Makuwerere Bwititi and the *Chronicle*, Bulawayo
John Conyngham and the *Natal Witness*
Marilyn Eaton and the Gauteng PDSA
Vera Elderkin
Gillian Forbes and Who's Who of Southern Africa
Dominic Gibbs and the Cayzer Trust Company
Russell Hadley and Meikles Hotel, Harare
Adelaine and Peter Hain
Chenjerai Hove
Jock and Doreen Hutton
Lord Joffe
Dr Roger Leakey
Prue Leith and the Prue Leith Chef's Academy, Prue Leith Restaurant and Prue Leith Chef's Studio, Centurion, Gauteng.
Celia Mandlate and the Automovel Touring Club of Mozambique
Monica Mason
Wilf Mbanga
Festus Mogae
J. M. Ndegwa and Nairobi City Council
Matthew Parris
Rupert Pennant-Rea
Christopher Purvis
Jeff F. Ramsay and the Office of the President of the Republic of Botswana
Barbara and Tim Saben
William Saffery
John Sentamu, Archbishop of York
Sally Silius

Trevor Southey
Sylvester Stein
William Tekede and the National Archives of Zimbabwe, Hararc
Sheila Ware

Also available from Jeppestown Press

Where the Lion Roars: An 1890 African Colonial Cookery Book

The Bulawayo Cookery Book and Household Guide

The Anglo-African Who's Who 1907

Matabeleland and the Victoria Falls

With Captain Stairs to Katanga

The Ghana Cookery Book

Cooking in West Africa

See our web site at www.jeppestown.com, or order any of our books online from www.amazon.com or www.amazon.co.uk.